# My Garden Companion

# My Garden Companion

## *A Complete Guide for the Beginner*

*with a special emphasis on*
*Useful Plants*
*and*
*Intensive Planting*
*in the*
*Wayside, Dooryard, Patio, Rooftop,*
*and Vacant Lot*

by Jamie Jobb
illustrated by Martha Weston

*Sierra Club Books / Charles Scribner's Sons*

*San Francisco / New York*

Trade distribution is by Charles Scribner's Sons, 597 Fifth Avenue, New York, New York 10017

*My Garden Companion* was developed and prepared for publication at The Yolla Bolly Press, Covelo, California under the supervision of James and Carolyn Robertson during the fall and winter of 1976-1977. Production Staff: Sharon Miley, Loren Fisher, Gene Floyd, Jay Stewart, and Evelyn Swift.



Manufactured in the United States of America

1 3 5 7 9 11 13 15 17 19 MD/C 20 18 16 14 12 10 8 6 4 2
1 3 5 7 9 11 13 15 17 19 MD/P 20 18 16 14 12 10 8 6 4 2

Library of Congress Cataloging in Publication Data

Jobb, Jamie.
My garden companion.

Bibliography: p. 336
SUMMARY: A guide to planting vegetables, flowers, and other plants with information about soil, water, weather, and insects.
1. Gardening — Juvenile literature. [1. Gardening]
I. Title.
SB457.J6 635 76-57675
ISBN O-684-15018-2
ISBN O-684-15019-0 pbk.

# Table of Contents

## Part Four: Your Next Gardens

# Every Garden Has a Gardener

Anybody can start a garden just about anywhere. And anybody can learn how to become a gardener. Just by doing it. Gardeners are special people. They include kids, doctors, waiters, mothers, and others. They look at the world in special ways.

Most people don't see the sun, soil, bugs, seeds, plants, moon, water, clouds, and wind the way gardeners do. These are the jigsaw pieces of every garden.

A garden is an important part of the home and family. A place where people can relax or be busy. A place to learn about the magic of nature and the mysteries of life. Furthermore, it's a place to learn about yourself.

No garden happens overnight. It happens slowly. Little by little. Day by day. Every day a garden has something new — a new leaf, a new flower, a new bug, a new surprise to show you.

There is always more going on in your garden than you can ever know. Mostly because you can't be there all the time. Don't let this bother you. Just learn to look closer when you are there.

A garden can bring color, food, and spice into your life. But you can also grow brooms, shoes, soap, chewing gum, or almost anything else that grows on plants.

What a garden produces is not always as important as how it grows and changes every day. Many gardeners are happy just to *be* in their gardens. They don't always need to take something from the garden every time they visit it.

Bad weather, troublesome bugs, soil problems, or poor timing can hurt a garden. But nothing will ruin a garden faster than the gardener's big hopes and dreamy expectations.

There is no "right" way for you to garden. As you develop your own way of gardening, you will choose ideas from other gardeners' methods. Over the years, your own "method" will change because it is based on your own changing experiences. A garden is moved by influences you cannot see, fully comprehend or control. You are only part of the whole blooming thing.

# How to Use This Book

A book can start you thinking about a garden. But a book can't actually start the garden. Only you can do that.

You don't need to read this book all at once. Use it like you use a dictionary or catalog. Read it slowly, little bits at a time. Come back to it when you have a question. The book is divided into four parts:

*Part One "Before You Dig In"* — Important things you should do and think about before you actually begin to dig and plant. Includes chapters on finding space for a garden anywhere you live now. Learning the best times to plant and care for the things you want to grow. Finding out what soil is and how it supports plants. Ideas for getting help when you need it.

*Part Two "The Whole Blooming Thing"* — What you need to do to get the garden going. How to dig and prepare soil. What to do about weeds and seeds. Watching how air and water affect the garden. Learning how to live with bugs. And how to pinch, prune, and pick the things you grow.

*Part Three "Anyhow You Garden"* — If you really get excited about gardening, you'll want to know and do more. Here you'll find out about plant breeding by watching bees. Learn to recognize and respect the seasonal cycles of the earth, sun, and moon. And discover what else you may.

*Part Four "Your Next Gardens"* — A classified section of helpful information.

## Special Thanks

Any gardener and any writer is always indebted to neighbors, friends and other folks who help his garden and his book grow.

I am thankful for the California Academy of Sciences Pictures Collection and the Marin County Public Library. Special thanks to Ann Brown, Francis Davis, and the other librarians at the San Rafael Public Library.

Ideas, guidance and support came from many folks. Especially Lynn Ferar, Robert Kourik, Terry Porter, Jerry Testo, Mollie Rights, Deanne and John Lindstrom, Peder Jones, Richard Hobbs, Tom Schneider, Gene Andrews, Jerry George, Helga Olkowski, Doris Cellarius, John A. Dickerson, Jim and Alice Wilson of the Wide Skies Press, and the most helpful gardeners in our neighborhood, Mr. and Mrs. J. C. Meagor.

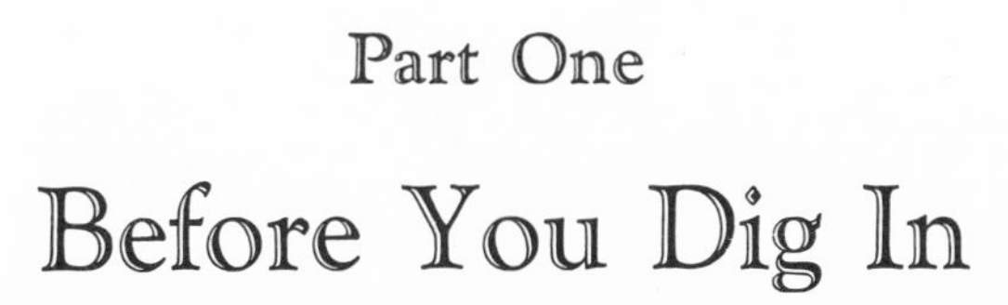

# Part One

# Before You Dig In

Chapter 1

# A Place for Everything

You now live in a place you call home. But you probably won't spend the rest of your life there. Especially as you grow older and change your ideas about what to do with your future. You will probably move and find new homes. You might move to another state or another town. You might even move to another country.

Anywhere you live you can find room for a garden somewhere. In fact, you'll probably find a garden of some kind there already. It might be overgrown and neglected. It might be only a few weeds growing out of the cracks in the sidewalk out front. But it's there, somewhere.

Anywhere you live you can have a garden: in a house, apartment, trailer, treehouse, or even on a sailboat. All you need is fresh water, soil, sunlight, and permission. You can have a garden that is very little and quiet, or very big and busy, or very in between.

This chapter tells where you can begin a garden at home right now. But it also has ideas about where you could put a garden when you move somewhere else.

# Where Should You Locate Your Garden?

Every single garden on earth is different and special. Each garden you see can introduce you to some new plant or animal you've never seen before. Sometimes it's even new to the gardener who lives there.

Because each garden is so different from the next, it's hard to talk about gardens as a group. It's not like talking about cars, trucks, or submarines. Every single garden is unique. And each one has its own story.

Just look at the gardens around you.

## Finding the Best Gardens in Your Neighborhood

Go on a walk or a slow bike ride before dinner this evening. If you can't go then, go early in the morning. Don't go looking for anything in particular. But look at your neighborhood in ways you haven't done before. Notice how it changes from home to home.

Slowly you will find what you weren't really looking for — the most interesting, colorful, busy, and magical gardens in your neighborhood. Some of them might even jump out and grab you! It's good to know the outstanding gardens in your neighborhood. These gardens and the gardeners inside them can help you learn a lot about starting your own garden.

Early morning and early evening is when most gardeners garden. These people may be willing to talk with you, answer questions, and otherwise help.

### Some Questions to Answer

After you take your tour of gardens in your neighborhood, come home and look around. Get a clear picture in mind of your entire home. The inside and the outside. Then sit down and think.

Think about where you could put your garden. Answer these questions.

Do you live in a house? Apartment? House trailer? Tall building? Houseboat? Yurt? Someplace else?

Do you have a yard? Patio? Porch? Balcony? A roof with an easy way to get soil and water onto it? A room with a window?

Does your home already have a garden? Who does the gardening?

Has anyone else at home ever had a garden before? Do they want to have a garden now? Will they help you start one?

Is there any part of your yard or neighborhood that is wasted, neglected, overgrown with weeds? Would it be possible to have a garden there? Could you get permission?

Do you know where north is?

## Nine or Ten Ways to Begin

Some gardeners have so much room that they need a small tractor to cultivate it all. Other gardeners live in tall buildings with gardens on patios, ledges, roofs, and windows. Or anywhere else one can fit. Anybody who really wants a garden will find a place for it somewhere.

If you have never gardened before, then it's best to start small. Pick a couple of plants you want to grow. Or six or seven. Don't try to grow more plants than you can care for.

### A One-Window Greenhouse

If you have no roof, no ground, no patio, no other room around home, you can still start a garden. In your own room.

A window is a little greenhouse. Especially a window that faces south, southeast, or southwest. A window facing these directions gets the most sunlight, especially in winter. But it doesn't matter if the window faces another direction. You'll just need to select plants that like shade or partial shade for these window gardens.

**Some Plants to Start in a Sunny Window**

| | | |
|---|---|---|
| squash | peanuts | popcorn |
| tomato | avocado | potato |
| grapefruit | rice | beans |
| watermelon | peas | |

You can get seeds for most of these in your kitchen. Let all the seeds dry first. Peanuts, peas, beans, popcorn, and rice are seeds themselves. Peanuts should be unsalted, unroasted, and otherwise untreated. Just slice a potato into two or three pieces, plant them, and they will grow.

## A Two-Window Garden

After a while you will outgrow your one-window greenhouse. It won't be enough room for everything you want to try growing. If you have two windows in your room, you can easily start another window garden.

Or you might want to start another window garden somewhere else in the house. The dining room or living room might be a good place, as long as it has good windows.

By putting plants around the house, you'll realize that each room has a different environment. A kitchen is usually hot and dry, unless something is boiling. A bathroom is usually warm and moist, but not always.

Different plants will like different rooms of the house. You'll find out easily, because the plant will tell you. If it grows big and healthy, it likes the room. If it doesn't do well, move it somewhere else.

### Some Other Plants to Try in a Window

| | | |
|---|---|---|
| lettuce | zinnias | carrots |
| broccoli | nasturtiums | beets |
| pansies | marigolds | |

You can get seeds for these at a garden supply store or a plant nursery. Or through mail-order seed catalogs.

### Greenhouse in a Bottle Garden

Even in a room without a sunny window, you can have a tiny garden. You can start a garden in a bottle. The bigger the bottle, the bigger the garden. Gardens in bottles are called terrariums.

It is usually easy to find big bottles. Sometimes restaurants and food stores throw away big bottles. Ask for them. Or check the garbage bins behind the store or restaurant. Also check the recycling center, if there's one nearby. They might have large bottles, if you get there before they're broken.

You'll also find bottles in your own kitchen. Big bottles of fruit juice are good. Look around. Or reserve a jar you see still being used.

The only trick: There must be an opening in the bottle big enough for you to pour soil and slide young plants through. Planting is done by dropping in seeds or using a bent coat hanger to slide young plants into the soil and to pat soil down around roots.

If you keep a cork or top on the bottle the plants will water themselves. But plants also need fresh air, so the bottle should be opened often to let fresh air in and to cool things off when the bottle gets too hot. If the plants in the bottle seem dry, water them with a fine mist spray. You don't have to water a bottle garden very often.

Many nurseries and seed companies have plants for terrarium gardens. You should look for plants that are small enough to handle. You should also get ones that are suited to the light conditions where the bottle will sit.

**Some Plants to Try in a Bottle**

| | | |
|---|---|---|
| African violets | aluminum plant | miniature roses |
| ferns | moss | oxalis |
| begonias | geraniums | Venus flytrap |
| miniature ivy | orchids | dwarf impatiens |

## Balcony, Patio, Porch, or Roof Garden

It is easy to start a small garden on a balcony, porch, or patio. Or even a roof! All you need are containers full of good soil. And a way to get water to the containers.

Just about anything that grows in a garden, will grow in a container outside, even small trees. Plants will not grow as as large as they usually would if they were in the ground because the roots can't grow beyond the container.

You can use all kinds of things for containers: wooden boxes, bathtubs, sinks, buckets, pots and pans, mailboxes, or any piece of junk. The bigger the container, the bigger the plants. Just be sure each container has a good hole or holes in the bottom so water will drain out.

**Some Plants to Try in Containers**

| | | |
|---|---|---|
| tomato | strawberries | any herb |
| lettuce | radishes | any flower |
| carrots | onions | anything! |
| parsley | cucumbers | |

Get plants anywhere, but be sure they stay watered enough. Some containers dry out fast.

### Soup and Salad Garden

No backyard is so small that it can't have room for a soup and salad garden. If you have a backyard, find some small corner for the garden. It's best if it's near the kitchen where soups and salads are made. This kind of garden doesn't need to have full sunshine on it all the time. In fact, it's better if it's partially shaded from the hot afternoon sun.

**Some Greens and Things to Grow for Soup and Salad**

| | | |
|---|---|---|
| lettuce | mustard greens | cucumbers |
| parsley | leeks | radishes |
| dill | peas | tomatoes |
| cabbage | carrots | kohlrabi |
| dandelion | onions | |

One thing to remember about a food garden. You must keep replanting things after you pick something. Otherwise, you'll run out of food.

Soup and salad gardens can also be grown in containers on a patio, porch, or inside the house.

### A Rose in a Nose Garden

Old-time gardeners plant roses and garlic together in the same spot. It seems odd, but they say the two plants improve the smells of each other. I've tried it and it seems to work in my garden.

You can take a small corner of any sunny backyard and plant a rose bush in the middle. Then you can plant garlic and other smelly herbs and flowers all around the rose. When this kind of garden is in bloom, try matching the many smells with the plants they come from. Think you can do it?

**Besides Roses and Garlic, Try These Smells**

| | | |
|---|---|---|
| violet | jasmine | pink carnation |
| chamomile | thyme | roquette |
| nasturtium | rosemary | citrus |
| hyacinth | sage | wistaria |
| gardenia | balm | |

### Secret Outback Wild Garden

There are several ways to have a garden if you can't have one anywhere at home. One way is to find a secret garden somewhere. A garden that no one but you knows about.

Start by looking for a place where you're sure very few animals, humans, or other creatures will bother things. You might find this place in a forgotten corner of a big vacant lot. Or along a river bank. Or in some unused weedpatch. You'll know the spot when you find it. Secret spots always call out.

Only the strongest plants will grow in a secret garden: native plants, wildflowers, and weeds. Things that could grow there even if you didn't plant them.

Big colonies of the same kind of plant will do better in a secret garden than just one of each kind of plant. So get a lot of seeds and broadcast sow them. Throw them out onto the soil after you have prepared it. Then rake the seeds into the soil and wait. The sun, air, and water will start the seeds moving.

Plants need moisture during the early weeks of their growth. So it's best to plant a secret garden when you expect rains will follow and help get the plants started. By the way, the career of one of the world's great geniuses, George Washington Carver, began in a secret garden.

**What to Plant in a Secret Garden**

dandelion
sunflower
prickly lettuce
wild buckwheat
little barley
watercress
kochia
red sorrel
lamb's-quarters
purslane
oxeye daisy
shepherd's-purse
tansy mustard
narrow-leaf vetch
common mallow
dogbane
yellow toadflax
bedstraw
curly dock
corn cockle

All of these plants are found throughout most of the United States. Ask experienced gardeners and native plant societies about weeds, wildflowers, and other hardy plants in your area.

### Renew a Lost Garden

When I look around my suburban neighborhood I see many houses that don't have gardens. They have trees and bushes and lawns. Backyards and sideyards. Lots of room for a garden. But everything is neglected.

Do you live in the suburbs? Maybe someone in your neighborhood would like to turn their neglected yard space into a garden, but they don't have time or energy. Maybe you could start a garden there for them and for yourself.

It will help if the neighbor is a friend or relative. But maybe you'll find someone who really wants a garden. They might even want to pay you for it.

**Plants That Can Renew Tired Gardens**

| | | |
|---|---|---|
| fava beans | millet | soybeans |
| peas | oats | barley |
| clover | alfalfa | vetch |
| sorghum | rye | green beans |
| buckwheat | mung beans | |

Plant these first. They help rebuild soil by digging deeply and renewing nitrogen.

### Adopt a Garden

There's another way to have a garden if you don't have space around home. You can adopt one. In many cities this is simple. Cities have conservatories, aboretums, public gardens, and other botanic wonders. You can "have" these gardens, too. Just go there a lot and spend time finding out about what grows there. When you aren't digging or planting this is what you would do in your own garden anyway.

Most botanic gardens are so big and full that it would take years just to learn the names and varieties of everything. These gardens usually have someone around to answer questions. Get to know one of these people and you will find a good guide for the garden, too.

### Whole Family Mixed-Up Garden

If you live in a home with front, back, and sideyards, you are lucky. You have lots of choices for places to put a garden. And room to expand it next year.

You're even luckier if you have a family that likes to do things together. If they're interested in improving the feeling of your whole home, they can help you turn the entire place into a garden. Inside and outside.

If you have a large family, it makes sense to have a large food garden. Food plants can grow anywhere outside and inside your home. But to have a healthy food garden you also need to have lots of flowers, herbs, houseplants, and lots of busy bug life.

**Seeds You Might Need for Family Food**

| | | |
|---|---|---|
| beans | corn | peas |
| broccoli | lettuce | tomatoes |
| carrots | melons | |
| celery | onions | |

Or anything else your family likes.

**Caution: Highway Hazards**

People who grow food in cities and suburbs are learning something. Certain vegetables grown near busy streets, highways, and especially superhighways may be dangerous to eat! These vegetables include lettuce, spinach, chard, cabbage, collards, and other leafy greens. Also think twice about eating any plant that grows with the edible part exposed to smoggy air — like broccoli, berries, fruit, and tomatoes.

The danger is due to high amounts of lead and other auto exhausts settling on the plants. Lead can poison people if they consume enough of it.

Be sure anything you do eat from a roadside garden is thoroughly washed before it gets to the table. Use a little vinegar when the smog is really bad.

# What Should You Put into Your Garden?

Once you decide where to put your garden, you'll need to decide what to put into it. You have a lot of choices, enough to make your brain spin, especially if you have lots of garden space.

People have always grown and used plants for all kinds of reasons. People were inventing and making tools, foods, and homes out of plants long before people had "history" to tell about it.

You can grow and use plants that don't grow in most gardens. You can grow chewing gum, sponges, brooms, just about anything you need.

## Some More Questions to Answer

Before you begin to choose plants to put into your garden, you should consider some things.

What size is the garden? How many planting patches? How wide and long is each planting space? Measure it and write the measurements down. What time of year is it? How much time and energy do you have for a garden? Where are the sunny spots in the garden? Shady spots? Windy places? Where are the trees around and in the garden? How big a shadow does each tree cast? How is the soil in the garden area? Is it loose, dark, and crumbly? Or is it hard, cracked, and dry? What grows best in your neighborhood? Do you know the names of the best local varieties of vegetables and flowers? How can you find out? How tall are the plants you want to grow? Seed catalogs usually tell you.

# The Sun and the Seasons

Earth doesn't spin
through space
straight upright.
It tilts.
This tilt is why
we have seasons.

Earth's tilt
causes sunlight
to hit your garden
at a different
angle every day.

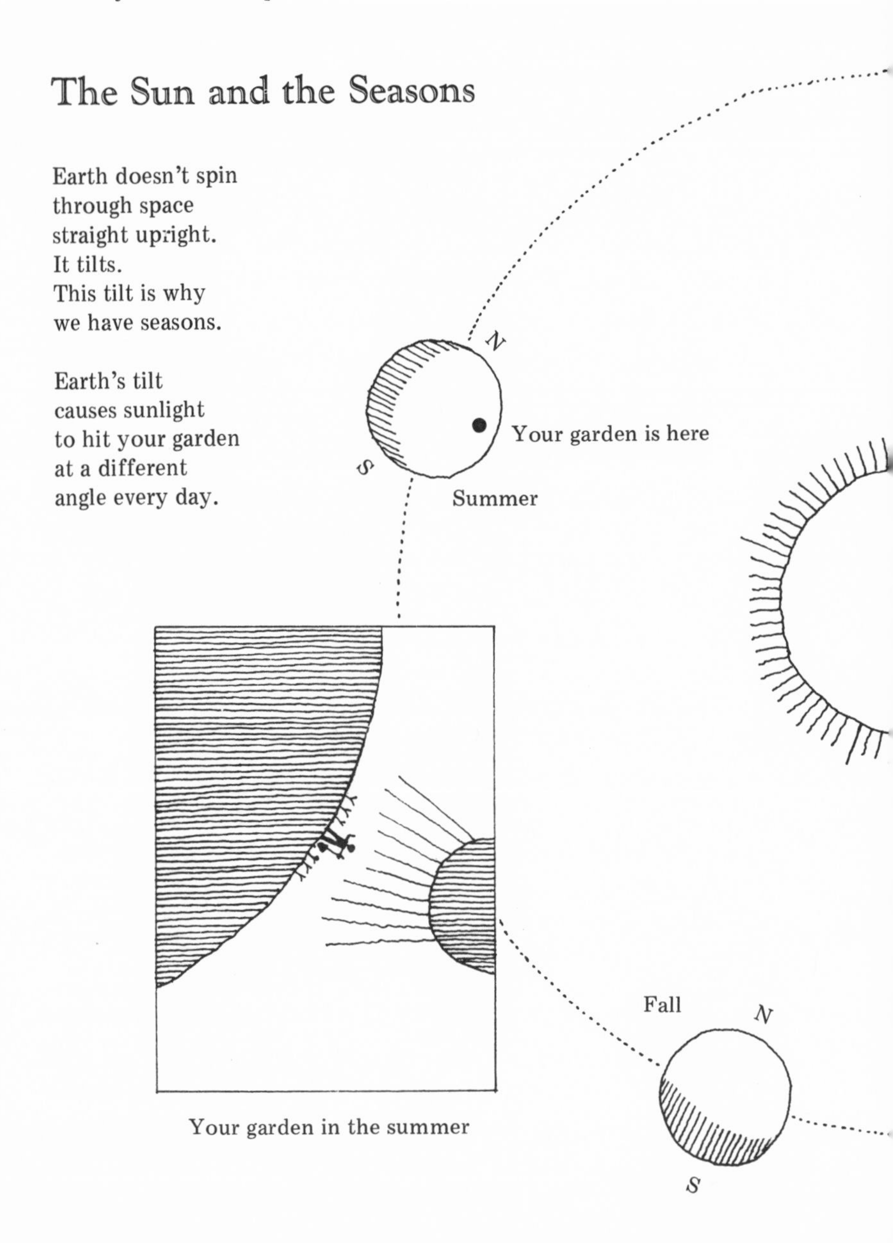


Your garden in the summer

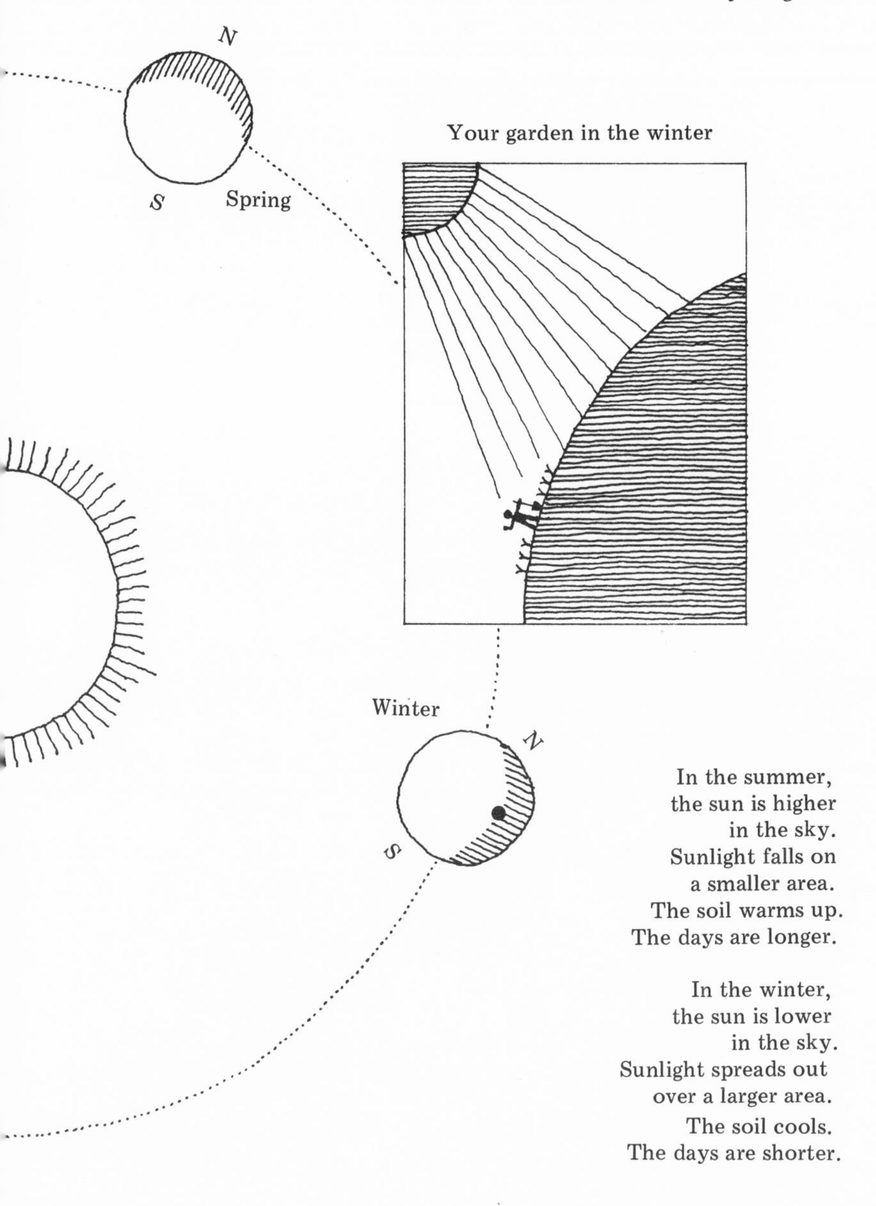


In the summer,
the sun is higher
in the sky.
Sunlight falls on
a smaller area.
The soil warms up.
The days are longer.

In the winter,
the sun is lower
in the sky.
Sunlight spreads out
over a larger area.
The soil cools.
The days are shorter.

## Sunny Spots and Shady Spots

Have you ever stopped to notice how the shadows move across your garden? Do you know what casts the biggest and longest shadows? How do these shadows change from one month to the next?

It will take a while to figure out the sunny spots and shady spots in your garden. They change from season to season. The change is slow, but regular.

You must know where these spots are in your garden, so you can put sun-loving plants in the right place and shade-loving plants where they belong.

## Tall Plants and Small Plants

Sunlight comes from the south much of the year in most North American gardens. Do you know the south side of your garden?

Small plants that need sunlight should grow on the south side, especially in early spring and late fall. Tall plants should grow on the north side. Otherwise a tall plant like corn will overshadow a small plant that needs sunlight later on.

It is usually easy to find out how tall a plant will grow. Most seed packages and seed catalogs tell how tall plants are expected to grow.

Varieties called "bush" or "dwarf" varieties are smaller versions of taller, longer plants. Be sure to check the size of the exact variety you're growing. Some beans are taller than others.

### The Importance of Varieties

Most seed companies list 30 to 40 varieties of tomatoes, 20 or so varieties of corn, countless varieties of roses, dahlias, and other flowers. Why are there so many varieties? Why is there so much choice?

Gardeners always want something new. And when it comes to food plants, they want varieties that produce sooner and longer than others. Plant breeders try to give gardeners the varieties they want.

Picking the right varieties is especially important if you live in a difficult growing area with a short growing season. Read seed catalogs completely and talk to gardeners in your neighborhood before you get seeds.

### Know What Grows Best in Your Area

You will save yourself a lot of trouble and disappointment if you find out which types and varieties of common garden plants grow best in your area. This is especially true for a food or flower garden.

The best gardeners in your neighborhood will probably be very willing to tell you which varieties to get. This is especially important with such vegetables such as: tomatoes, beans, corn, carrots, peppers, peas, melons, and onions.

## Talking with Gardeners in Your Neighborhood

You may not be an outgoing sort of person who can just go up to any door, introduce yourself, and begin talking with someone you don't know.

It's easy for me to introduce myself and talk to people I don't know. I have worked as a reporter and an usher. These are two jobs where you are paid to talk to complete strangers to do your work.

Some people are friendly sometimes. Other people are unfriendly some of the time. Everyone isn't always acting the same way, all the time. Generally people have friendly and unfriendly moods. And you usually can tell when someone is in one or the other mood, just by paying attention.

If you're afraid of talking to gardeners in your neighborhood, pick out one who looks friendly. Then ask about their garden. Usually, most gardeners are flattered to know that somebody notices their garden and appreciates it enough to want to ask questions. Friendly gardeners love to talk about their gardens.

## Beware of Bragging Gardeners

Be careful with information you get from other gardeners. Some people like to brag. Some people like to tell about tomatoes that sound big enough to swim in. Some people stretch and bend the truth without thinking about it.

Don't believe anything until you've heard it from three or four other people. The more folks you talk to, the clearer picture you'll get about what you can and can't do gardening in your neighborhood.

### Don't Be Afraid of Neighbors

If you feel really uncomfortable about talking with total strangers, even though they are your neighbors, try this: go to their door with a good friend. Take a potted plant or something else from your garden that would make a good present. Gardeners usually like it when somebody gives them something new to grow.

## Planning It or Letting It Plan Itself

Planning a garden and writing it all down on paper sometimes may seem like a waste of time, especially if the garden is very small. After all, the garden doesn't grow on paper. It grows on soil. Although planning a garden seems simple, it is important if you want to have a large reliable food garden or a blooming all-year-round garden.

### How to Do a Scale-Sized Garden Layout

Get some lined notebook paper and something to use for measuring: yardstick, ruler, tape measure, meter stick, your elbow, your foot, or your arm.

Measure the spaces you have chosen for your garden. Write down the measurements. Now, which plants do you want to grow and how much room do they need? How many plants can you squeeze into the garden? When you find out, write the position of each plant on a drawing of your garden. Use a pencil so you can erase easily. Do you know about scale-sized drawings? You can make one of your garden easily. Your drawing might look something like the ones on the next three pages.

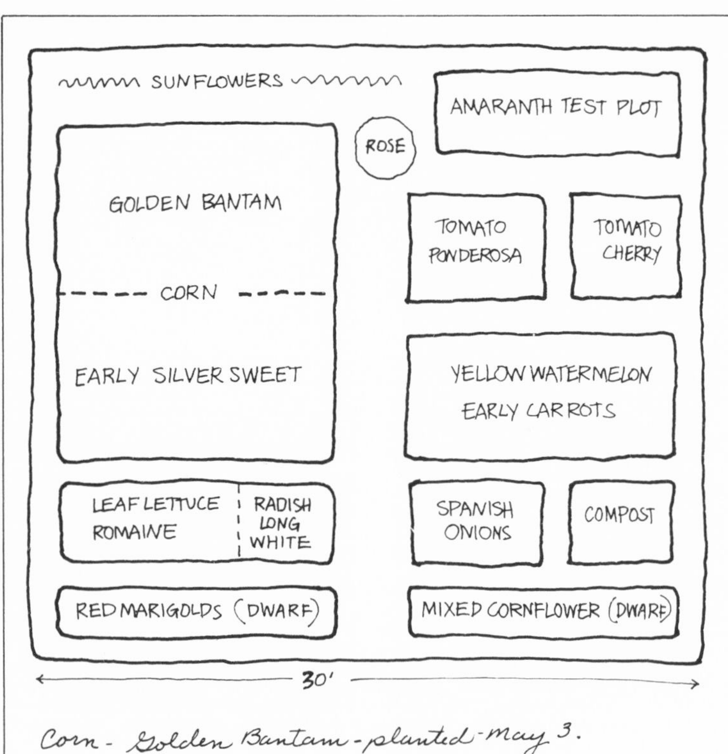


Corn - Golden Bantam - planted - May 3.

Corn - Early Silver Sweet - planted - June 1.

Leaf and Romaine lettuce - planted - March 10.

Radish - Long White - planted - March 10.

Tomato - Ponderosa - planted - June 6.

Cherry tomato - planted - May 21.

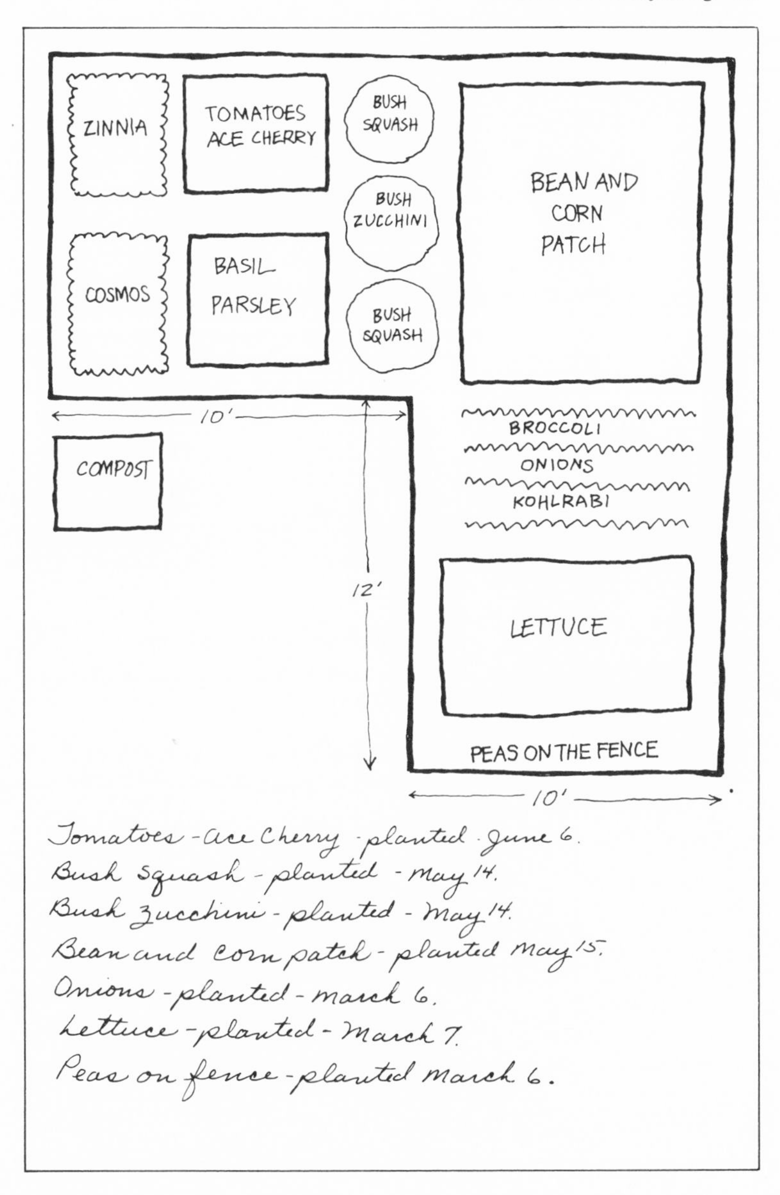
ZINNIA
TOMATOES ACE CHERRY
BUSH SQUASH
BEAN AND CORN PATCH
BUSH ZUCCHINI
COSMOS
BASIL PARSLEY
BUSH SQUASH
10'
BROCCOLI
COMPOST
ONIONS
KOHLRABI
12'
LETTUCE
PEAS ON THE FENCE
10'
Tomatoes - Ace Cherry - planted June 6.
Bush squash - planted - May 14.
Bush zucchini - planted - May 14.
Bean and corn patch - planted May 15.
Onions - planted - march 6.
Lettuce - planted - March 7.
Peas on fence - planted March 6.

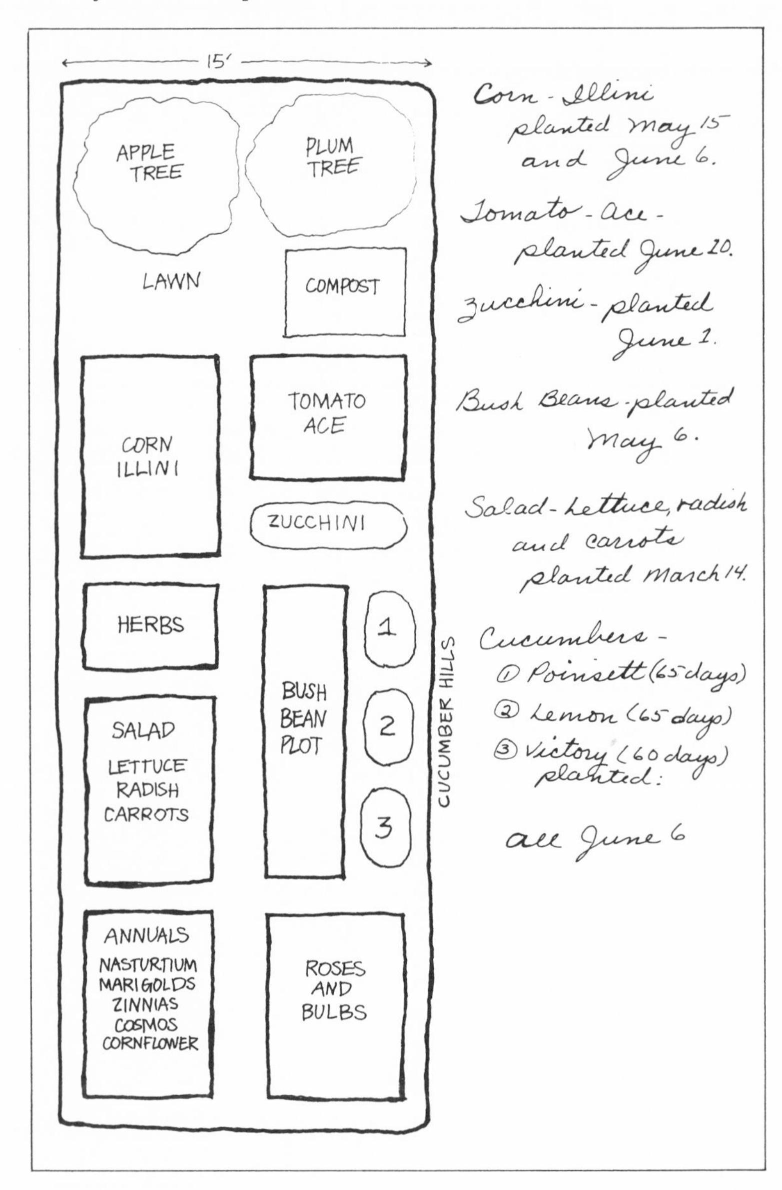
15'
APPLE TREE
PLUM TREE
LAWN
COMPOST
CORN ILLINI
TOMATO ACE
ZUCCHINI
HERBS
BUSH BEAN PLOT
1
2
3
CUCUMBER HILLS
SALAD
LETTUCE
RADISH
CARROTS
ANNUALS
NASTURTIUM
MARIGOLDS
ZINNIAS
COSMOS
CORNFLOWER
ROSES AND BULBS
Corn - Illini planted May 15 and June 6.
Tomato - Ace - planted June 20.
Zucchini - planted June 1.
Bush Beans - planted May 6.
Salad - lettuce, radish and carrots planted March 14.
Cucumbers -
① Poinsett (65 days)
② Lemon (65 days)
③ Victory (60 days)
planted:
all June 6

Measure your garden, then figure that one foot of real garden ground is one inch of ground on the paper plan. One inch of plan equals one foot of garden, in other words. If you want to be very exact, use graph paper.

### Some Things to Consider When Planning Your Garden

What are your seed needs? What do you want to grow? What does everyone else want? Are you sure you know the best varieties to grow in your neighborhood? How long does each variety take to mature? Do you have enough planted to last all season?

Can you put varieties that mature at the same time together in the same planting patch? Do you have enough room to overplant so you can give food and flowers away? Will you have seed ordered and soil ready well ahead of the time to plant?

### Leave Room for Volunteers

On many traditional American farms, the family garden has a special section reserved year after year for "volunteers." These are the herbs, flowers, and vegetables that managed to sprout from last year's garden. These plants clearly say to the gardener: "Don't pull me out!"

Gardeners who let volunteers grow usually have a reserved section for them. Often they are transplanted into this section. Each year the volunteer patch becomes the home of special plants that would otherwise be pulled out. A volunteer patch is almost a weed patch. It doesn't need a lot of attention, just occasional watering. Volunteers can take care of themselves.

How do you know if a volunteer should be saved or pulled up? Watch it grow for a couple of days. It should tell you quite clearly.

Chapter 2

# A Time for Everything

Things seem to move very slowly in a garden. But nothing ever remains the same. Moment to moment. Day after day. Plants, bugs, birds, and animals are alive and growing. Everything moves. Everything changes.

Every plant in your garden has its own time, its own rhythym, its own way of growing. Daffodils come up in spring, not fall. Watermelon is ready to eat in fall, not spring. Corn, beans, sweet alyssum, and other plants must be planted each year. Roses, berries, and fruit trees are planted once in one spot where they come back year after year.

Gardeners must know the right time to dig, plant, water, weed, pick, and replant for anything they decide to grow. They must find out the best time of day, time of month, and time of year to do things. Good timing and care are what keep the garden going.

## Knowing When to Plant What

The toughest problem for most beginning gardeners is knowing when to plant everything. The next problem is actually doing it on time. Planting everything on time — especially food and flowers — is necessary so each plant will grow to its fullest.

It hurts to watch late-planted corn grow for a couple of months, and then begin to grow abnormally when the weather turns suddenly cold. Strange ears of corn come out the top of the plant instead of the side where they belong.

The most active gardens in your neighborhood are planned out months in advance. People who plan their gardens well, usually get everything in on time. And everything comes out on time.

## How to Tell When to Plant Almost Everything

If you want to find out the best times for planting anything, think about these questions first.

How long is your growing season? This is easy to figure out, if you know the usual dates of first and last frosts. In what generation does the plant belong? Plants can be annual, biennial, or perennial. What is the plant's growing season? Some like the "cool season," some like the "warm season." How long does the plant take to reach maturity? Different varieties of the same plant take different times. Is your growing season long enough for the variety of plant you want to grow? When you know what you want to plant, think about these questions. How warm or cool is the soil? Warm season plants won't sprout in cool soil. Is the soil otherwise ready for planting? Weather and moon must be right for digging.

# The Garden's Growing Season

The growing season is the busy time between spring and fall when garden plants grow without danger of freezing on a cold night. Every garden has a different growing season, even gardens that are less than a mile apart.

A long growing season can last from all year to ten months in "frost-free" zones. Places with this long growing season are the Mississippi River delta, the bottom half of Florida, most of coastal Texas, the southern coast of California and the high southwestern deserts.

Most gardens in the United States have a growing season of five to seven months. But if you live in high mountains or cold northern areas, the growing season can be as short as three months. Gardens in these places take lots of care and preparation.

## Four Fast Ways to Find Out

If you want to learn how long your growing season is, ask someone who really knows. There are lots of poeple in any area of the United States who know about the growing season. Some of them are: experienced local gardeners, county agricultural extension agent, garden editor of local newspaper, district conservationist of Soil Conservation Service, nearest U. S. Weather Bureau, local nurseries and farm supply stores, area seed companies, nearby garden centers and public gardens.

Use the Yellow Pages of the phone book to find names and phone numbers of these people in your area. Then call someone and find out.

# The Plant's Growing Season

"Warm season" plants are watermelon, tomatoes, corn, sunflowers, zinnias, cucumbers, cosmos, beans, and on and on. These are planted from early spring to midsummer.

"Cool season" plants are peas, potatoes, onions, broccoli, kohlrabi, daffodils, tulips, and on and on. Cool season plants are planted midsummer to fall and late winter to early spring.

How long a warm season you have depends on many things. One of the most important is how far north you live. The farther north, the colder and less sunny a garden will be.

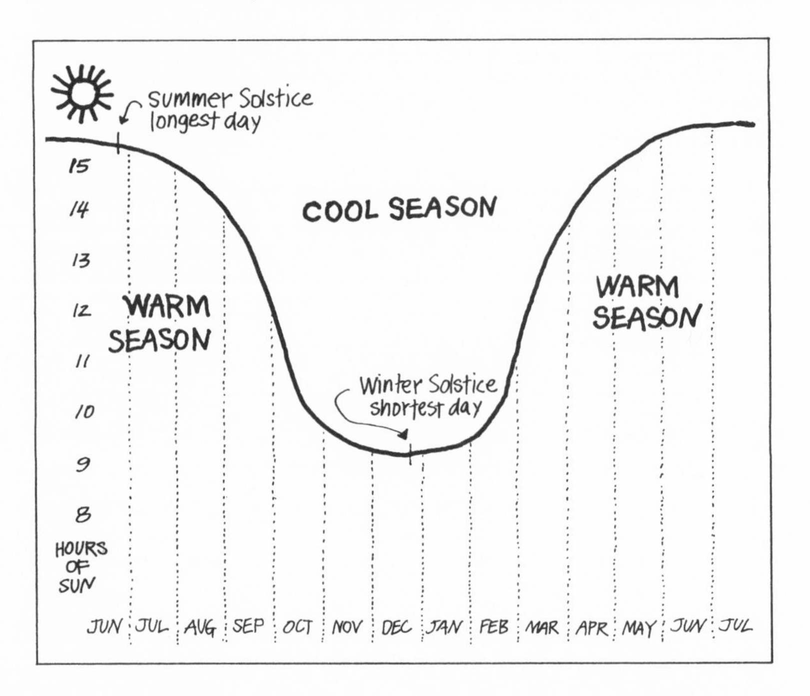

Many garden plants die during the first hard freeze. But a few, like Brussels sprouts and cabbage, love the cold. Plant and bug growth slows in the deepest darkest days of winter; seeds don't sprout. Many plants hibernate like animals.

## When Does the Plant Reach Maturity?

Plants grow up and mature. Just like other living things, including yourself. Maturity is the plant's time to produce flowers, seeds, and fruit.

Different varieties of the very same plant can mature very differently. Early Girl hybrid tomatoes take 54 days to mature. Ponderosa tomatoes take 83 days, or one month longer than Early Girl. Ponderosa would not be a good choice for a garden with a 90-day growing season. Do you know why?

Seed packs and seed catalogs are usually very good at telling how long a plant needs to mature. Vegetable varieties are called "early" if they mature earlier than is normal for that plant. Varieties are "late" if they mature a month or more later.

Knowing the maturity date is especially important for northern gardeners who want to grow melons, peanuts, popcorn, or other warm season plants. Northern gardeners always get early varieties and plant them on time.

## How Warm Is the Soil?

Before they can sprout, seeds need water, air, and time. But most of all, seeds need soil that is the right temperature. The temperature of the soil is how a plant knows if the growing season is right. Warm season plants won't sprout in cool soil. Cool season plants won't sprout well in hot soil.

In spring, the parts of your garden that get more sun will heat up first. Go into the garden at noon on a sunny early spring day. Feel the soil in a spot where the sun hits it. Feel the soil in a shady spot. How much difference is there in the temperatures?

*Note:* When you feel the soil with your hands, dig down a couple of inches. Soils warm up from the top down. If the soil is warm on top but cool an inch down, warm season seeds like corn and beans will wait before sprouting.

### How to Prove a Point about Soil Temperature

In early spring before trees "leaf out," get some seeds for warm season plants like corn, tomatoes, or zinnias. Plant five seeds in a milk carton with holes punched in the bottom and soil filled almost to the top.

Put this planter in a warm window in a heated room inside the house. Keep the soil moist. On the same day, plant ten seeds outside. Five in a sunny spot and five in a shady spot. Keep these spots moist also.

Where did the seeds sprout first? Where did they sprout last, if at all?

## Plant Families and Plant Generations

Plants have families just like people. Usually the shape of a plant's flower tells which family it belongs in. But scientists do not always agree on which plant belongs in what family.

Some families include plants that you wouldn't think could be grouped together. Did you know that bell peppers, potatoes, tomatoes, and eggplant are all in the same family? The nightshade family.

Some families include plants that seem very much alike. Watermelon, cantaloupe, pumpkin, squash, and cucumber are in the same family. The gourd family.

In each family, plants also have generations, just like people. But plant generations are very different from people generations. Some plants never live longer than a year. Some last no longer than two years. Others live many years. These common generations of plants are called annuals, biennials, and perennials.

## Annuals

Annual means yearly. Plants that are annuals will sprout, grow, flower, and make seed all within one growing season. Annuals are like a high school yearbook. They come out once a year.

An annual's most important job is to make its seed, so another generation of plants can live next year. Most, but not all, flowers grown from seed are annuals. Usually the seed pack will tell whether the plant is annual or something else.

These common flowers are annuals:

| | | |
|---|---|---|
| marigold | zinnia | cornflower |
| nasturtium | cosmos | strawflower |
| alyssum | aster | candytuft |
| poppy | sunflower | calendula. |

Some, but certainly not all, vegetables are annuals. Usually they are ones that make seed in one growing season. Sometimes we eat the seeds (corn, popcorn, peanuts, beans, peas, tomato, cucumber). Sometimes we don't eat the seeds (watermelon and apples).

Wildflowers and weeds that scatter their seed each year are annuals.

## Biennials

Biennial plants need two growing seasons to flower and make seed for the next generation.

Often the seeds of biennials are small and hard to get sprouted. The plants also seem to take longer to grow than annuals.

Biennial flowers like hollyhock, carnation, and sweet William are planted late in spring for flowers next year. Others like pansy, forget-me-not, and English daisy are planted in fall for flowers the next year.

Many root vegetables are biennial. These include carrots, turnips, beets, onions, leeks. However, these plants are usually grown as annuals and picked long before they flower. Gardeners do this because the nutrition stored in the root of the plant is used when the plant flowers. A carrot is dry and tough after it flowers instead of big, juicy, and sweet as it should be.

## Perennials

Perennial plants are planted in one place and they usually stay there, year after year. Unless the gardener decides to move them. Sometimes that isn't easy. Trees are perennials. Most berries and fruits (not melons) are perennials. Roses, columbine, iris, many other bushes, shrubs, and flowering plants are perennials. They flower year after year in the same place.

Perennials can be grown from seed, but they are usually started by some other way of propagation. These include hardwood cuttings, softwood cuttings, root division, or layering.

A few vegetables — asparagus, artichoke, rhubarb — are perennials. Balm, mint, and rosemary are perennial herbs. Many of the strongest native plants in your neighborhood are perennials. You should get to know them.

## Be Certain Before Planting

Some varieties of the same plant can belong to different generations. Dahlias are usually perennials, but some varieties are annuals. Asters are usually annuals, but some kinds can be perennials.

How to be sure a plant is annual, biennial or whatever: Check seed pack, check seed catalog, ask whoever gave you the plant, look up the variety in a good garden book, or call someone at a local plant nursery.

## Trees and Time

During your lifetime as a gardener, you will see many plants pop out of the soil, grow to their limits, then die. As a human who is not "annual" or "biennial," you will stand apart from these rhythms of the seasons. You will see many flowers come and go. Your life will move to a different beat.

Trees see and hear a garden in a time and tempo that's like yours. Trees are usually the largest and most influential life forms in your garden. Their shadows are bigger. Their roots spread farther.

Each tree in your garden is someone special. In spring you should congratulate your trees with a bucketful of compost dug into the soil around each tree trunk.

# Time Guides: Almanacs and Daybooks

Many gardeners use a farmer's almanac to help them plan their gardens. An almanac is about time. At first glance, almanacs seem mysterious. But they're not, once you get used to them. Most almanacs have an index and a section telling how to use the book.

All almanacs have a section on gardening. Basically this means vegetable gardening, but they also include information about herbs and some flowers.

Almanacs predict the best days to go fishing, the best and worst days to plant, dates of upcoming eclipses, sunrise and sunset times, moon phases, dates of first and last frost. A current calendar is also included.

This is what a page from your garden daybook might look like:

| variety | where | planted | number | days to mature | due | first harvest | last harvest |
|---|---|---|---|---|---|---|---|
| Carrot • Nantes coreless | B | mid-May | 1 row | 70-75 from seed | Late July | Late July | Mid Sept. |
| | better sprouting under black plastic. Total harvest: HHT HHT HHT IIII | | | | | | |
| Celery • Utah green | S | June 21 | 1 hill | 120-130 from planting | late Oct. | Following spring | |
| | slow but steady. loves lotsa mucky soil volunteers nicely Total harvest: HHT | | | | | | |
| Corn . Golden cross Bantam | B<br>B | May 4<br>May 15 | 1 row of 7<br>1 row of 9 | 82 from seed | July 30 to Aug. 10 | Aug. 10 | Aug. 30 |
| | July 1 - tasseling / July 15 - silks Golden cross wastes space - only 2 ears But IT IS SWEET !! CORN. WOW. Harvest: HHT HHT HHT HHT HHT HHT | | | | | | |
| Corn • Country Gentleman | B<br>B<br>B | May 15<br>June 15<br>July 1 | 1 row of 8<br>2 hills of 5+6<br>2 rows of 7 | 92 from seed | Aug. 15 to Sept. 14 | yellow Aug. 30 | late Sept. |
| | Didn't do well - picked too early. Row 7 - on the east side of the fence - slow growers. Harvest: HHT HHT | | | | | | |
| Cucumber . Spartan Valor | B | June 1 | 2 plants | 58 from seed | July 31 | July 23 | mid-Sept. |
| | not enough water Harvest: HHT II | | | | | | |

There are several national almanacs. Check a newsstand in the fall to find the one you like. They cost about 75 cents. Or go to the library and ask to see one.

When you have a large garden, it's easy to forget what you did last week or what you should be doing next week or exactly where and when you planted those Kentucky Wonder beans.

A good way to remember everything you do in your garden is to write it down the day you do it. Keep a garden daybook, diary, journal, notebook, scrapbook, or any other book that is easy for you to write in.

Once you have the book, you'll figure out a good way to organize it. You might want to have space to write something every day, like a diary with the dates printed in it. Or you might want to reserve pages for each plant you try to grow. Pictures you draw, take with a camera, or cut out of seed catalogs can be included.

In your daybook, you should keep track of these facts: when you planted everything, where you planted it, what variety you planted, where you got the seeds or plant, how long the plant needs to grow to maturity, and when you should expect to pick it.

## Year after Year

Don't plant a whole lot of one plant in one place year after year. Do you know why?

When bugs have had a good year feasting on one kind of plant, they lay more eggs for next year. If the same plant is there in large numbers again next year, the bugs will have a feast. And they'll lay more and more eggs for the following year.

This will go on for a few years until there are so many bugs waiting to eat that the big colony of plants won't stand a chance. The bugs will destroy the entire planting. Most of the big farmers in the world have learned this lesson the hard way. If you keep growing the same plant year after year in the same spot, you will someday doom the plants to an insect invasion.

The way to prevent this kind of insect invasion: Put in a different kind of plant each time you replant any part of your garden.

## Chapter 3

# Down to Earth

The entire earth is a garden, a natural garden, especially when you look at it from near space: warm land, water, clouds, and air. It all takes care of itself. Certainly the earth is more of a garden than the moon or Mercury or Mars. Those places are dry and full of holes.

Parts of the earth may not seem like a garden: many cities, for example, or highways, or lands ruined by wasteful digging. But these parts are small compared with the vast jungles, prairies, marshes, mountains, and other natural gardens all across the earth.

When you are in a city, it may seem like a lot of land is being wasted under concrete. But when you see a picture of earth from near space, you see oceans, trees, and open land first. Most of the earth really is a garden.

The most important part of any garden is the soil. This chapter and the next tell how you can make your own soil out of what other people throw away.

# The Story of Soil

Understanding soil is difficult because you usually only see the top of it. Most of what happens in soil happens underground, out of sight. This is where the roots go. This is where all the soil life lives.

Soil scientists who look at it under a microscope don't completely understand soil. That's why they study it. To learn more about how it all fits together to support the life within it and on top of it.

One thing is certain about soil. Different plants need different types of soil. As a gardener, you must know the kind of soil each plant needs.

### The Main Ingredients of Soil

*Minerals* (nitrogen, phosphorus, potash) and trace elements from underlying rock and the air.
*Humus* from dead and decaying plant and animal parts.
*Air* that can move freely through small open pores in soil.
*Water* and moisture to plants in amounts they need.

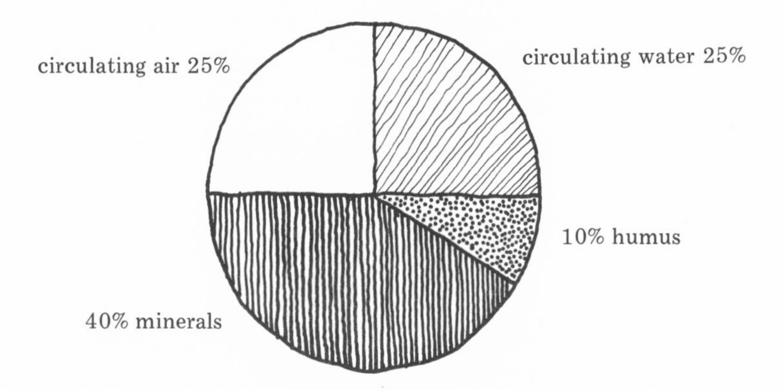

## Mountains

What does a rocky spine of mountains have to do with the story of soil? Everything! This is where the story begins because this is where the soil begins.

Look at the landslide at the base of the mountain. What do you notice about it? Why are most of the big rocks and boulders at the bottom of the landslide? Why are the smaller fine pieces of silt and minerals on the top? Why are plants growing on top of the landslide but not on the bottom?

Seems simple, doesn't it? The big rocks broke off the mountain. Gravity pulled the heavier ones down the mountain side. Silt and small pieces of rock don't weigh so much and they don't slide as far.

## Landslides

Any time you dig a large amount of dirt, you can see this landslide action as you toss dirt into the pile. Big pieces end up on the bottom. Silt stays on top. If you look around, you'll see landslides in every pile of dirt.

*The trouble with clay:* It sticks together so roots and water can't get through.

*The trouble with sand:* It doesn't stick together so water drops right through, slipping past dry roots, and the plants are starved for water.

*The trouble with loam:* There's never enough!

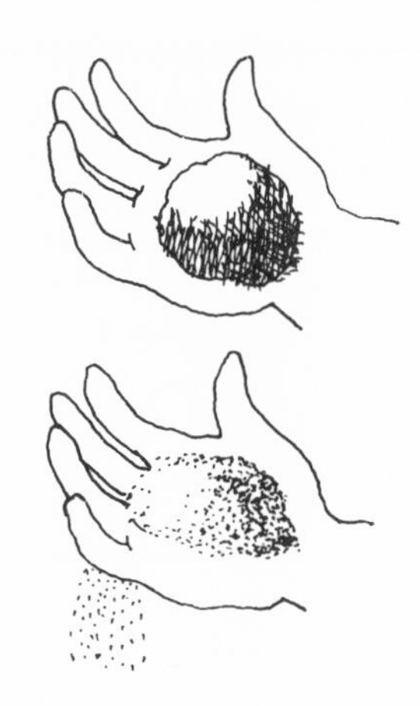

## How to Tell a Native Soil

Trees are usually the largest and most telling plants in any area. Big forests of trees tell what soil is native to a place. Trees also drop billions of leaves onto the soil each fall. The leaves turn into humus that is balanced in favor of the tree. The tree feeds the soil and the soil feeds the tree.

Many soils in the United States were once hidden under thick forests that were cleared out by early settlers and farmers. This is the nature of many soils in the northeast, southern, and midwest states.

But soils change over time, depending on what else grows there or doesn't grow there. Some soils on large farmlands have been drained of their life because the farmers did nothing to replace the humus-building cycle of fallen leaves that happened under the forests.

The earth is not quite 8,000 miles thick. The earth's atmosphere is about 20,000 miles high to its thinnest reaches.

But all life on earth is found in the thin eggshell layer of soil, water, and air at the surface of the planet. This layer is known as the biosphere. It is the shallow zone of earth with all the life in it and all the creatures in it.

Like an eggshell, the biosphere is very thin. But it isn't as thin as the layer of topsoil which covers the one-fifth of earth that isn't under water, pavement, or floors. Topsoil can be as deep as five feet in some fortunate places. Elsewhere topsoil can be shallower than one inch.

No matter how deep it is, this layer of soil is what most creatures in the biosphere (including you and me) need to make our daily living.

Your garden is in this thin eggshell zone of the biosphere. Anything you do to improve the texture, circulation, drainage, fertility, and smell of your soil will also improve life in the biosphere.

## Bringing Good Soil into Your Garden

If you want a big and busy garden, it will take a big and busy effort to get good soil into it for the first two or three years. Especially if the land has been misused or mistreated.

### Soil Is Not Dirt

Just any old dirt will not suit most garden plants. Soil (not dirt) is what every gardener wants. Soil is the stuff of life! Dirt is perfect for weeds, native plants, and other hardy plants. But dirt won't grow most of the tender food and flowering plants. Soil will.

## Soil Is Not Cheap

Good garden soil does not come without effort. In the beginning, a lot of shoveling, tossing, hauling, and moving of heavy rock minerals, composts, and manures. When people talk about the "work" involved in gardening, this is usually the part they are talking about.

## A Spoonful of Soil and a Planetload of Bugs

All fertile soil is full of tiny life forms you can't see, unless you use a microscope. Even then, you can't see all the small and strange bugs, plants, and animals that live in the soil. These animals and plants are called microorganisms or microbes.

One spoonful of healthy soil contains at least 100,000 protozoa, 30,000,000 fungi, and 2,000,000,000 bacteria. More or less. That's a lot of "life" in one little spoon. In fact, there are more microbes in two spoonfuls of soil than there are people on earth.

Although you can't see them, you must realize that these microbes are necessary for any good garden soil. The best way to get these life forms into your soil is to use compost and manure.

## Humus Condition: Decaying but Not Dead

Humus is the decaying parts of plants and animals that have already lived their lives. Now they are giving themselves back to the soil, in the form of humus.

Humus returns old life to the soil so that new life can follow. This is the way plants and animals put back into the earth what they took out.

Any soil has some amount of humus in it. How much depends on its location. You'll find very little humus on a desert or mountain peak. But you'll find a lot of it on a forest floor covered with leaves or in good garden soil.

A good gardener always looks for fresh sources of humus. Here's where to find some:

fallen leaves from nearby trees
every dead plant and leaf in your garden
scraps of fruit, vegetables, and other real food
clippings from the lawn
sawdust from home, neighbors, lumberyards
hay and straw from stables and farms
aged manure and stable sweepings.

## How to Make a Heap of Compost

The food that your family doesn't eat at any meal is still good food — food for your garden. Don't throw away fruit peelings, vegetable parts, plate scraps, or any other real food that would otherwise be tossed in the garbage. Save them for your compost heap. And keep the heap covered.

Compost is decomposing plant and animal remains from the garden and kitchen. When a compost heap has finished decomposing, you will have the perfect fertilizer for dressing your topsoil. And every bit of it is free and homemade.

Every day, usually after dinner, take out kitchen scraps to the heap. Also add lawn clippings, weeds, and the unused parts of plants.

A corner of your garden should be set aside for your compost heap. You can build a bin or box. Or you can dig a pit. Or you can just pile it up and cover it. Anyway you look at it, it's a heap of compost.

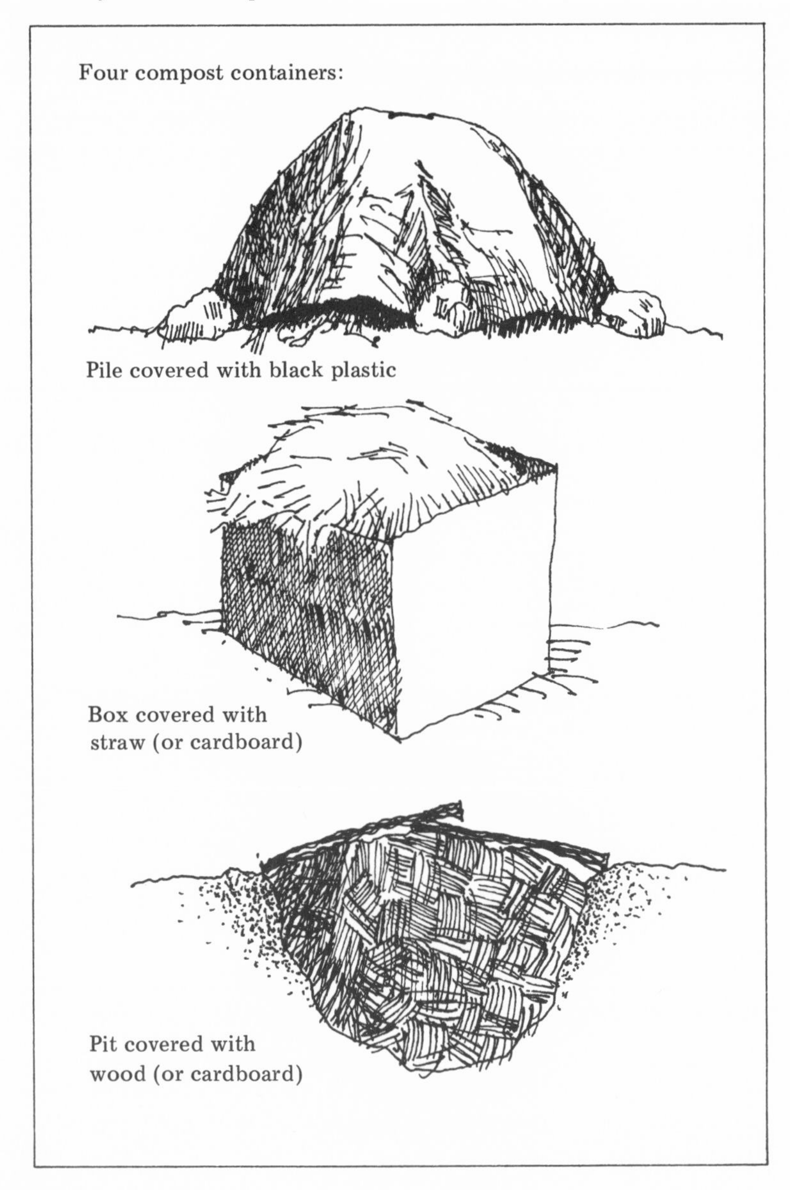
Four compost containers:
Pile covered with black plastic
Box covered with
straw (or cardboard)
Pit covered with
wood (or cardboard)

Always keep compost covered. Use straw, lawn clippings, tired soil, or some other layer of humus building material. This looks better and reduces smells. And it keeps flies away.

Don't add a lot of artificially flavored "foods" into your compost heap if you can help it. These products contain chemicals that don't belong in your garden. Throw this stuff into the garbage where it belongs!

## A Secret of Fast Compost

A compost heap must heat up to do its work and break down everything into a form that can fertilize plants. Compost naturally heats up in the spring and again in fall when microbes are most active in the heap. Make sure you have compost collected and piled at least three feet high (or deep) during spring and fall.

To help speed up the heating action in compost, add a high-protein, high-nitrogen fertilizer to the heap. Some of these fertilizers are: fresh manures, bone meal, blood meal, soybean meal, alfalfa meal, cottonseed meal, and fish scraps.

## Earthworms in the Compost

Earthworms are also very helpful in compost production. They help break down the garbage as they tunnel through it. And they add their castings to the whole heap.

Before you fill your compost heap, break the soil underneath it so the worms can easily climb into the pile and get to work. If your soil or compost heap doesn't have enough worms, find some, in vacant lots and weed patches, under boards and flat things, in soil around manure piles at stables, at a bait shop.

### City Compost

If you live in the city, you can also make compost. But you should take extra care in keeping it covered. So it doesn't draw flies or rats and offend neighbors.

Some city people use large garbage cans with tight-fitting lids for composting. They add fallen leaves, other old parts of plants, vegetable scraps, and any other decaying vegetation they can find. Others add soil, earthworms, old compost. They always keep it covered.

Also they must turn the compost often (at least once a week). Adding blood meal, bone meal, or some other fast-compost fertilizer helps. Meat and fish scraps attract dogs and cats. Many people won't add these to compost but throw them in the garbage instead. Just be sure to put this compost can in a place where the garbage men won't pick it up.

## Don't Be Afraid of Manure

Growing food and other plants in soil mixed with manure may seem awful to some people, but manure can be found in garden and farm soils all across the earth. To many farmers and gardeners, manure is more precious than gold.

Manure is just another word for dung, feces, excreta, excrement, guano, droppings, or "wastes." Whatever you call it, it's a great fertilizer for the soil.

Some common complaints about manure are: it smells bad, it's messy, it's hard to handle.

However, it only smells bad when it's very fresh, but not after it has begun to air out, decompose, and turn into aged, composted manure. Use a pitchfork or pointed shovel for more ease in handling. Choose only manures that are old. They're lighter, cooler, and less sticky.

### Fresh Manure and Aged Manure

Manure may be hard to find in some places. Use the phone book to find stables, dairies, ranches, farms, zoos. Or other places you think should have manure because they have animals.

Once you find a source for it, you will probably have two kinds of manure to choose from.

Fresh manure is hot! Reach into the pile with a shovel and see. It is hot because the microbes are busy. Put it in topsoil and fresh manure will burn seedlings. But dig it into a deep layer of subsoil and fresh manure will warm up the soil so seeds sprout earlier.

Aged manure is old manure that has cooled off. It can be worked right into the soil.

How can you tell the difference between aged and fresh manure? Piles of fresh manure will be higher, heavier, wetter, and smellier than aged manure. Before you load up any kind of manure, poke around the piles. If you want to use it right away, get aged manure. If you are going to wait before you dig, get fresh manure.

### Green Manure

Wise farmers don't let a field sit empty during the fall and winter. Instead, they plant "green manure" crops following the regular summer crops.

This is not "manure" like animal manure. Green manure is plants. A green manure crop is not grown to be picked. It is grown so it can be turned under the soil in spring. Farmers use only certain plants for green manuring. They know that these plants will improve the soil.

Some gardeners, especially those who want big food gardens, use green manure, too. Here are some plants used for green manure: fava beans, crown vetch, clovers, rye, alfalfa, soybeans, mung beans, oats, buckwheat, and peas.

## Balanced Soils: Three Main Nutrients

People and animals need a balanced diet for good health. Garden plants need a balance in their diet too.

### Nitrogen

*What it does for plants.* Provides energy for fast growth, makes dark-green leaves, forms strong healthy stems.

*How to bring it into the garden.* Grow legumes (peas, beans, peanuts). Also, grow clovers and vetch. Dig in compost, manures, stable sweepings, sewage sludge, blood meal, bone meal, cottonseed meal, chicken feather meal, fish scraps.

### Phosphorus

*What it does for plants.* Speeds overall growth, helps root growth, makes more blossoms, matures seeds.

*How to bring it into the garden.* Dig in compost, stable sweepings, raw phosphate rock, colloidal phosphate rock, bone meal.

### Potassium

*What it does for plants.* Helps overall health and strength, aids forming of plant sugars, protects from dry and cold.

*How to bring it into the garden.* Dig in compost, stable sweepings, hardwood ashes, green sand, granite dust, cottonseed meal, fish scraps. Also grow alfalfa as green manure.

## Two Sides of the pH Scale

Soils on earth range from ones that are highly alkaline to those that are highly acid. Alkaline soil is bitter like baking soda. Acid soil is sour like a grapefruit.

Highly alkaline soils are usually found in dry salty desert areas. Most of the high-altitude deserts of the West have alkaline soils.

Highly acid soils can be found under evergreen forests. Most of the soils east of the Great Plains are moderately acid. These include soils of the Central Prairies (Iowa, Missouri, Arkansas, Oklahoma), the South, the Midwest, and New England. But not all soils in these areas are acid.

A soil is acid or alkaline depending on: the chemical nature of the native rocks that made most of the soil, the types of trees that grow there, and the kinds of plants that live and die on the soil. The best garden soil isn't too acid or too alkaline, but somewhere in between.

### How Can You Tell If Your Soil Is Acid or Alkaline?

You can make a pH test of the soil. Cheap and expensive pH test kits are available at nurseries and garden supply stores. Or you can mail order them through seed catalogs.

Or you can do a simple pH test yourself. The scale used to determine pH in soil is the same one used to tell pH in other things like vinegar and baking soda. Most food and flowering plants like a soil with pH 6.5 to 7.0, or very slightly acid soil.

### A Measure of More

Soil is not the only thing measured for pH level. Blood, tomatoes, ammonia, soda all have pH levels that can be measured. So do lots of other things.

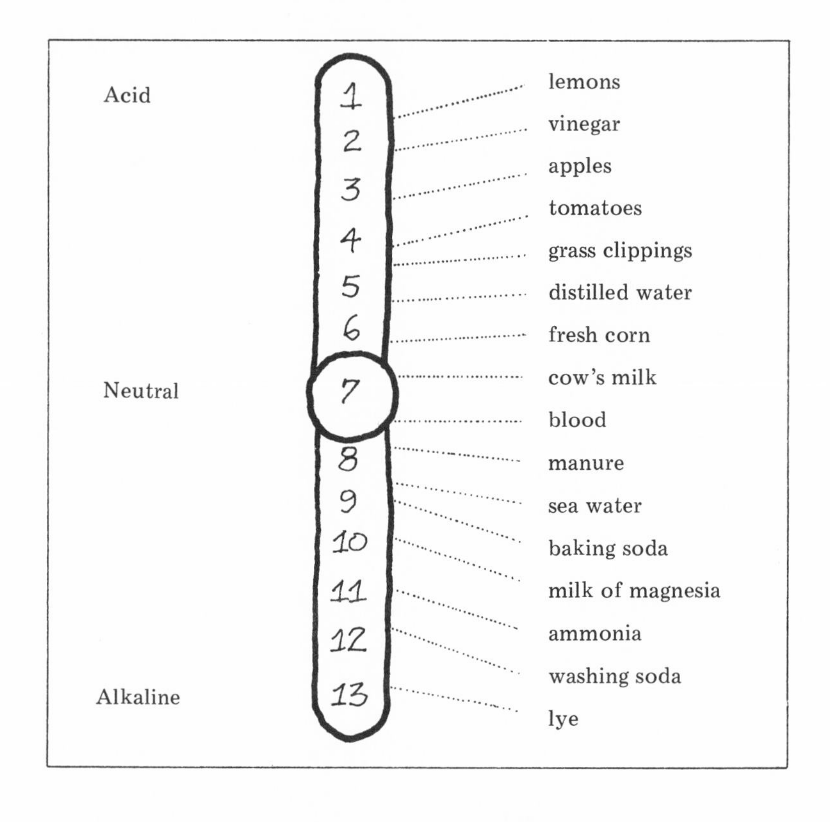

# How to Do a Quick pH Test

Have you ever used litmus paper in school? Go to a drugstore and ask for some. Litmus paper is good for doing a quick pH test of your soil.

*Here's how to do the test:* Wash your hands before you start. Go to garden and pick spot you want to test. Take a spoonful of soil from the top seven inches of soil, all mixed together. Do not take soil from the very top of the bed because it is richer than soils below. Mix topsoil with all soil down to seven inches.

Grind up soil into a clean glass jar. Add water to make wet mixture. Put litmus paper into mixture and wait half a minute. Then pull out paper and rinse it in clear water.

If paper turns pink right away, your soil is very acid. The pinker it gets, the more acid it has. If it turns blue, your soil is alkaline. If paper is neither pink nor blue, your soil is neutral. This is a rough method. If you want exact pH results, order a pH kit from a seed catalog or nursery.

### The Old Farmer's Taste Test

What's the quickest way to tell if you have good soil? Pick up a handful and taste it. That's right! Just put a bit of soil gently on your tongue and see how it tastes. Is it sweet? Is it bitter? Or sour? This is how farmers used to tell if their soil was good enough for vegetables, grains, and other food crops. Some farmers still taste test their soil.

How does your soil taste? If it's too bitter like salt or soda, your soil is too alkaline. If it's too sour like lemons, your soil is too acid. If the soil is sweet, it's just right! A farmer knows that very bitter and very sour soils don't taste good to plants either.

## Find Out First: Who Needs Poor Soil?

Not all plants need manured, composted, trenched, and pulverized soil. Nasturtiums prefer poor clay soils. Alpine plants like rocky soils where carrots and cantaloupe wouldn't last a day.

Find out first what kind of soil the plant needs before you dig and prepare the soil for it.

Chapter 4

# Getting Help and Doing It Yourself

Throughout this book I am expecting that you are smart enough to start a garden by yourself without a lot of help from grownups and busybodies. But sometimes you'll need help. Every gardener needs help sometimes.

Gardeners need help shoveling manure, hauling mulch, digging, hoeing, or watering early on hot days. The list will be as long as your ambitions.

This chapter is about what kinds of help you might need. And when, how, and who to ask for it. You will know those times when you need help in your garden. If you don't know when they are, then you probably don't need help.

| *Things You'll Need Help With:* | *People Who Might Help:* |
| --- | --- |
| finding information about plants, bugs, weather, anything | plant nurseries<br>libraries<br>seed companies<br>other gardeners<br>government agencies |
| digging soil and other heavy-duty work | your family<br>relatives<br>friends<br>acquaintances<br>anyone else |
| transportation for hauling manures, fertilizers | your parents<br>relatives<br>friends who can drive<br>anyone who'll barter with you |
| finding tools for digging and pruning | other gardeners<br>parents<br>relatives |
| money for seeds, supplies. | anyone who'll barter with you. |

## Who and When to Ask for Help

With some people, asking for help can be tricky; with others, it's easy. It depends on who you're asking. Some people naturally like to help. Others wouldn't help you if you paid them in milkshakes.

The trickiest part is knowing when to ask. If your dad has just broken the windshield trying to repair a tire, it's a bad time to ask him to drive you somewhere, right? Wait until the best time to ask for favors. Even if it means putting off the work you have to do.

# Help at Home

Are your parents shocked by supermarket prices? Do they talk about ways to save money on food bills? If they do, they might be willing to help you with a food garden. This includes help with finding seeds, supplies, tools, and manures. Help with hauling and lugging fertilizers around. Help with paying for things. Help with planning.

It's also helpful to know someone who has a pickup truck or some old station wagon for hauling loads of manure, stable sweepings, and stuff.

## How to Decide What to Plant

This year our family tried a new way of planning our vegetable garden. I made a book with cut-out pictures of all the fruits and vegetables I know how to grow.

Then I got out a box of colored stick-on stars. Everybody in the family picked a favorite colored star.

Everyone voted for their favorites as I turned the pages and we marked them with stars. In the end, the fruits and vegetables with the most stars were the ones I planted.

## Barter for Help

Before people invented money as a way to get things they wanted, they used something called "bartering" or the "barter" system. Barter is just a half-dollar word for trade. When an acquaintance or someone you don't know helps with your garden, offer something in return. Offer to help them with something anytime. Or give them something from your garden.

Your garden can produce many fruits, vegetables, cut flowers, house plants, and things that are valuable to many people. When you plant anything, put in extra for bartering.

## Have an All-Day Help Party

The fastest way to do a big job is to invite lots of people over to help. This is how many of America's frontier homes and old barns were built. Everybody helped with the work, ate well, had a good time, and partied into the night.

You can have an all-day help party if you need assistance in digging the soil, hauling fertilizers, planting and transplanting, or anything else you need people to help with.

I have friends who put in last year's garden this way. We had a party last spring when we put up our greenhouse. If it's warm enough, you can barbeque or enjoy an outdoor supper after the day's work is done.

### Two or Three Things to Remember About Help

When someone helps you it is nice to return the favor. Give them a gift and offer to help them when they need it. Also you could give them flowers or food from your own garden to show how much you appreciate their help.

Don't disappoint yourself by counting too much on anyone to help you after they said they would. Sometimes people can't help because their plans change. Don't complain to them and say, "But you promised!. . ."

Know how to tell people thanks when you realize they're doing more harm than help. Politely send them home. Then finish the work yourself.

## Six Ways to Help Yourself

When no one around home or anywhere else wants to help you — you can still help yourself. Here are six ways to help yourself and your neighborhood.

### Recycling before Recycling

Maybe your town has a recycling center where you can take glass, aluminum, tin, paper, and other things form your garbage. The recycling center sends the separated stuff back to the separate manufacturers who need it. Aluminum and glass goes back to the bottle and can manufacturers, for example.

Good gardeners are good recyclers. They recycle everything that can be used in the garden. They seldom return a bottle, can, or other container to the recycling center unless it is totally used up. That means broken bottles and rusted cans.

Here are the things I recycle at home: coffee cans with plastic tops, small glass jars and containers, cardboard milk cartons, plastic bags, old kitchen utensils.

### Weed Watch

In spring and fall when people are clearing out weeds from their yards and vacant places, you will have another good source of compost.

If you ask for those weeds, your neighbors will probably give them to you gladly. In fact, they might even have more weeds for you. But you might have to pull them out yourself. If you see weeds piled up outside someone's house, don't take them without asking. They might be saving the pile for their own compost or someone else's.

### Neighborhood Leaf Mold

In autumn, in many towns and cities with elms, maples, oaks, and other big trees, people always have a problem. You can help them with it.

Their problem is falling leaves. First there's the problem of raking them up. Most people are willing to do this themselves, usually because they think leaves look ugly all over the place. But the next problem people have with leaves — getting rid of them — really shouldn't be a problem.

Gardeners know that leaves make the best compost. Any compost pile in the fall should have lots of leaves mixed through it. You can get as many leaves as you need by going around the neighborhood when you see them piled up. Just ask people if they'd mind if you took the leaves for your garden.

Besides putting leaves in compost, you can also pile them up and enclose them with chicken wire or some other covering. Let them sit until spring. Then you'll have another kind of garden gold: leaf mold.

### Supermarket Scrap Hunt

Go with your parents the next time they go shopping for food. But instead of looking for food, look for garbage. Ask the manager of the store or supermarket employees if they have any "spoiled" vegetables, fruits, or otherwise unwanted produce. Tell them you are a gardener and you want the garbage for your compost heap. If they don't understand, you might have to explain compost to them.

Usually supermarkets throw out lots of spoiled vegetables and fruits from their produce departments. You can find it boxed up in trash bins at the rear of the store. Try to pick ones that aren't smelly. Put them in the trunk of the car.

When your parents go home you can take home fresh garbage for your compost.

### One-Kid Compost Collective

Most of the people in your neighborhood probably don't save the daily food scraps from their kitchen. They probably throw this valuable stuff in the garbage. The same goes for lawn clippings, trimmings from plants, and weeds that people in your neighborhood think are a waste problem.

You can help these people and yourself if you collect and compost their kitchen scraps and other plant "wastes." Tell them you'll take this garbage off their hands. Start a compost collection service.

Ask people to save kitchen garbage after every meal. Tell them to keep scraps in an old milk carton, a plastic bag, or some other container. Be sure to pick up the container every night after dinner, so they won't be bothered by food scraps in the kitchen. Keep the scraps covered as soon as you put them into the heap. Otherwise they'll get smelly and draw flies.

Do this in spring or fall for about a month. Or as long as you need to build up a big compost heap.

### Roadside Produce Stand

If you have a big vegetable garden with lots of room you might be able to open a small produce stand in front of your house. You can sell any surplus food that you can't use at home or give away.

This will be easier if you live on a busy street. Make big signs so people can see them from cars. Open up your stand in the evening when people are returning home from work.

Some towns might have laws against kids selling garden produce. Call city hall or the county courthouse and find out before you set up your stand.

Also, before you sell anything you should check the prices of produce at the supermarket so you know how much things cost, then, sell yours for less than the store. That way, people won't be able to pass up your bargain: fresher food at a lower cost.

## Your Garden Doesn't Have to Cost Much

You could walk into a garden supply store or large nursery with a handful of hundred-dollar bills and you could spend it all there in that spot.

Greenhouses, greenhouse supplies, ready-made cold frames, plant starter kits, weed-killing devices, thermometers for the soil, thermometers for the air, thermometers for the water, growing lights, fancy sprinklers, baskets, pots, nets — everything — and it all costs money.

You can make just about everything you need for a garden out of scraps and other things people throw away. So don't worry if you can't afford to buy something. Figure out how to make it yourself, or make a trade with someone else for it.

### Necessities Free or Cheap

*Tools.* Make your own. Use other things for tools. Trade something for good used tools. Look for tools and tool scraps at the dump.

*Seeds.* Other gardeners might give them away. Maybe your parents would consider vegetable seeds a food expense.

*Plants.* Other gardeners may give you cuttings and small plants if you ask. Nurseries often throw out plants that can be rescued like wounded birds. Check the nursery's garbage bins.

*Pots and planters.* Save milk cartons, cans, or other containers around the house. Make sure they have drain holes. Thrift stores may have used pots.

*Fertilizers.* Make compost. Get manure.

## Join a Community Garden

In the last few years large gardens have been started in vacant lots of many towns and cities. These gardens have been called "community gardens" because people from a neighborhood share the garden.

Some of these gardens will let kids join. Some won't. The trouble is finding a community garden before everybody else joins and takes all the space.

What is the best way to find a community garden near you? Use the Yellow Pages of the phone book to find these numbers, then call one.

City hall
Park and recreation department
Garden editor of local newspaper
School board
Local library
Nurseries and garden supply centers

## Part Two

# The Whole Blooming Thing

Chapter 5

# Doing the Digging

The people who first gardened and farmed the earth realized that many fruits, vegetables, and other useful plants grew best in soils that were loose and light. People understood that by digging and cultivating, they could make loose, light soil.

But to dig the earth, people need tools. When people needed a tool in those days, they usually made it themselves from things they could find around, like rocks, sticks, horns, and bones from animals.

This chapter will help you figure out how to find, make, and use tools that fit you. Then we will discuss when to dig, when not to dig, and when to rest with the soil.

You'll probably have a hard time finding garden tools made to suit you. Tools sold in garden supply centers will probably be too long, too heavy, or too expensive for you. Unfortunately, the best digging tools usually cost the most. A well-made rake and shovel can cost $30. What should you do?

*If they're too long.* Cut down the handles to a size that feels comfortable. But don't get carried away! Next year you may need those extra six inches of handle if your body is still changing and getting longer. Anyway, as a regular-sized grownup, I think most garden tool handles are too short.

*If they're too heavy and too expensive.* Find old tools and rebuild them. This is simpler than it seems. Or make your own. What do you think the first farmers and gardeners did centuries ago? They certainly couldn't buy them at a store!

## Four Basic Tools

The first farmers and gardeners made their tools out of animal horns, bones, rawhide, sticks, and anything else that was nearby and served a useful purpose. These tools were free but they didn't last forever. Ancient gardeners always knew where they could get a new tool when they needed one.

You probably won't find many animal bones and horns around. But you can still make your own tools by using parts of old tools and machines that you can find thrown away in your town.

This certainly makes more sense than spending a lot of money for tools that don't fit you. There are four basic tools you'll need to start and maintain an outdoor garden.

*Dibber*

A planting stick for poking holes in topsoil for seeds; a transplanting stick for putting soil gently around roots.

*Rakes*

Bow rake for leveling and loosening topsoil, removing rocks, improving texture.

Yard rake for sweeping up leaves and other yard messes for composting.

*Hoe*

For opening up topsoil, breaking up soil clumps, weeding.

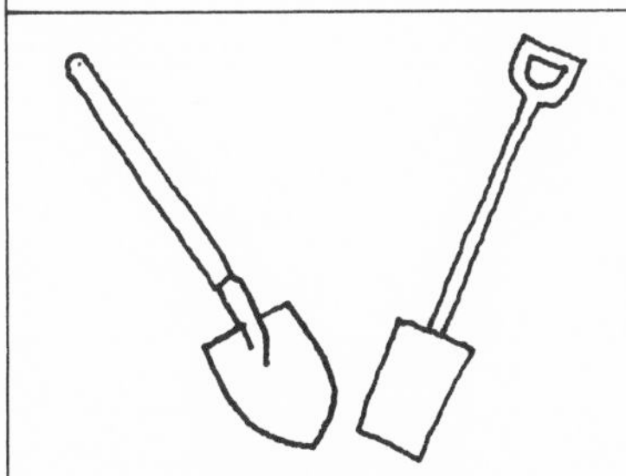

*Shovel or Spade*

For deep digging or double digging and for moving large amounts of soil.

| | | |
|---|---|---|
| *Dibber* | Any old stick that was around. They whittled end into a point. | Pencil<br>Popsicle stick<br>Tinker toy stick<br>Corn dog stick<br>Chopstick<br>Any other six-to twelve-inch long stick |
| *Rake* | Tied reeds to stick with rawhide for broom rake.<br><br>Tied antlers or other horns to stick with rawhide for bow rake. | For a broom rake you can grow several kinds of reeds or bamboo. Or you can split corn stalks. In the South, use palm fronds. For bow rake, hammer three-inch galvanized nails through a piece of one-by two-inch hardwood. Old broom handles are strong enough for most rakes. |
| *Hoe* | Tied an old flat bone or a flattened stone onto a strong stick with rawhide. | Find a hard piece of metal with a sharp end. Be careful. Hammer or bend it into a hoe shape. Screw, nail, or have it welded onto a strong handle from the town dump. |
| *Shovel*<br>*Spade* | Not many Indians had shovels. Those that did, usually carved them out of a piece of hardwood. And they didn't use them to break heavy soils. | Check the dump or junkyard first for old shovels. You'll probably find a handle there too. Be sure it's strong wood. Sand off the rust and oil the metal. Screw or nail it or have it welded to the handle. |

Indians and other ancient gardeners always made their own tools. So can you. Opposite are the same tools — how an Indian might have made them, and how you can too.

## Do-It-Yourself Digging Tools

Tools invent themselves sometimes. Visit nearby garden centers, nurseries, plumbers, auto wreckers, farmers, or any other place with scrap metal, broken parts, and pieces of junk. Look for things you could use to make a digging tool. Handles, pointed pieces of metal, things that can break up the soil.

Get all the parts together in one place. Spread them out so you can see each one. Sit and look at these parts until you start to put them together in your mind. Think of many ways to put them together.

Do you see a tool in those pieces of "junk"? Put it together the best way you can. If it doesn't work, try again. That's how the first gardeners and farmers did it.

Do you know anybody who is a welder? If you do, maybe you can ask them to do you a favor and weld together metal parts that are hard to fit together. Any parts you don't use you can save for the scarecrow.

## Three Hand Tools You Probably Have on Hand

Not every tool you need for your garden has to be made, found, or bought. You have a few garden tools in your kitchen right now.

You probably don't think of them as garden tools, because you usually use them for something else. But they are especially useful for transplanting or repotting. And they are perfect tools for miniature gardens.

*A spoon.* Can become a little shovel or small trowel. Soup-spoon size is best. But any size spoon can be used for scooping up small anounts of soil when planting and transplanting in small containers, miniature gardens, or terrariums.

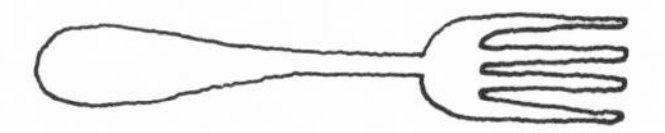

*A fork.* Can be a weeder and hand rake. Can be used to pat down loose topsoil in flats. Lifting out plants while transplanting. Weeding in tight places. Or as a rake for finishing topsoil in miniature garden.

*A knife.* Use an old steak knife or other sharp hand or pocket knife. Be sure it can make clean cuts. Use in trimming dead leaves, removing difficult weeds, pinching, pruning, or cutting flowers.

## Start a Tool Co-op

Do you know other kids and other gardeners who need good tools but can't afford them? Maybe you all could get together and start a tool co-op.

Everyone could split the cost of a good hoe, bow rake, and shovel or spade. But they would also have to split the cost of replacing damaged tools. And everyone would need to be responsible for cleaning and storing each tool after they use it. This is how tools are sometimes shared in a community garden.

## Digging Shoes

Ready to do a lot of digging? Be good to your feet first. Sneakers, sandals, and other lightweight shoes can't stand too much digging. Wear shoes or boots with thick soles; thick enough to absorb the repeated shocks of a spade or shovel. And thick enough to stop a shovel or hoe that wants to dig your toes instead of the soil.

## Digging Clothes

If I don't tell you this, your parents probably will: Wear pants with no cuffs when you dig. Cuffs will catch soil and sneak it into the house. Take off your digging shoes at the door when you're through. Shoes will smuggle soil into the house too. Clean shoes and tools after you're through with them. Wash off soil in the garden where it belongs. Keep tools stored out of the wind, sun, and weather.

# When to Dig and When Not to Dig

*When to dig:* early morning or late afternoon, when soil crumbles in your fist as you squeeze it, when the moon is in fourth quarter (week before New Moon), when the moon rises in Zodiac signs of Leo, Aries, Virgo, Aquarius, Gemini, or Sagittarius, or when you have time.

*When not to dig:* right after a long and heavy rain (when soil is cold and wet), when soil forms into mudball as you squeeze it in your fist, when soil is dry and dusty, or during midday heat.

**Digger's Advice: Be Good to Your Body**

Always dig in a comfortable position. Legs neither too wide apart, nor too close together. Keep a low center of gravity. Bend your knees and keep your pelvis near the weight you are lifting. Let your muscles work and rest in rhythm.

Full back and forth movements are best for any set of muscles. Quick, short movements waste energy. Use only as much energy as you need for each move. Don't rush yourself. Spread the weight of any heavy load over as many muscles and joints (knees, hips, back) as possible.

Breathe in rhythm to the movement. Take in air as you bend down to pick up soil or move something. Let air out as you toss away soil or drop a heavy weight. Feel good about what you're doing for your garden, its plants and bugs.

Rhythm is important when you're shoveling lots of soil. Smooth rhythm. The rhythm of any heavy work is usually controlled by breathing.

*Do these two as one movement.*

1. Use foot and dig in.

2. Bend down, keep back straight.

3. Stop and breathe in.

*Then do these two as one movement.*

4. Keep legs apart. Lift up with legs, pull shovel back while breathing out.

5. Throw in full swing. Follow through.

One good thing about anybody's body: Once you practice using a tool long enough, it will become automatic, a habit. It will become a good or bad habit depending on how you learn to do it in the beginning.

## Lasagna of Life

Good garden soil is like lasagna, an Italian dish that is made with noodles, meat, cheese, and tomato sauce in different layers. Each layer of soil is distinct and different. If you dig a hole deep enough, you'll usually find these layers in your garden.

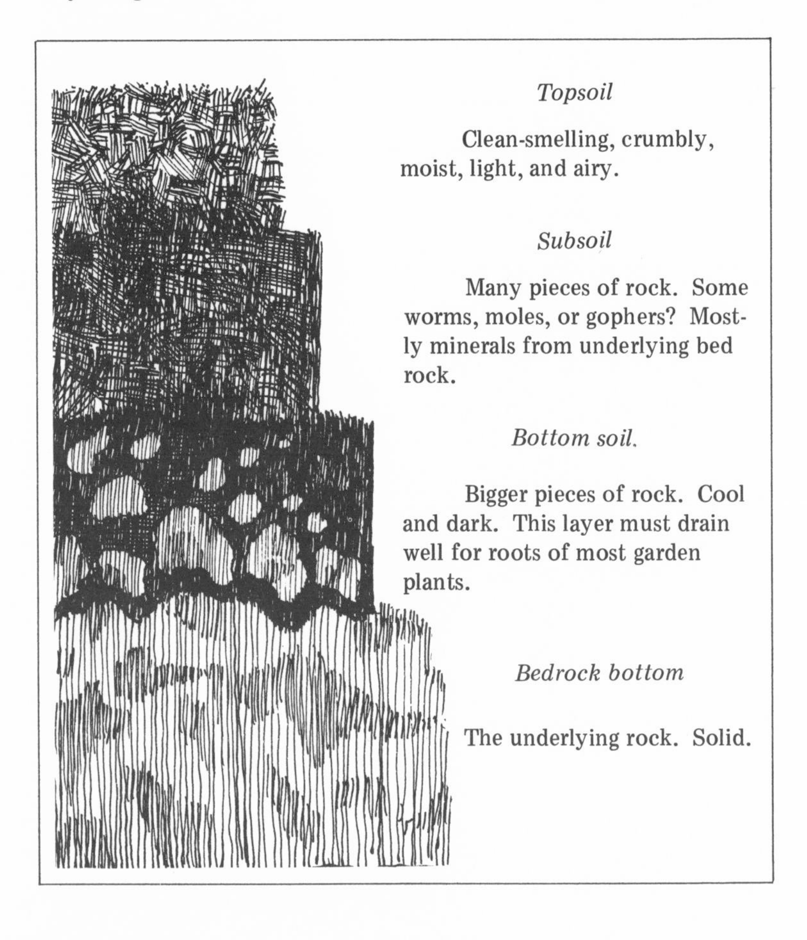

### Brownies of Life

Making good garden topsoil is sometimes like making a good brownie. All the ingredients need to be mixed well. No lumps of this. No bubbles of that.

The texture or feel of topsoil should resemble a baked brownie — light, moist, open, loose, and crumbly. Roots love this kind of soil because they can slide through it.

Use a bow rake to smooth out the surface of topsoil and remove the rocks, especially if you plan on growing carrots, beets, potatoes, turnips, or other thick-rooted vegetables.

## Double Digging

If you plant a big food garden or a few beds of tender annual flowers, you should consider double digging. It's a lot of work, but it pays off..

Double digging is done with a shovel or spade. The soil is dug as deep as possible (usually 18 to 36 inches) without mixing up different layers of the soil. Topsoil is smoothed with a bow rake. Double digging is especially good for gardens in areas with bad drainage caused by hard clay subsoil.

### One Way to Do Double Digging

Eat well and give yourself time to digest the food before you start. You'll need a lot of energy.

I do not double dig by the traditional methods described in many vegetable gardening books. I use a half-and-half method which is simpler and faster.

Here's how to do it:

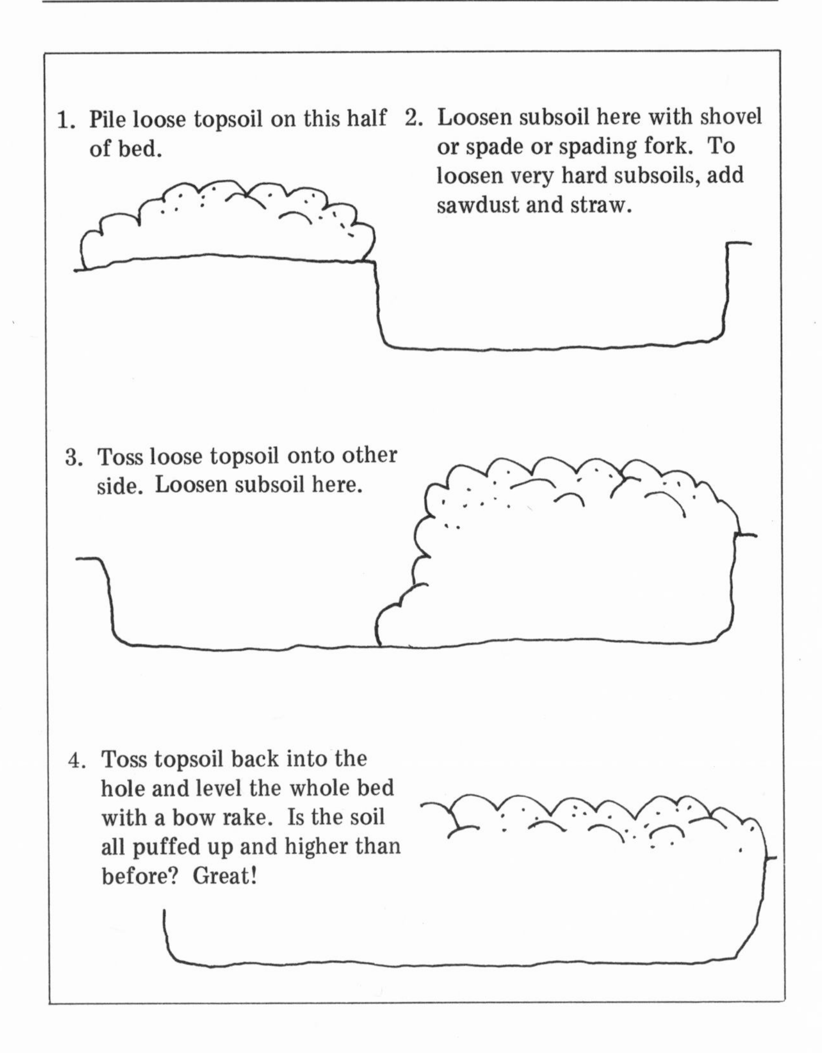


You should figure out your own method of double digging. Make it easy. Dig as deep as you can. And keep the layers of topsoil, subsoil, and bottom soil separated.

## Adding Manure, Compost, and Other Fertilizers

*To fertilize a bed*, add to topsoil: sifted compost, aged manure, aged stable sweepings, and rock minerals. These can also be added to subsoil to increase the depth of the topsoil.

*To warm up soil*, add to subsoil: fresh manure, fresh stable sweepings, blood meal, hot compost, tankage, and bone meal.

Put a piece of cardboard or newspaper between the layer of manure and the topsoil. This way young roots won't dig into the manure layer and burn.

## Other Garden Supplies

I don't think anybody needs to buy any dangerous chemicals, pesticides, and poisons that overcrowd the shelves of most garden supply stores. If you haul manures and make compost, you won't need any of these poisons. They're expensive anyway.

Most garden poisons kill other animal and plant life along with the bugs that are causing the problem. This is stupid because it hurts the whole garden instead of helping it.

### Rest Stops: Letting Soil Settle

After you dig anywhere in your garden, you should water the soil and let it "rest" for a day or two.

Digging, especially deep digging, is a very shaky experience for the earthworms, microbes, and other small life in the soil. They need to get used to their new places in the ground after the digging stops and the soil starts to settle.

After you dig, let the soil sit. Always. Both you and the earth need rest.

### After Digging

After you finish digging, get under your favorite tree in the garden. Take off your shoes and your socks. Let your feet enjoy the fresh air for a minute.

Then stick your toes and feet into the soil. Do you feel the tension pulsating out of your body? Rest for as long as it feels good.

## Earthworms: Help with the Digging

You may dig your garden only once or twice a year. Earthworms dig your garden every day.

Earthworms pass soil through their bodies as they dig their tunnels. The worms digest the soil and return it in the form of "castings." Earthworm castings are really earthworm manure. Besides adding fertilizer to the soil, earthworms are constantly opening the soil and loosening it so air and water can pass through.

Whenever you dig into your soil, don't kill, throw out, or otherwise hassle the earthworms. They are the best friends you have in the soil.

## No-Dig, Just-Mulch Garden

Some gardeners have soil so rich and loamy that they never dig their gardens. Instead they put down thick blankets of mulch. Very thick — 8 to 12 inches. Straw is commonly used, but other mulches are fine. You just need to find enough.

Each year this thick mulch breaks down into the soil and adds to its fertility. Sometimes aged manure or compost is spread onto the soil before the next layer of mulch is added on top of it.

But these "no-dig" gardeners do not cultivate or otherwise upset the soil's fertile texture once it has become established.

Usually these folks have been gardening in one spot for several years. Their soil is nothing like the crusty unfertile stuff most people find when they start a garden in a place that never had one before.

When planting a garden like this, the mulch is usually pushed away and seeds planted directly into the soil. Then, when the plants are big enough, the mulch is pushed around them. Some day you may be fortunate enough to have this kind of garden.

## Chapter 6

# Seeds and Weeds

What would happen if you didn't plant anything after you dug your garden? What would grow there?

If you are in no hurry to get your garden in, why don't you find out? Don't plant anything for 10 to 15 days. Wait and see what plants come up. Do you know what they are?

Some people might call them weeds. But is that really what they are?

There's nothing really "wrong" with weeds. Except they won't stop growing everywhere you want something else to grow. A weed is a plant trying to live in the wrong place at the wrong time. But it's only "wrong" as far as the gardener is concerned.

How do you feel about weeds? Maybe you think you could do without them. You might even be one of the many gardeners who thinks weeds are the worst part about gardening. Or you might be one of the rare gardeners who understands weeds and finds out about them and learns how to use them.

Some weeds (dandelion, purslane, lamb's quarters) taste good in salads. Some make excellent teas (mint, yarrow, clover). Some fertilize the soil (clover, vetch, nettle). Some have powerful roots (dandelion, buckwheat, wild oats) that keep digging the soil long after you've hung up the spade.

Just like bugs, birds, and other wild life in your garden, weeds have a place. They are the strongest, fastest-growing plants around. They deserve your respect.

### When Weeds Were the Only Plants in the World

Imagine how life must have been on earth in the days before jets and fast travel. Before supermarkets and fast foods. A time with no towns, no streets, no roads. Nothing on the landscape except trees and plants.

At that time *every plant was wild.* It grew there because it planted itself there. Nobody was a gardener or a farmer. Because nobody thought they could move a plant from where it naturally grew. Where did people live? What did they take with them when they moved to a new place?

Scientists believe the first people on earth were hunters and foragers. Nomads who roamed around in families, in tribes, or alone to find food, clothing, tools, and the other things they needed.

People could only get these things from animals and plants. Because there was nothing else around. People thought animals and plants were special beings, especially plants. Plants were everywhere people went. In all shapes and sizes. They were alive. But they didn't have to move around to find food like people and animals.

## Where Did the First Gardens Grow?

Slowly people realized they could move plants. Rather, they realized they had been moving plants all along. Someone probably noticed a grain-like barley or flax growing along a trail where they traveled each year. Perhaps it was along a hilly trail where no grains normally grew.

Certainly they wondered how the plants got there. Until somebody remembered that grains from one of their packs had spilled at that spot earlier. Not until then had anyone known that the grains were actually seeds. Magic little things that made new life out of almost nothing.

From then on people grew their own food, their own medicines, their own clothes. Anything they needed. People learned how to cultivate plants by doing it and watching what happened.

Slowly plants changed. They became used to growing in soils that were rich in animal and human manures. People learned other ways to propagate and crossbreed plants. Plants kept on changing. And so did people.

1
2
1. Central American highlands
2. Northern Andes
3. Abyssinia
4. Mediterranean
5. Southwest Asia
6. Southeast Asia

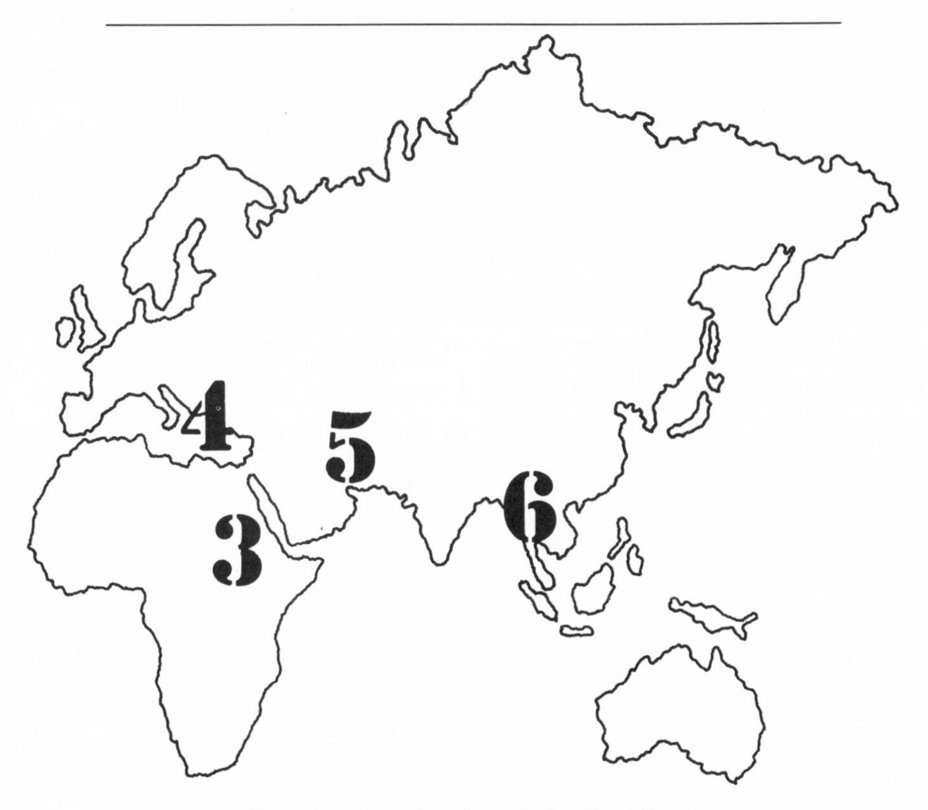


Real Roots: Origins of Garden Plants

Gardening and farming began very slowly in many different places all over the earth. No one place was the "cradle of civilization." There were at least six centers of cultivation where people realized they could grow plants and raise animals themselves, instead of following the plants and animals around. So they settled down in these places and began great civilizations.

These six centers were where most of today's garden plants originally came from.

## Six Gardening Centers

*Zone One:* Central American Highlands (Mexico, Guatemala)
*Climate:* hot and moist summers; warm and dry winters
*Plants:* corn, common beans, pumpkin, summer squash, chayote, marigolds, nasturtium, dahlia, cosmos, zinnia, avocado, papaya

*Zone Two:* South American Andes (Peru, Columbia, Bolivia)
*Climate:* hot and dry summers; warm and wet winters
*Plants:* tomato, potato, pepper, sweet potato, winter squash, lima beans, nasturtium, peanuts, morning glory, pineapple, petunia

*Zone Three:* Abyssinia (Ethiopia, Upper Egypt)
*Climate:* very hot, wet summers; warm and dry winters
*Plants:* watermelon, basil, dates, okra, hibiscus, sorghum

*Zone Four:* Mediterranean (Israel, Italy, Greece, Spain, Syria)
*Climate:* mild, dry, and balmy year round; no harsh winters
*Plants:* alyssum, daffodil, snapdragon, gladiolus, hyacinth, summer savory, sage, kale, collards, broccoli, asparagus, beets, celery, turnips, figs, thyme

*Zone Five:* Southwest Asia or Near East (Persia, Kashmir, Turkestan)
*Climate:* very hot and dry summers; cold and dry winters
*Plants:* lettuce, carrots, onions, peas, melons, rye, wheat, tulip, spinach, apples, pears, plums, grapes, balm, chervil

*Zone Six:* Southeast Asia (China, India, Malaysia)
*Climate:* hot and wet summers; mild winters
*Plants:* bamboo, cucumbers, flax, soybeans, rice, radish, green onions, Chinese cabbage, celtuce, eggplant, black-eyed peas, apricots, peaches, oranges, lemons, grapefruit, mango, limes, banana, purslane, hollyhock, mums, peony, regal lily, camellia

### How Do Seeds Travel Around So Much?

Seeds were one of the first things an explorer, traveler, or trader carried from the Old World to the New World. Seeds were valuable and everyone knew it. Besides, they didn't take up much room in anyone's traveling bags.

Seeds of lettuce, cauliflower, watermelon, soybeans, and all the other Old World plants are now able to grow in your garden because someone brought them across the ocean many years ago.

## You Can Grow Almost Anything

You can try to bring any plant on earth into your garden But if you want the plant to live, you must learn about it.

Find out how to grow it before you plant it. Know what the plant needs. Find some way to propagate it. By seed division, cutting, layering, or whatever. If you see the plant in someone's garden, they might help you find some way to get it into your garden.

Realize that you're not the one who's really growing it. The garden grows itself. The plant grows itself. You're only part of it.

## Some Things You Might Find in Your Garden

How many ways can any plant be used? This is a question wise people have asked themselves for centuries.

How well they answered it meant how well they lived.

Flax is one plant early people knew how to use many ways. They ate the seeds along with other grains as a cereal. Seeds were used for oil. Fibers inside the stalk were woven into linen.

Bamboo is another useful plant that has been used for centuries. People use bamboo for food, fences, heavy construction work, almost everything.

When you grow any plant, find out about its parts and what they have been used for. Then figure out how else you can use it. What you don't use can always go into the compost.

There are 50 plants listed in the Planter's and Picker's Pages (see Part Four of this book). Here are some of the uses people have made of those plants.

| | | |
|---|---|---|
| clothes | soap | furniture |
| shoes | musical instruments | fences |
| rugs | chewing gum | plumbing |
| brooms | skin salve | containers |
| sponges | medicine | housing |
| compass | food and drink | bridges |

## Watchacallit?

Sometimes nothing can be more confusing than the names people give to plants. "Daisy" and "lily" are two words that are often given to many flowers that are neither daisies nor lilies in the proper sense of the words.

One plant might have many different names in many different places. Or one common name might be used to mean many different plants. This just adds to the confusion.

Scientists try to unmuddle the mess. They give each plant a Latin name and put it into a family. Plant families are grouped into orders. Orders are divided into classes. Classes make up divisions, which make up subkingdoms of the entire plant kingdom.

Botanists want to give each plant a place and a name that can be understood all across the world. But plants don't easily fit into the scientists' categories. Sometimes the scientific names and organization just adds to the confusion.

Most gardeners never learn scientific names for what they grow. Besides, "snapdragon" sounds better than *Antirrhinum majus.* And it's easier to say.

Sometimes you might need to know the scientific name of a plant. Especially if you want to identify it exactly. Or if you want to clear up confusion about how to grow it.

## Getting Clues from a Scientific Name

The scientific name for a plant can often give you clues about how the plant grows. The biggest clues are in the plant's species name. Which is always the second word of the two-word scientific name.

*Lobularia maritima* is the proper name for sweet alyssum. Does the scientific name give you any hints about where the plant originally grew?

If you don't have any idea, look up the word "maritime" in a dictionary. Or look up the history of alyssum in the Planter's and Picker's Pages.

Here are some species names which tell where a plant originally grew as a native weed.

*agrarius* - of the fields
*alpinus* - of the mountains
*aquaticus* - on water
*australis* - southern
*borealis* - northern
*exoticus* - not native
*nivalis* - near snow
*occidentalis* - western
*riparius* - on river banks
*saxatilis* - with rocks
*silvestris* - of the woods

## The Thrill of Not Knowing a Plant's Name

It's nice to know the names of things in your garden. But it's also nice to forget a plant's name. After all, the name probably doesn't mean that much to the plant. (Or does it?)

I don't know the name of everything that grows in my garden. I like it that way. There's always something new to find out.

If something starts growing by itself, I let it grow to see what it is. If I don't know what it is, I still let it grow. I wait until someone tells me its name. Or I find it listed in some book or something. Even then I don't always know its right name for certain.

This way your garden always has a few surprises in it.

# Garden Window Shopping

Are you confused about what to plant in your garden? Why don't you go window shopping for plants? Go to a public garden near you or visit a garden supply store, a house plant store, or a nursery. Bring paper and pencil with you so you can write down the names of plants you like. You can learn a lot just by looking around a nursery. Especially if it's spring and all kinds of new plants and rootstock are on display.

## Good Seeds Grow, Cheap Seeds Are Slow

Stores that sell hardware, groceries, drugs, and cosmetics sometimes sell seeds. All the seeds are in one rack; all are from the same company. Sometimes the seeds are on sale or for sale very cheap.

If you're serious about having a good garden, don't buy seeds from these stores. These are apt to be poor seeds. They may be old and were probably not selling well at another store. That's why they're so cheap.

Get seeds from a store whose main business is gardening. Not selling nails or drugs or hair spray. Check the date on the back of the pack. Get seeds from someone who knows about them and can answer your questions about which seeds will grow best in your area.

## Pick a Seed House in Your Area

Wise gardeners always start with good seeds. Seeds that are suited to their area and climate. The best way to do this is to mail order seeds from a good seed house in your state or area.

If you live in the South, you will be able to grow many varieties that can't grow in the North. So don't order from a northern seed house. Likewise if you live in the North order from a northern seed house because it has more seeds to suit your short growing season.

See a Catalog of Seed Catalogs in Part Four of this book to find a seed house near you. Send for their catalog.

### Who Needs to Read a Seed Catalog?

In winter, most gardening is done inside the pages of seed catalogs. Sending away for next year's garden seeds is the most enjoyable garden "chore" for many gardeners. Turning pages is certainly easier than turning soil.

I love the pictures of bright flowers and perky vegetables in seed catalogs. But I realize these pictures show the very best plant the seed company has to offer of that variety.

Most seed catalogs also contain long-worded descriptions which try too hard to sell you a variety of seed while burying the real information you need.

You should appreciate the seed company's success. But you shouldn't be disappointed if your seeds don't grow into the living wonders seen and described in the catalog pictures.

### Shopping for Seeds

When you shop for seeds in a catalog, here are some things you should look for:

*A variety of seed suited to your area and climate.* Check for growing season, usually written in this form: "75 days." This is especially important for vegetables. "Early" varieties grow faster, "late" varieties need more time.

*Plants that will fit into your garden.* Find out how much room the plant will take. "Pole" or "climbing" varieties need stakes, fences, or other support. "Bush" and "dwarf" types can support themselves. "Trailing," "runner," and "vine" varieties with big fruits (pumpkin, melon, some squash) need lots of room to roam on the ground.

*Will they otherwise fit into your plans?* Have you picked the kinds of vegetables everyone likes?

## How to Read a Seed Pack

Some seed packs come with nothing written on them except the name of the seeds. Others have instructions on them. But the instructions are the same for most of the other seed packs they sell. Other packs have what seems to be complete instructions.

No seed pack can tell you all you need to know about planting whatever's inside it. Here's what to look for on seed packs:

when and where plants should be started
how deep to plant them
how far apart plants should be after thinning
how much time they need to grow
exact name of variety.

### Seed Packs You Can Eat

Did you know that an apple is also a seed pack? You can try to grow any seeds that come wrapped inside fruits and vegetables for sale at your local market.

These seeds might not always grow into healthy plants, but some will. As far as the seeds are concerned, anything is better than the garbage can. Which is where most seeds from the market end up.

Some market seeds you might want to try as tropical house plants are papaya and mango.

Papaya seeds make happy, fast-growing trees if you give them enough room in front of a sunny window. But they don't transplant easily, so start them in a big container with holes for drainage.

Other fruit seeds will sprout and make nice house plants. But they probably won't bear fruit.

## Collecting Plants in the Wilds

Luther Burbank, George Washington Carver, and many other naturalists collected seeds and pieces of wild plants while they were on hikes, and brought the wild plants back home to plant and study in their gardens. You can do this too. But you must be sensible and honest. All it really takes is common sense and consideration.

Whose land is the plant on? Do you have permission to be there? Do you have permission to collect seeds and plants? Who gave you permission?

If it's on public land (national forest, state park, county lake, whatever) are you certain you have permission to collect anything? Who gave you permission? (It is illegal to move even rocks in many public parks.)

Do you know the easiest way to propagate the plant? Do you know when and how to collect seeds? Do you know how to remove a cutting or stolon from a plant without making it seem like anything is missing?

Can you understand the plant's wild environment enough to know what kind of home it will need in your garden? Sunny or shady? Wet or dry? Hot or cold? Have you figured out a good way to label and store seed you find in the wilds?

## Starting Seeds

Many gardeners want to get their plants off to an early start. So they soak the seeds. This speeds up the germination or sprouting process of the seed.

This is especially true of slow germinating seeds like carrots, many annuals, and most herbs. The soaking helps soften the seed's shell. And it tells the tiny taproot inside the seed that the time is right.

Here's how to give seeds an early start: Soak seeds for 15 minutes in fresh water. Wrap seeds in a paper or cloth towel. Soak the towel, put it in a plastic bag, and let sit overnight. Next morning, plant the seeds and water them. Some seeds do not benefit from this treatment. They need sunlight and air to germinate instead.

### Sunbather Seeds

Some seeds do not need to be covered in soil and moisture to germinate. In fact, it is unwise to cover them with soil. Why?

These seeds need sunlight and air to germinate.

It sounds a bit odd. But it's true. And it makes good sense when you think about it. Native plants and weeds manage to plant themselves without anyone putting soil over them. The seeds don't need it.

Here are some plants that need sunlight to germinate:

| | | |
|---|---|---|
| lettuce | African violet | wax begonia |
| petunia | Alpine strawberry | Cape primrose |
| snapdragon | yarrow | clarkia |
| stock | scarlet sage | most evergreens |
| salpiglossis | gloxinia | and |
| coleus | tobacco | most grasses. |

When you plant any of these, just rake the soil smooth, then toss the seeds. Don't cover them.

### Headstart Window: Starting Slow Plants Indoors

If you live in a place with a short growing season, you can still grow plants that need a long growing season. Just get a head start by planting warm season plants indoors. Some people start as early as February. Any window with at least six hours of sunlight can become a small greenhouse when you need it.

Here are some plants gardeners commonly start early indoors:

| | | |
|---|---|---|
| cosmos | sage | pumpkin |
| zinnias | other herbs | tomatoes |
| marigolds | cucumbers | peppers |
| other annuals | watermelon | other vegetables. |
| summer savory | luffa | |
| thyme | chayote | |

These seeds will sprout early only if the soil is warm enough. Be sure sunlight warms soil through the window. Otherwise they won't germinate quickly. And you won't get much of a head start.

## What Is Companion Planting?

Excuse me for mentioning school at a time like this, but. . . . You know how it is when certain people like to sit next to certain other people in class. Plants are the same way. Certain plants like to grow around other certain plants.

The only difference is plants can't leave "class." They're stuck in the garden, usually in one spot all the time. They don't mind really. But any plant likes it better if it grows next to a friend.

Do plants really have friends? It seems so. Many old time gardeners believe peas and carrots like each other, but they say peas and onions can't stand each other.

Some gardeners test old timers' claims about companion plants. They use a process called chromatography which is similar to photography. They get interesting results that sometimes prove old timers are right.

But a lot is still unknown about companion plants. How can you tell which plants like to grow with other plants? By experimenting and trying companion planting ideas you hear or read about. The plants will let you know if they like growing with each other. (See the Planter's and Picker's Pages to find companions of 50 common and uncommon garden plants.)

Besides planting friendly plants together and keeping unfriendly plants apart, there are other ways to think about companion planting. One idea is to grow more plants in less space. By companion planting root vegetables, tall plants, and climbing vines, you can grow several times more food in the same soil. Beets, corn, and pole beans can be combined this way.

However, this type of companion planting requires a very rich, deeply dug soil and lots of pruning away of dead leaves so the plants get enough light and aren't bothered by insects. Another kind of companion planting is based on the belief that certain herbs and other special plants repel or distract pesty bugs from the garden. Sometimes this works and sometimes it doesn't. Bugs are a lot wiser than most books believe.

### The Best Kind of Companion Planting

Planting seeds is the best part of gardening. But it's not always fun to do it alone. When you plant your garden, plant with a friend or someone you enjoy being with. In a couple months, you both can come back and see what happened to those little seeds you planted together.

# Putting Plants to Bed

Do you like it when someone steps on your foot? Of course not! How do you think plants feel when someone steps on their roots? That's what happens when anyone steps on the soil around a plant. Especially someone who weighs a lot. The soil presses down on their roots. The plant feels it all over.

This is why some gardeners plant everything in "beds." These are nothing like the beds you sleep in. But they are soft. The soil is light and loose. The whole point about beds is to keep the soil loose so roots don't have trouble digging through it.

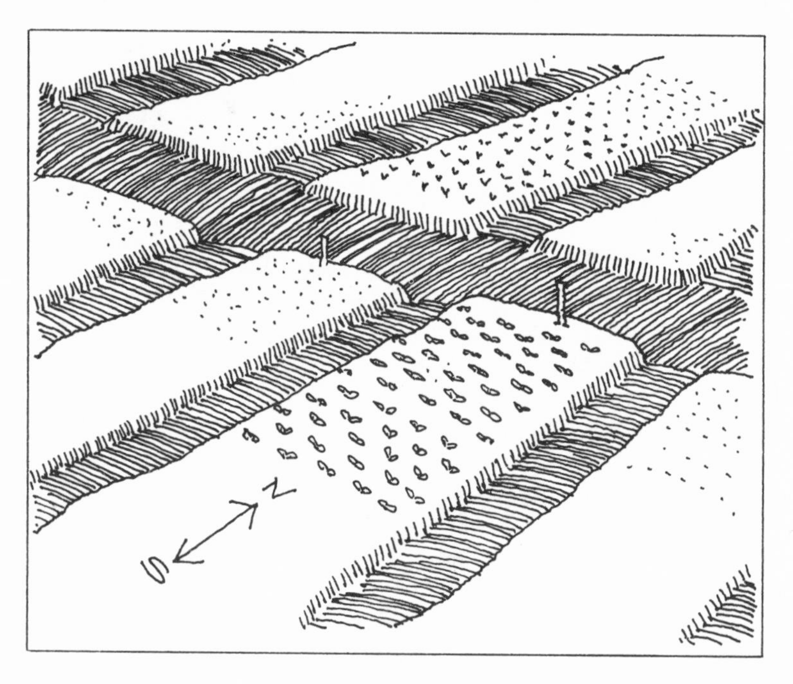

The beds can be as long as you want, but they shouldn't be wider than you can reach from either side. If you have a "boardinghouse reach," the beds can be 36 to 42 inches wide. Or they can be narrower. It depends on you. The beds should run north and south for best sunlight. But on hills, beds should run along the contour of the land. Pathways run between the beds.

### What's the Matter with Planting in Rows?

Many gardeners plant their gardens like farmers. They act like they have all the room in the world. They plant in long rows with wide spaces between the rows. This is OK, if you have the space. But if you have a small garden it's a big waste of valuable soil. This includes most city and suburban gardens. And also many town gardens.

Forget what the seed packs say about the distance between rows. That information is for farmers who need to get farm machines through the plants. It's better to plant in "offset rows" or triangle patterns like the diagram shown.

The distance between each plant, in any direction, is the same. To tell this distance, look on the back of the seed pack for the "distance between plants."

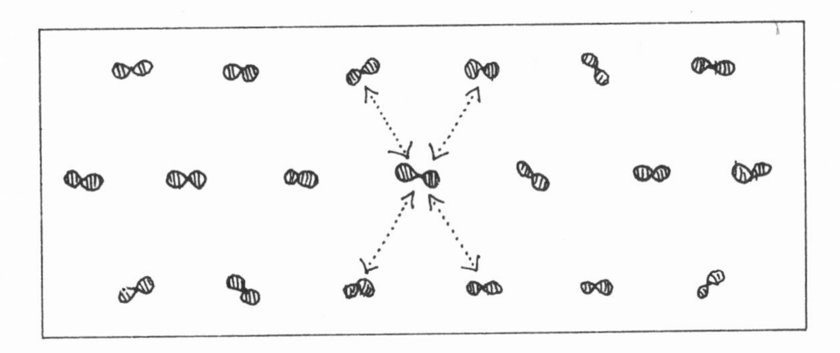

## The Phantom Underground High Jumper

To properly root themselves, many seeds need to do some underground gymnastics when they sprout and become seedlings. The seed's taproot must bend into a big arch before the seed can find energy to break out of the soil.

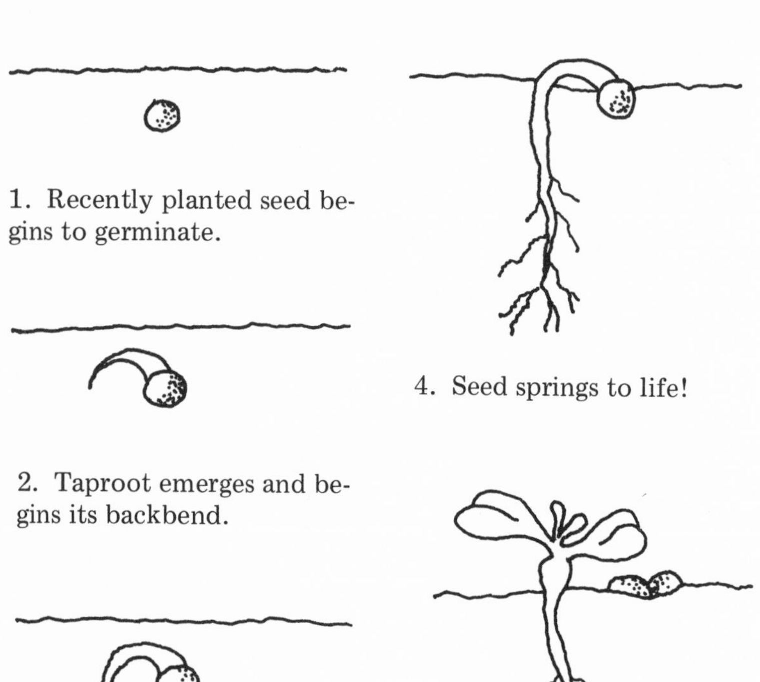

1. Recently planted seed begins to germinate.

2. Taproot emerges and begins its backbend.

3. Taproot arches to create tension.

4. Seed springs to life!

5. First leaves (cotyledons) open to meet sunlight.

It's easy to see this happen. Find a clear plastic container and punch a hole in the bottom for drainage. Fill the container with soil. Wrap black paper around the outside of the container. Black paper keeps out light that would confuse the roots about where "up" is.

Plant radish seeds near the walls of the container. Water them and wait a day. The next day remove the paper every four or five hours to watch for progress of roots. Do this every day for a week. Be sure to replace the paper around the container after you've looked.

Later you might try other kinds of seeds. Do some seeds send out a taproot that spirals crazily? Why do you think this happens? How can you tell the top of a seed from the bottom?

## Planting: One Rule of Thumb

Often, plants don't come up in a beginner's garden because the seeds are planted either too deep or too shallow. Seed packs usually tell how deep the seed needs to be. But if you don't have that information, you can still tell how deep to plant most seeds. Here's the rule to remember:

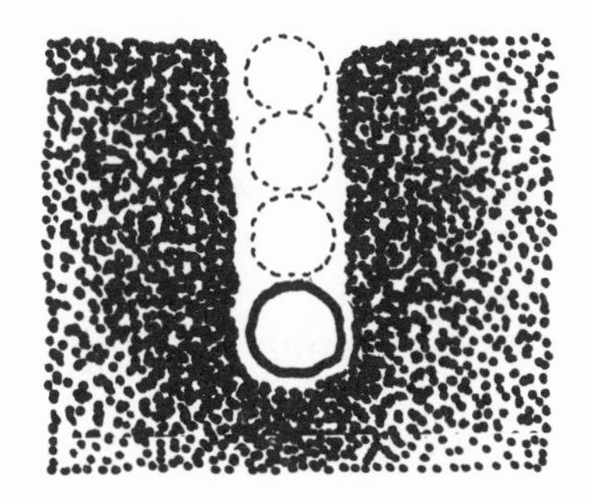

Plant each seed so that three more seeds exactly the same size could be placed on top of it.

You'll need to guess more for odd-shaped seeds (watermelon, squash, bean, pumpkin.)

## Another Way to Do It

If you can't remember how deep to plant a seed, figure out the depth using the three-for-one rule. Then mark the depth on your thumb with a ball-point pen. Then push your thumb into the soil up to the line, like this:

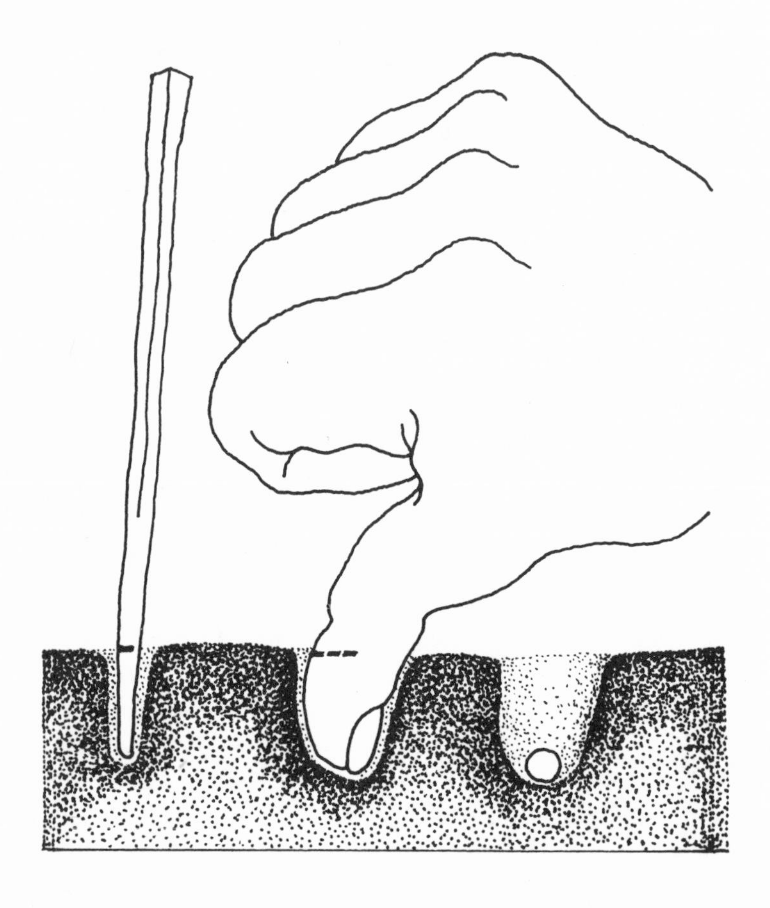

Fill in with soil, tamp down firmly and give the seed your good wishes.

P. S. If you can't press a hole into the soil with your thumb, the ground is too hard. You'd better dig it again, and add compost or manure. Most garden plants can't grow in hardpan.

Don't peek where you planted. Seeds need time to germinate. Don't go poking around, trying to find out how they're doing. Leave them alone unless they are a week past their normal germination time.

## Don't Be Afraid to Thin Out

One of the most important things a gardener does is thinning out. This means pulling up all the slower growing, too skinny, too small, and too sick seedlings and composting them. Or putting them in salads.

Thinning is done as soon as possible after plants have popped up and have shown you whether or not they will grow well. If you don't thin out, all the plants will suffer. They will grow longer and skinnier as they stretch to catch the light. Their stems won't be strong. They will spend most of their strength trying to stand up during even the slightest winds.

## Thinning Tool

Tweezers are a good thinning tool. Get the kind with slanted tips. It will make thinning out easier. Just be careful not to injure the plants you decide to save. *A rule of thumb:* Don't let leaves of any pair of young seedlings overlap and begin a battle for sunlight.

## How to Get a Plant Out of a Pot

1. Put your hand over the opening of the pot. Let the plant's stem rest between your two fingers.

2. Tell the plant "Look out!" Turn the pot upside-down.

3. Tap the pot on the edge of something if the plant won't come out by itself. Gently.

4. Or poke something through the drain hole and push hard.

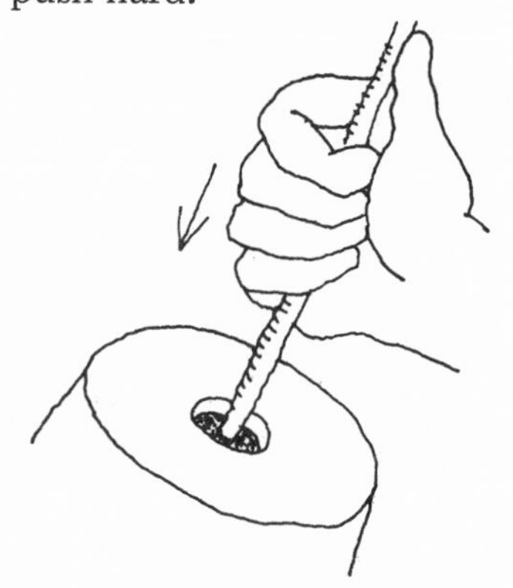

# Transplanting

If you start seeds in flats and in cut-off milk cartons on sunny windowsills, you will learn how to transplant and when to transplant. Transplanting is not hard, as long as you do it gently and not hurt too many roots.

When do you know a plant is ready to be transplanted? Roots will peek out through the drainage hole of the container or flat. The plant will stop growing so fast and it will dry out more often.

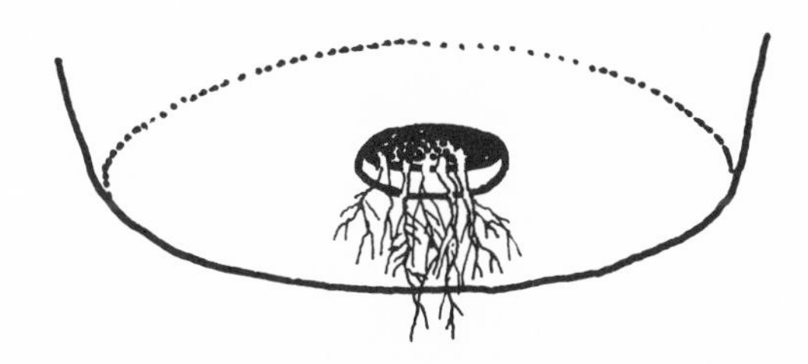

Plants can be transplanted into the garden or into bigger pots. This should be done when the sun is going down and the garden is cooling off for the night. If the next days are hot and sunny, be sure to shade the plants with newspaper hats or cardboard boxes or something that will keep the sunlight off them.

Roots of transplants must be free to spread out in all directions into the soil. If the roots are pinched into the soil too tightly, or if too many of them are torn, the plant will have trouble growing in its new place.

Beans, melons, cucumbers, and squash are tender when transplanted. So handle them with care. Don't try to transplant carrots, turnips, beets, or other big-rooted plants.

## Transplant Trick

Even when they are very small, plants know where north and south are. They know because they're used to the sunlight. And their roots are used to the earth's magnetic forces. So when you transplant young plants, the first thing you should try to do is keep the plants aimed in the same direction as they grew in the house or planthouse. This way plants will be less confused or shocked by the transplanting.

Note: If you buy plants from a nursery, forget all about this. The plants have been turned. Try to keep them as lined up as you can.

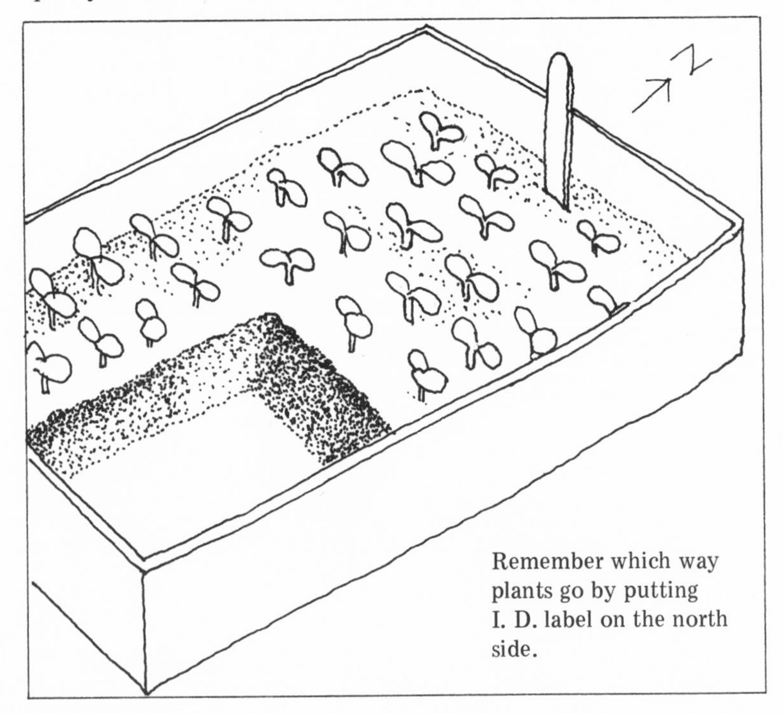


Remember which way plants go by putting I. D. label on the north side.

# Seedless Propagation

Seeds are everywhere. So you probably know quite a bit about them. But did you know that many garden plants are not seeds when they're planted? Some are bulbs, corms, tubers, or rhizomes. People have bred and crossbred these plants so many times that the plants have forgotten how to make seeds.

Other garden plants, especially fruit trees and most perennials, reproduce in ways no animal can. And they aren't started from anything that even looks like a seed. They are propagated by cutting, budding, grafting, layering, and dividing pieces from a "parent plant." Gardeners who learn all the many ways to propagate plants also learn how to make more plants without spending very many pennies.

## Bulbs

Tulips, daffodils, lilies, and other popular garden plants grow from bulbs. Most bulbs are planted in the fall and bloom in the spring. Bulbs usually reproduce themselves through tiny bulblets that grow around the base of a parent bulb. Or as bulblets that grow inside the leaf axils of some lilies.

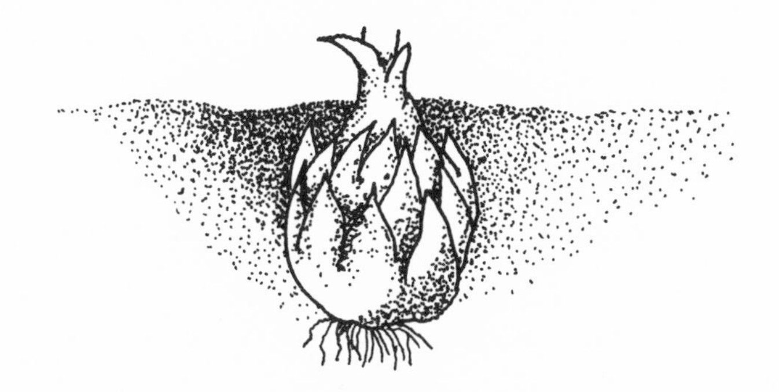

A bulb is actually the whole plant — leaves and flower bud — wrapped up tightly. It has all the nourishment it needs for the next blooming season also wrapped inside it. But the bulb must fully flower and die back to the ground before you dig it up. Otherwise the bulb won't produce all its nourishment for the next season. After the plant withers and dries up, you can dig up the bulb and pick off the bulblets to start new ones. But when you dig, dig carefully. It's easy to ruin a bulb by chopping it with a shovel or trowel.

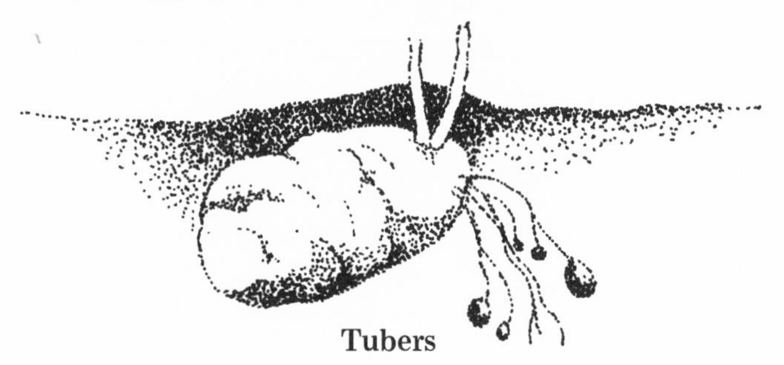

**Tubers**

Potatoes, sweet potatoes, dahlias, calla lilies, Jerusalem artichokes, and some begonias propagate themselves by tubers. A tuber is an underground swollen root and food storage organ of a plant. Tubers come in many sizes and shapes. Often they dry out before being replanted. Some tubers can grow very quickly. One type of desert plant *(Chamaegigas intrepidus)* has a dry tuber that begins to grow the minute after the first rain. And in two days the plant is flowering.

**Corms**

A corm looks like a squashed bulb. But actually it's a swollen storage root and underground stem. It does not have a flower bud inside. Gladiolus and crocus are the most popular plants propagated by corms.

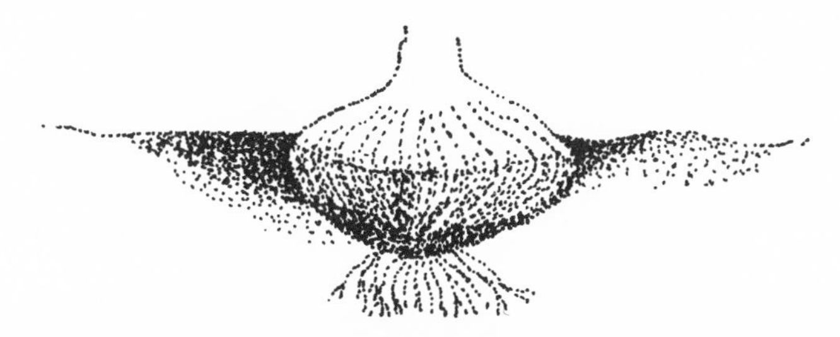

The corm is used up after the flower blooms each year. But a new corm grows on top of the shrinking old one. To make sure the new corm does not climb out of the ground, the plant has a contractile root. After the plant dies, this root contracts and pulls the new corm down into the soil until it is firmly anchored. Sometimes a corm also makes tiny cormlets underneath the new corm.

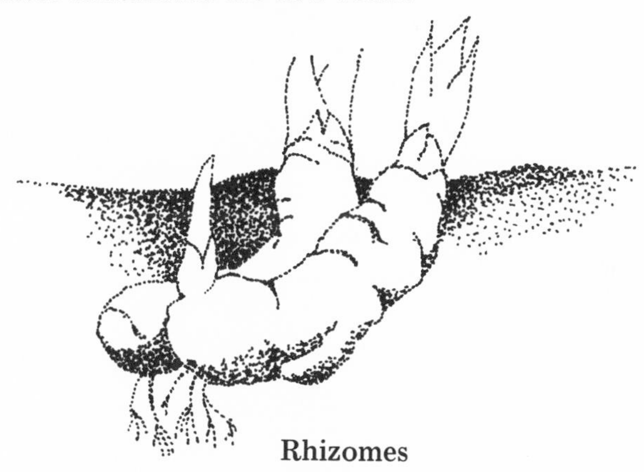

**Rhizomes**

Iris, orchids, and bamboo grow from rhizomes. A rhizome is a creeping, underground stem or rootstock. But it does not always stay underground. After a few years rhizomes overcrowd each other. There is no place crowded rhizomes can go but up. They do not have contractile roots, like corms, and some bulbs, to hold them down.

Rhizomes are propagated by division. Every two or three years, an overgrown clump of rhizomes is divided by cutting some of them off the main stem. The cut rhizomes with roots attached are replanted in well-drained soil. But they are not covered completely. The top of the rhizome usually sits slightly above the top of the soil.

## Other Kinds of Propagation

Propagation is all the many ways plants get started. Anytime you plant anything you are propagating it, whether you plant seeds, bulbs, tubers, corms, or rhizomes. But the new plants can also be propagated by other ways besides planting. These ways include cutting, layering, division, and grafting. Any plant propagated these ways comes from a parent plant, one that has already been growing for some time.

### Cuttings

One of the easiest ways to propagate many plants is to cut off a piece of the plant and put it into water. That's it! Cuttings can be started from leaves, leaf buds, stems, and roots cut from a healthy "parent" plant. Cuttings are usually taken off trees, shrubs, and perennials (both hardwood and softwood).

When placed in fresh water, the cutting will prove how much it wants to live. Like magic, roots will stretch out into the water. A new plant will be born. But not quite yet. First the cutting must develop enough roots.

You can speed up this process by putting plastic bags and glass jars over cuttings. This conserves moisture and protects the plants like a small greenhouse. Some gardeners use growth hormones and liquid vitamin $B_1$ to speed up cuttings. But it isn't necessary. When a cutting has several roots ¾-to one-inch long, they are ready to transplant into pots or into the garden.

You can also use a rooting mix instead of plain water to start cuttings. Good rooting mixes are made of anything that will stay moist: clean river sand, vermiculite (heated chips of mica), perlite (heated and crushed volcanic rock), peat moss and sand, crushed styrofoam, peat moss, and sand.

## Layering

Purslane, chickweed, ground cherry, wild strawberries, and many other weeds or native plants grow well because they are masters at propagating themselves by layering. Layering is similar to making cuttings, except the layered part is not cut from the parent plant until the roots have completely developed. And the layered plant is a separate plant.

Although it is a natural propagation method of many plants, layering can be an art form in the garden. Its history has been traced to ancient China. Modern gardeners use layering as a way to propagate berries. There are many kinds of layering: simple, trench, mound, mulch, compound, continuous. In each case, a stem or branch of the plant is bent to the soil and held there until roots develop. Then it is cut from the parent plant and remains in the soil, or is transplanted.

## Division

A few shrubs and many softwood perennials are propagated by division of roots. This is done by carefully cutting them with a sharp knife or spreading them apart with a spading fork. Root division must be done during a dormant time in the plant's life. If the plant blooms in early spring, its dormant time is fall. If the plant blooms in late spring or fall, it should be divided in spring. Hard asters, chrysanthemums, Chinese larkspur, foxglove, lupines, peony, summer phlox, artichokes, and many other perennial plants are easily divided if you do it at the right time.

### Grafting

Experienced gardeners can take small buds from hardwood plants and graft them onto other hardwoods. It's sort of like carving a small part of one plant onto another one. But "carving" is actually too rough a word for it. Grafting is a delicate operation.

Grafting takes advantage of the tree's natural need to heal itself. Slowly tissue from the tree is able to grow around the grafted piece and make it a part of the tree. This is also why a single tree can give more than one variety of the same fruit.

Grafting is hard to learn by yourself. If you know any neighbor gardeners who have grafted any of their trees, ask them to show you how they did it.

## Ancient and Foreign Seeds

At least 3,000 different kinds of plants have nourished people throughout history. But now the world relies on only 20 crops for most of its food. Potatoes, sweet potatoes, tomatoes, beans, peas, peanuts, soybeans, corn, wheat, rice, oats, barley, buckwheat, millet, sorghum, sugar cane, sugar beets, coconuts, bananas, tapioca, and very few others feed the world.

More people live in cities now. They rely on bigger farms to make lots of one kind of food and haul it long distances. Much is known about how to grow the major crops, but little is known about the old food plants. Farmers usually can't afford to experiment. And people don't demand variety in their diet. At least, not enough people to change the farmers' minds.

Many valuable food plants still grow wild or are cultivated in the six ancient centers of cultivation. Have you heard of taro root, amaranth, winged beans, Asian wax gourds, chaya, buffalo gourds, quinua, or pummelo? Maybe someday you will.

## The Search for Heirloom Seeds

Do you have parents, relatives, or family friends who sometimes travel to other countries? If you do, maybe they can become an explorer for you. Ask them to bring you seeds of strange vegetables, fruits, flowers, herbs, or other plants that might grow in your garden.

This isn't as hard as it may sound. Seeds from squash, corn, beans, tomatoes, melons, and other plants can be found wrapped inside their natural packages at rural markets in many countries. Often the people who sell them are the people who grow them. Seeds from these farmers usually have been passed from one generation to the next. Many gardeners call these "heirloom" seeds, because they are valuable.

Some heirloom seeds may be very old varieties, nothing like the varieties sold by seed houses. This is especially true in countries with long gardening and farming traditions — Mexico, Guatemala, Peru, India, China, the Near East, and countries around the Mediterranean Sea. However, anyone who wants to transport seeds from one country to another must check with local customs officials to be sure the seeds aren't restricted.

### Foreign Seeds and Customs Inspections

Foreign pests can be imported along with foreign seeds. But generally, there are few restrictions against Americans bringing foreign seeds into the country as long as they are seeds for fruits, vegetables and other garden plants. Some plants are restricted by the Plant Quarantine Section of the Department of Agriculture. Many of these are exotic plants. If you want your explorer-friend to import anything exotic, you should write this address to find out if the plant you want is restricted: Import Permit Office, Plant Quarantine Section, Room 638, Federal Building, Hyattsville, Md. 20782.

## Saving Seeds

Many gardeners save seeds just to give them away or trade them with other people. One plant usually makes lots more seeds than one garden needs. In this tradition, many small, select seed houses are sprouting up all over the United States. They have a new vision about what a seed house should be.

What separates them from older seed houses is their attitude about home-grown seeds. They are willing to trade seeds with gardeners. And they are willing to help gardeners learn how to save their own seed. (See page 322 if you want to order a catalog from a seed trader or a select seed company.)

### Should You Save Your Own Seeds?

Seeds are smart. They know how to create life out of almost nothing. But most garden books and seed catalogs give the same silly advice about seeds. They say you should not save seeds that come from your garden.

Experts say seeds are usually from hybrids, special plants invented by plant breeders. Hybrids are supposed to grow fast and "vigorously." But seeds from hybrids are not supposed to be vigorous. They won't "breed true" according to the experts. This means the seeds of hybrids won't produce plants with all the exact traits advertised in seed catalogs. Seeds from a hybrid tall pink chrysanthemum will not produce all the same tall pink flowers next time. Instead, the seeds will grow into many different chrysanthemums. Some tall. Some short. Some pink. Some red. Some strange.

The experts act as if every gardener grows nothing but hybrids. But that's not always so. Besides, they also forget to mention that one or two special seeds from any hybrid could develop into a strange new plant. If it gets a chance.

## Homemade Seeds Are Tough

The seeds that sprout first, grow fastest, and live to become the healthiest plants in my garden are seeds I saved from last year's garden. Some seeds are from hybrid parents. Most are from "open-pollinating" or "standard" varieties. All of them seem to know my garden better. They seem more at home than seeds and plants from a nursery or big seed company. Bugs don't bother them as much.

If you have lots of room in a volunteer patch, or if you have a special interest in a certain plant, or if you have an experimental garden, you should save the seeds that interest you most.

## How to Save Seeds for the Future

It's easy to save seeds from plants you grow. Many gardeners save the first seeds from their best open-pollinating tomatoes, beans, peas, melons, pumpkins, squash, cucumbers, sunflowers, and other annuals. Here's how you can save your seed.

Be selective. Decide what kind of seed you want, then select the best single plant among all the others. It should be the healthiest, fastest-maturing, most colorful, or whatever. Find the part of the plant that makes the seeds. It may be a fruit, pod, cob, or boll.

Tag the seed-making part of the plant with a ribbon or string or something else so you'll remember to save it. And other people will know not to pick it. Pick the first fruit or pod when it's ripe, or let the plant complete its life cycle in the ground. Let it die and start to dry. Then pull it out and hang it upside-down in a cool place.

Remove the seeds. If they're dry, keep them dry. If they're wet and pulpy like melon seeds, rinse them in cool water. Then dry them on a dish towel in an open room out of direct sunlight. Eat or compost the fruit, boll, pod, or whatever held the seeds.

## Seed Storage Hot — Seed Storage Cool

Until you are ready to plant them, seeds and seed packs should always be kept dry and cool. Tear off only a small corner of the pack when you open it. Don't rip it because you'll need it to hold leftover seeds. Once you've opened seed packs, store them in an empty coffee can with a plastic seal top. Do this on a dry day so you don't seal in too much moisture.

Be especially careful with seed storage if you live in the Deep South or another place with high relative humidity. If it's too moist around the seeds, molds will form. Seeds will be destroyed while you're waiting for the next year's growing season.

Chapter 7

# Air, Water, Weather, and Degrees

Good gardeners always get to know the climate and weather in their gardens. But it takes a while. First they have to know a few things about air and water.

## Water: The Elementary Ingredient

Water shapes the world around us. Water enlivens everything. Without water, the earth would be like the moon or Mars or any other barren place without gardens. Water is such a daily part of our lives that people usually don't stop and watch it or think about it as it drains down the sink.

Water is almost always moving. It is most alive when it is moving, because fresh air bubbles through it and enlivens it more. Water that doesn't move becomes stagnant. Dead. On land, water is always seeking a lower level. Gravity pulls water down mountains, hills, streams, and rivers toward the sea. Or gravity pulls water down into the soil, to the water table.

## Air: The Perfect Companion

The sky is also an ocean. One big ocean with many currents of air mixed with water droplets all flowing through it. Air moves in many of the same ways water moves. But because air is thinner, it can also fly! Air isn't as weighted down by gravity as water.

Air is everywhere — not just in the sky, your body, your room. Air is in water and in soil too. Water is also everywhere — not just in oceans, rivers, and lakes, but also in the air and in the soil. Air and water are easier to understand if you know how they move. Most of the time they move together, but not always in the same direction.

### Three or Four Things to Know About How Air and Water Move

*Warm air* expands and rises, tries to escape gravity. *Cool air* contracts and must obey gravity.

*Hot air* holds more water vapor than cold air. *Cold air* holds little water vapor; "squeezes" moisture out of hot air to make rain.

*Very hot and moist air* forms clouds and sometimes rain but only when it meets cool air. *Very cold and dry air* freezes water vapors into ice clouds (Cirrus or highest clouds).

*Very hot water* boils and becomes steam. *Very cold water* expands as it freezes and becomes ice.

## When Does Water Hide in the Sky?

Air and water hang out together most of the time. In the soil. In the sea. In the sky. But we usually only notice them together in the sky when the weather changes for the worse. Water is hiding in the sky most of the time. When does this sky water come out of hiding?

*Humidity* is water in the air — in the form of small droplets that form invisible water vapors. Air moisture is another term for humidity.

*Clouds* are water vapors that become visible in the air. Except the highest clouds, which are ice because the air around them is so cold. Vapors are like steam — they aren't really water. They can fly!

*Rain* is water that becomes visible in the air. And falls to earth, where it runs off and disappears into rivers, lakes, oceans, or soil.

## Why No One Really Sits at the Water Table

The water table is underground. Nobody sits at this table. But water is there all the time. All garden life depends in some way on the water table. When the table is too low, the climate is dry and it is a time of drought. When the water table is too high, everything floods and plant roots drown.

The water table is high or low or in between, depending on how much rain and run-off have been flowing at the surface of the soil and draining down to the water table. The water table is important to gardeners because plants stretch to get water from it when they can't get moisture from the topsoil. You won't have to worry much about the water table if rains are regular and you water your garden completely in dry weather.

# Get to Know the Wisdom of a Stream

Go watch water in a stream sometime. Watch how the water flows. See where it runs fast. See where it flows slow. What happens to the water between fast water and slow water in the stream? See how the water in the middle forms a sort of moving blanket between the conflicting fast and slow currents in the stream. See how this "blanket" changes shape as the currents change. Where else have you seen water act like a moving blanket and cover a big area?

## More Water Blankets

What happens when water is sprayed on a window screen? The water drops join together and form a thin skin or blanket of water across the screen. There's still another place you can see this water-blanket effect. On top of garden soil.

But you can only see it if it rains for a while. Or if you sprinkle it with a hose in one spot long enough for the layer of water to form. It won't form if water from the hose is scattered all around for only a short time. Plants rely on this steady blanket of water on the topsoil for most of their water. Plants need this water to get nutrients out of the soil.

## How Soil Breathes Air and Water

You know how a sponge gets wet. Water fills all the holes, drains out, and remains in the fabric of the sponge. Air then fills the holes. Water and air act the same way in good soil. The soil and the sponge stay wet until gravity and evaporation dry it out.

Thin moving water blanket covers one big area.

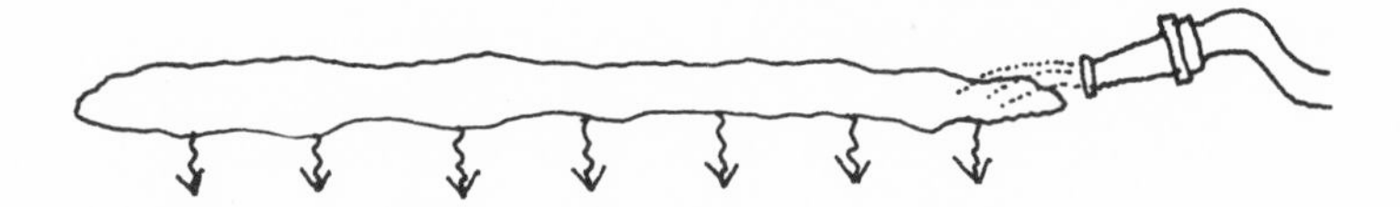

Water drains down evenly through topsoil.

Like a wick, the plant's surface roots and taproots draw water up from the watertable.

Turn off hose when blanket begins to puddle. After watering, gravity reverses the flow. Water returns to the watertable.

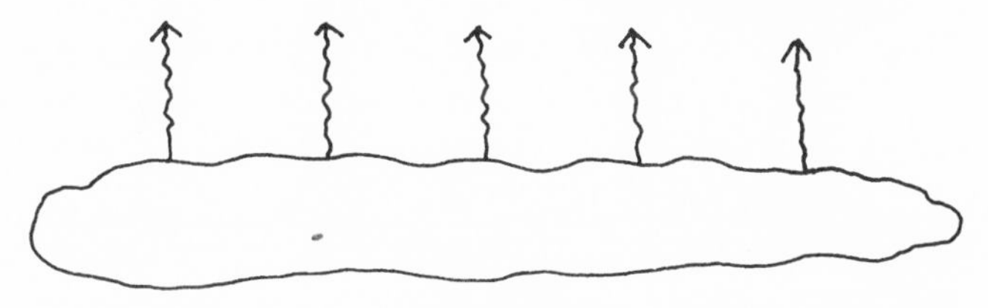

Water Table

Water falls from the sky or a hose and drains down through the soil, neatly obeying the laws of gravity. Plants work against gravity by pushing and pulling water from the soil upward into the plant. This is the mysterious magical way plants grow.

Plants have two parts to their root systems — surface roots and taproots. Surface roots get water from the capillary water blanket on the topsoil. The taproot stretches down to tap the water table. Most water enters the plant through the surface roots. By the process of osmosis, the roots bring in fluids and swell up. The swelling of roots forces fluids upward into the stem of the plant. This root pressure sometimes gets fluids rising as much as two inches above the ground; in some plants it can go higher.

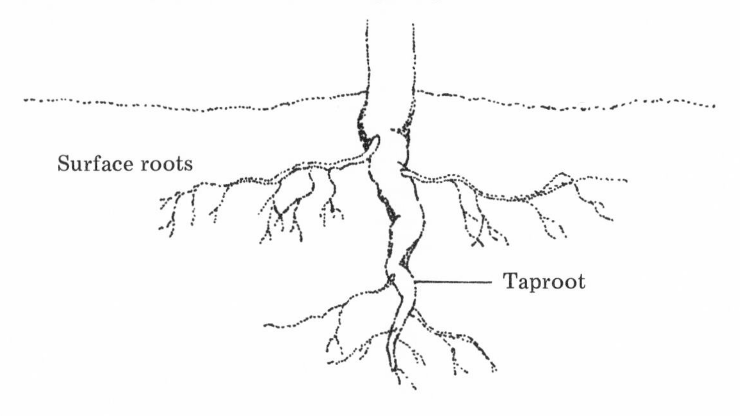


## How Plants Defy Gravity Again

In the stem of the plant, other forces take over to defy gravity once again. These forces are ruled by the sun. They pull the fluids up to the leaves where photosynthesis is taking place. Photosynthesis is a mysterious process. It turns sunlight into energy that the plants use for growth. Plants are the only form of life on earth that can do this.

Under each leaf, plants have thousands of microscopic mouths or noses called stomata. Plants take in carbon dioxide and give off oxygen and moisture through these stomata. This loss of water through the stomata creates a pull in the stems of the plant. This force is what moves the fluids on up into the plant. The fluids carry nutrients from the soil to the leaves where sunlight provides the energy for growth. At night the sun goes down in the west, and the processes of osmosis and photosynthesis slow down. Everything waits for the next day.

# Water Tools: Get a Good Hose

Do you live where there is a long dry spell every summer? Or where the rains are unreliable and the ground dries out if it isn't watered? If you live in one of these places, you should have a hose. A hose is probably your most important garden tool. Get a good one. People at home may be willing to help you pay for it.

## Three Kinds of Hoses

*Rubber.* The standard regular old garden hose — heavy but usually bendable. It will kink sometimes. Keep rubber hoses out of sunlight and harsh weather when you're not using them. Then they won't wear out so fast.

*Plastic.* I hate plastic hoses! They're hard to handle, especially on cool mornings when they don't bend or unroll. Unbendable and hard-to-handle hoses hurt plants.

*Radial.* This is a real racing hose — expensive but more bendable and the longest lasting. It has steel reinforced walls. Radials are easy to handle and won't bother plants as much as a frozen plastic or rubber hose.

Note: Be sure your hose has a good rubber washer to stop leaks.

## Hose Attachments

Water should spray onto plants in soft rain-size drops. It shouldn't blast plants or soil with a drilling stream. And it shouldn't spray onto them in such a fine mist that it blows away in the wind. To spray plants well, you need at least one of these water tools.

*Nozzle.* Use for hand watering. Nozzles aren't very expensive. Get a good one that won't jam up. Be sure it has a washer where it connects to hose so it won't drip.

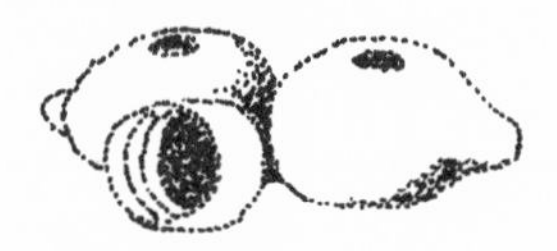

*Sprinkler.* There are many kinds of sprinklers. The best seem to be ones without moving parts. Get metal sprinklers. Plastic ones break and jam up too easy.

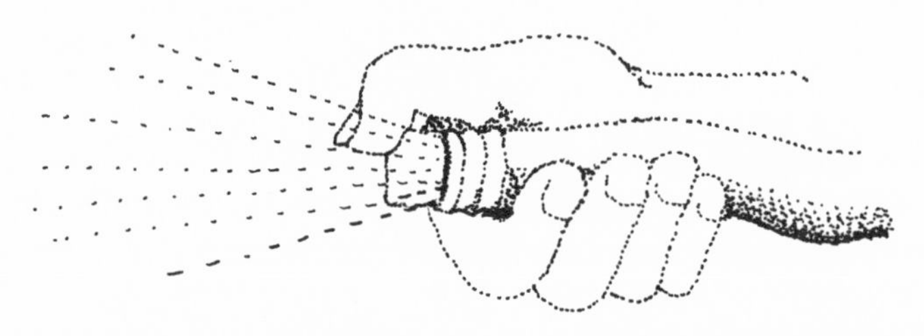

If you don't have a nozzle or sprinkler, find a short stick that will fill most of the hose's hole. Turn on water, put stick in hose, keep it in with your thumb. Turn water up or down to make a fine rain spray.

*Sprayer.* For finer misting of potted and house plants, especially those plants that grow in humid climates and need more moisture on their leaves. The sprayer can be used for pepper, garlic, pyrethrum, or other bug control mixtures. You might be able to recycle an old window-wash bottle for a sprayer. Clean it completely.

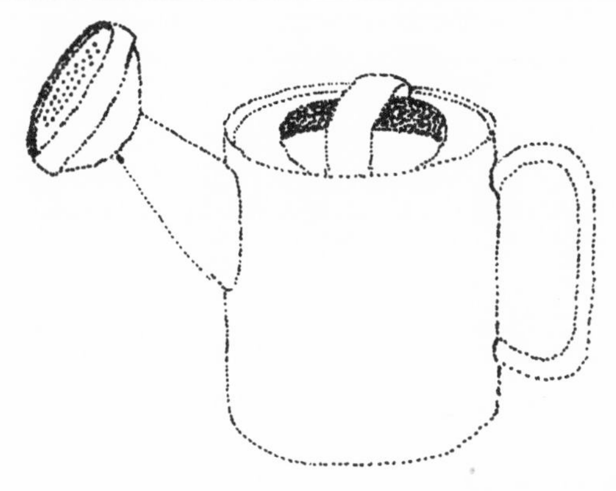

*Water Can.* Most useful for watering houseplants, potted plants, and flats. Always best if it has a sprinkler head on the end, and is made of metal. You can use an old glass bottle if it has a small spout. Be sure water poured from it won't hurt plant or soil.

*Drip system.* There are two kinds of drip irrigation, cheap and expensive. Expensive kinds can easily cost $500. Do you have a rich uncle? The cheapest drip irrigation happens when you drip water from a hose at the base of a plant. This is deep soaking. Some hoses are made especially for drip irrigation. They have holes all down their length.

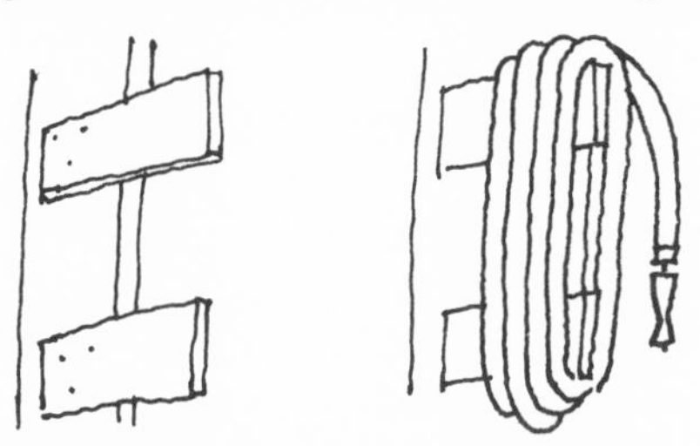

This is the best way to keep your hose clean and safe by keeping it out of the way. You can make your own hose holder out of wood. Nail it near the faucet, but in a sheltered place.

# Watering the Garden

People always seem to think that watering a garden is like washing dishes, or anything else that is done on schedule, like every Monday, Wednesday, and Friday. There is no way to schedule a time when the garden needs water. Clouds, wind, humidity, air pressure, temperature, and sunlight together determine how much water the garden needs. These things change every day. So how can you tell when your garden needs water?

## How to Tell If You're Watering Enough

The best way to tell if you're watering enough is also the simplest. Just poke your little finger into the soil and see if it's moist, light, or just right. Be careful! Make a small hole so you don't bother anybody's roots.

If the soil is dry or slightly dry, water it until it is moist (not muddy) for the top four inches of soil. Wilting is the obvious way plants tell you they need water. The leaves and and sometimes the stems will droop and look miserable. The whole plant seems to scream: "Water me!"

## Harvests and Water

Garden vegetables and fruits need lots of water if you want them to taste their juicy best. Steady moisture is especially important as the plants mature and demand more water. This is simply because they're bigger and they can hold more moisture. When the weather is hot, you may need to water every morning.

Vegetables and fruits are best when watered in the morning and picked in the afternoon. Corn, peas, beans, tomatoes, melons, cucumbers, squash, carrots, beets, lettuce, and other greens always taste best when their fluids are running high. Think ahead and water your garden on days you expect to pick something for dinner that night.

### Make a Water Map

Sometimes you might go away for a weekend, a week, or a six-week summer vacation. Someone will probably need to water your garden while you're gone. To make things easy and simple for your friend, make a water map of your garden like this:

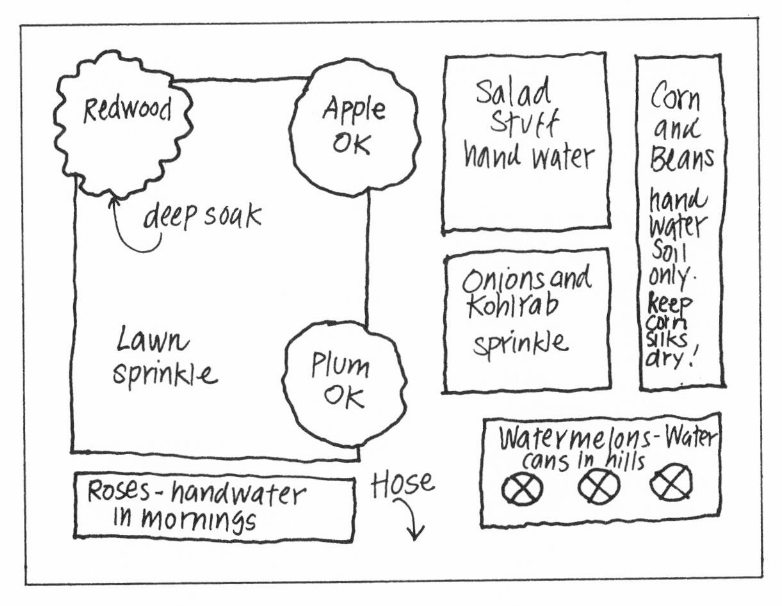


Then talk over the map with your friend so it's all clear. Give the garden one good long good-bye soaking before you go.

# How Water Gets Wasted

Someone has estimated that a modern city person needs 1,200 gallons of water to stay alive. An Indian or a wise camper living in the wild needs only a gallon a day. Clearly, modern people use tons of water. Most of the water seems wasted.

People waste water by letting faucets leak, by letting water run into the sink, and down the drain while they tell someone a story. Toilets waste water; showers waste water. Forgotten sprinklers waste water. Water is one of the most precious gifts you can ever bring to your garden. All the plants need it. How can water be saved?

### Five or Six Ways to Save Water

It's easy to save water in your garden. Here are three ways.

Keep fine mists and sloppy sprays out of the air, especially on hot or windy days.

Water a lot in one spot; don't skip around with the hose all over the garden.

Water that one spot until water begins to puddle up, then move the hose to another spot.

These water-saving ways are important in dry areas of the country, especially in the West and Southwest where no plant can rely on rain. Here are three more ways you can save water and cut down the time you spend watering the garden.

### Magic Mulches

A mulch is a blanket of anything that covers the soil around plants. The idea of mulching is to stop the loss of soil moisture through evaporation. Mulches also keep many weeds from sprouting and competing with the other plants for moisture.

The best mulches are made with leaves, straw, aged manure, compost, or anything else that will slowly break down during the growing season and add humus to the soil.

Some mulches are six to eight inches deep. The deeper the better. Here are some more things you can use for mulching: wood chips, stable sweepings, old rugs, lawn clippings, rocks, sawdust, cocoa bean hulls, and old weeds.

### The Sunken Can

If you grow watermelons, cucumbers, luffa, corn, or other plants that grow in hills, you can try this trick. Get a used two-pound coffee can from the kitchen. Around the

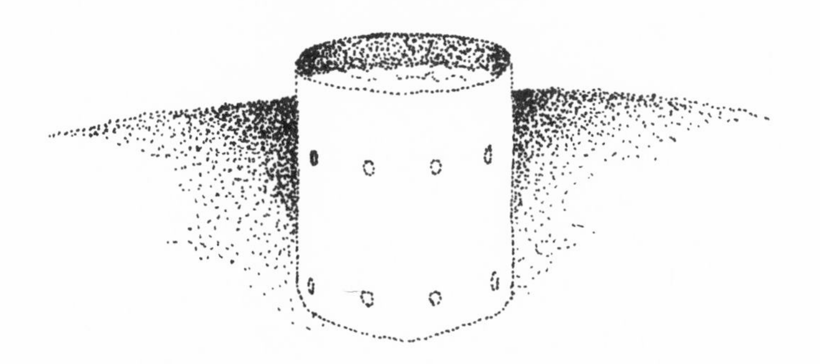

sides of the can, punch 12 to 20 small holes with a hammer and nail. Then put the can in the middle of the hill and plant seeds around it.

When it comes to watering these plants, all you have to do is put the hose in the can and water as long as necessary to moisten the roots around the can. This way, no water gets wasted by sprinkling it onto the ground where the plant isn't rooted. Also the fruits and vines stay dry so bugs don't bother them.

### Deep Soaking

Many plants appreciate deep soaking. You can do it, if you are around the house long enough on watering days. Just put the hose up to the base of the plant and let it drip there for an hour or so, or until the soil gets moist. But don't let it flood or puddle up around the plant.

Plants usually turn very green and look very vital when watered this way. The best thing about deep soaking: no water is sprayed into the air, so no water gets wasted by evaporation. Just be sure to remember you've got the hose dripping. Otherwise you might go off and leave the plant soaking wet all day.

## Weather and Climate

After you understand how air and water move and act in your garden, it's a lot easier to understand weather and climate.

The sun, moon, and stars play big roles in the earth's weather and climates. But air and water are the main movers of weather.

Weather, by the way, is what's happening outside right now. Whether it's sunny or funny or cloudy. That's weather. Climate is the overall weather patterns in your area for a season or other long period of time. It's not always easy to tell the weather based on what you know about a climate.

Right now I can look out my window and see rain. That's the weather. But our climate is normally dry and hot this time of year. Weather changes every day. But climate changes come slowly.

### Climate: Know Your Own Region

The kind of garden you have depends largely on what kind of climate you have. Most of North America has what is known as a "temperate" climate. That means it's not too hot and it's not too cold.

In the United States you can live in almost any kind of climate except tropical. But some summer days seem tropical in subtropical places. Climate only means how the weather is generally in a place. Where do you live? What type of climate do you have? How's the weather today?

## What's the Weathergirl Talking About?

Understanding weather can get very confusing sometimes. Weather maps and TV weather forecasts seem to be secret codes. The weathergirl seems to talk a foreign language. Here's what she's talking about.

*High and low temperatures.* How hot or cold the air is. The day's hottest and coldest air temperature readings from a thermometer measuring still air in the shade.

*Barometric pressure.* A measurement of air pressure. Tells whether we are having high pressure (30.2 inches of mercury or above) or low pressure (29.8 inches or below). Or something in between.

*High pressure area.* A center of high air pressure. Usually a place with fair weather. In high pressure areas, air is gently falling and pressing down on things more.

*Low pressure area.* A center of low air pressure. Usually a time of storms. Some low pressure systems are storms themselves. Storm "fronts" happen where winds from lows meet winds from high pressure areas. Air is gently rising in low pressure.

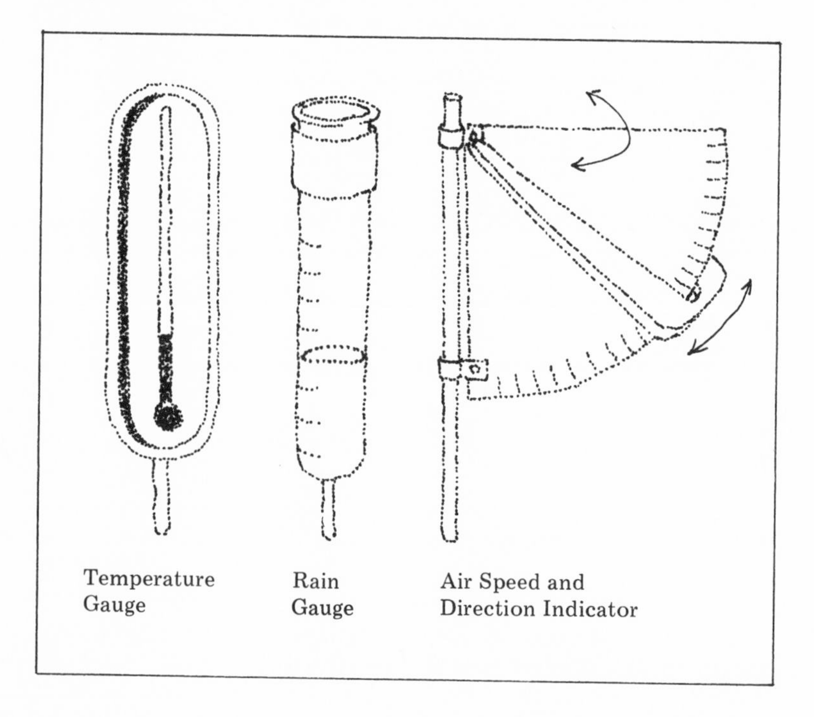

*Relative humidity.* A measure of the amount of water vapor or moisture in the air. A relative humidity of 30 percent is very dry. Humidity measuring over 80 percent is very moist air.

*Wind speed.* How fast and in what direction the wind is blowing from. Measured in miles per hour. Gentle breezes blow up to 12 mph. "Gale" winds start at 32 mph. Hurricane winds measure more than 75 mph.

## Weather You Should Watch For

To be sure you and your garden aren't surprised by quick changes in the weather, watch for these three things in weather reports.

*Winds.* Any wind storms, dust storms, or "gusty" conditions that might be ahead. Winds over 30 mph are rough on gardens.

*Storms.* Any rain, thunderstorms, or rough weather that might be coming. Know where low pressure areas are.

*Frosts.* Listen for the late-night low temperatures in the latter part of your growing season. Be sure Jack Frost or quick freezes don't sneak up on your garden.

### Wind Watch

A change in the weather usually comes after a change in the wind. But the wind can also cause other changes, especially in garden plants. Most of these changes aren't good. Dry winds will speed up soil evaporation. Winds whisk away moist air and replace it with dry air, which in turn is ready to take on more moisture. On windy days you need to watch the soil more closely to see if it needs water.

A strong gusty wind can break and burn plants. The effects of wind burn are clear. The outer edges of many leaves are scorched and brown. This even happens to plants with tough leaves like tomatoes, corn, melons, and calla lilies. Winds also knock down plants, blow away pollen, and keep the garden colder. In most places, the winds that cause trouble come from one direction almost all the time. Find out what direction that is. Talk to people in the neighborhood. Watch for the wind. When you have the winds figured out for your garden, grow trees, or a hedge, or put up a fence to slow it down and keep it off your plants.

## Storm Watch

Sailors, farmers, and old timers told the weather by watching the sky. Here are some of the ways they knew when to expect bad weather.

A dry morning means rain; morning dew means fair. Red sunrise means rain; red sunset means fair. Steady wind from east, northeast, or southeast means rain. Low clouds mean fair. Distant smoke falls and lingers before a storm. Birds won't fly before a storm. Earthworms come out of the ground before a storm. Bugs swarm and bite before a storm. Odors rise and linger before a storm. Sounds travel farther in low pressure and high humidity. Colors become more vivid before and during storms. When you face the wind, the nearest storm is to your right. If there are no clouds and no wind, the weather won't change. A halo around the moon means warm rain the next day.

Now people trust TV forecasts, satellite pictures, and newspaper maps rather than trusting the sky to tell them about the weather. You should trust anything that tells you the truth.

### Frost Watch

The first hard freeze marks the end of the growing season for most gardeners. Most everything in the garden dies or becomes dormant. Annuals and tender vegetables spend their last day in the garden. Plants, which are composed mostly of fluids, cannot take freezing and thawing. Their bodies and roots aren't made for it. In fact, very few of the natural things on earth can take very much freezing and thawing. This includes the hardest mountain rock which cracks, splits, and breaks away after many nights of freezing and many short days of thawing. After the first frost, some gardeners move their gardens indoors. Other gardeners just pile up lots of mulch and keep their garden going outside through the winter.

## Gardens in Winter

Do you live in Alabama, Arizona, California, Florida, Georgia, Louisiana, Mississippi, New Mexico, or Texas? Some gardeners in these states still have gardens going outside when most other gardeners are dreaming in seed catalogs.

The temperature may drop a few points below freezing a few nights, but their gardens keep going. How do they do it?

They plant cold-hardy varieties that can stand a slight frost. These include peas, radishes, lettuce, turnips, Brussels sprouts, spinach, cauliflower, and other things that don't like hot weather. They plant things slightly farther apart than the seed packs say. There is less sunlight in winter so plants need more room. They use a thick mulch as soon as the plants go in. This keeps the soil warmer and won't let it freeze so much. They get their winter garden in before the end of October. After that, seeds are very slow to germinate outside.

## Moving Your Garden Back Indoors

If you live in the northern part of the United States, you won't be able to garden outside because the weather will be too harsh. And the ground will be frozen solid for many days. But this doesn't stop many gardeners. They simply bring their gardens indoors for the winter.

You can grow lots of things in a warm sunny window. You can take cuttings from the tops of your tomato plants and root them in a pot of loose soil. Just pinch back a few leaves and keep the soil moist until new growth starts. Cherry tomatoes look great hanging down in a winter kitchen window. Seeds can also be started indoors in winter, if the soil is warm enough. Try nasturtiums, marigolds, zinnias, or anything that pleases you.

Chapter 8

# Don't Let Insects Bug You

One thing that will surely grow in everyone's garden is a crop of bugs. No matter where on earth the garden is located, indoors or outdoors. No matter what the gardener does. Thank goodness! Gardens would be dead places without bugs. Bugs that you can see all over the place. And ones you can't see because they're too small and they're hiding in the soil.

I know bugs drive many gardeners crazy. Crazy gardeners use lots of chemicals and poisons trying to drive the bugs out of their gardens. Crazy gardeners don't know very much about bugs.

## The More Bugs in the System, the Better

When most gardeners talk about bugs, they usually talk about the bugs that cause them problems. These people overlook the genius bugs that perform miracles in the garden every day. Many times people accuse the wrong bug of doing the damage.

The trouble with garden bugs is simple. People don't know enough about them. Most beginning gardeners hate bugs or are afraid of them. They don't understand that having a garden means having bugs. Most bugs in your garden are good for the garden. Get to know them. Watch them. Enjoy them.

## The Trouble with Good Bugs and Bad Bugs

People are used to thinking of bugs as either good bugs or bad bugs. It's like a cowboy movie where everyone is a good guy or bad guy. One or the other. But not both. That's not always how bugs — or people — are. Bugs, like people, can be good sometimes. And bad sometimes. And neither good nor bad a lot of the other times.

### Think about Ants for a Minute

Right now there are probably more ants on earth than any other kind of animal life. They are among the most indestructible, energetic, and organized creatures on earth. But are ants good or bad? Certainly, ants are amazing and often beneficial. They pollinate flowers. They scavenge and keep the garden clean. Some ants eat pesty insects like aphids, scale, and mealybugs. They also have a social order that seems more organized than those of most other animals. But ants can also do harm. Some ants eat seeds and grains. Some bother roots. Some ants carry diseases that harm plants and soil.

# Getting to Know Six or Seven Great Bugs

The first bugs you should get to know are the ones that are most interesting, most helpful, and most beneficial to your garden. Praying mantids, ladybugs, lacewings, assassin bugs, spiders, and bees are among the most fascinating and beneficial bugs around. In fact, they're great!

Of course, they're not always great. Praying mantids eat all kinds of bugs including other mantids. Spiders catch harmful bugs as well as beneficial ones. And bees, of course, sting. But only if you bug them first.

## Spiders

Spiders might look weird and scare many people in movies. But they are the super heroes, gymnasts, and acrobats of your garden. Spiders aren't really insects. They don't have wings or antennae. They have four pairs of legs instead of three. Spiders belong to a class of creatures that includes daddy longlegs, ticks, mites, and scorpions.

This class is called *Arachnida.* It is named after Arachne, a maiden of Greek myths. Arachne was such a good weaver that she made the gods jealous and was turned into a spider. This was supposed to be a punishment. But the gods didn't seem to realize what good lives spiders have.

Not all spiders spin webs. Some are hunters. Some are scavengers. They eat all kinds of insects, including beneficial ones. Whatever they do, they're all over your garden.

Don't be afraid of most spiders. Don't harm them or mess up their hard work. Watch them weave their webs and spin their sails while you're waiting for the circus to come back to town.

### Bees

Bees are the best garden bugs of all. Without them, there could be no gardens. Bees are the key to pollination of many plants. And pollination is the key to many plants' survival. Some people are afraid of bees because they sting. But a gardener respects bees and moves slowly around them. The bees seem to know that without the gardener, they wouldn't be there. We'll find out more about bees and how they pollinate plants in Chapter Ten, "Being a Bee and Being a Burbank."

### Ladybugs

*Ladybug, ladybug fly away home.*
*Your house is on fire, your children will burn.*

You know the nursery rhyme. But do you know what it means? In Old England, ladybugs were well respected creatures who were said to cross the English Channel and save the hops crop. Hops are important for making beer and ale. Ladybugs always came on time to eat the aphids which threatened to destroy the hops.

After the harvest of the hops' flowers, the British farmers burned the vines. Ladybugs and their babies were still in

It's best to begin with plants that have big flowers because they're easier to work with. Cucumbers, squash, gourds, pumpkins, chayote, and melons all have big flowers and belong to the same family, Cucurbitaceae. All of them can be cross-pollinated. But before you try to cross anything you should get to know what you want to grow.

## Good Inventors Don't Always Know What They're Doing

Plant breeders work two ways. Both ways are mysterious. They involve forces of life outside anyone's control.

*Cross-pollination* — Taking pollen from the male flowers of one plant and putting it onto the female flowers of another plant. Usually the plants are in the same family. Often they are different varieties of the same plant like corn.

*Selection* — Seeds from the cross-pollinated plants are sown next season. As the seedlings grow, the breeder selects the best of them according to the type of plant he has in mind. If none of the selected plants are exactly what he wants, he might cross them again. Or he might not. Anyway, he selects the best plants and plants the seeds from them each year until he finds what he wants. Sort of on purpose and sort of by accident. He doesn't always know what he's doing. He'll just do what feels right until he gets the plant he wants.

## But How Do You Actually Cross the Plants?

Have you decided which plants you want to cross? Then get a lot of good seeds for those plants and plant all of them at once. Thin out all but the best-growing seedlings. When these mature, you will select the two parents. The plants you want to cross.

The "pollen parent" is the father. The "seed parent" is the mother. Collect pollen from the pollen parent any time before the seed parent's flowers open.

Then watch those unopened flowers of the seed parent. And watch the bees. Be there with a knife when the flowers first open. Carefully cut away the petals and any anthers.

All that should remain are the seed parent's pistils, which are now ready to receive pollen.

Be sure to get to the seed parent's flowers before the bees do. Otherwise they'll pollinate them first. But once the petals and anthers have been cut away, bugs won't be attracted to the flower.

Brush, sprinkle, or dust the collected pollen onto the pistils. Once this happens, the flower is pollinated. It is fertilized.

## After Pollination

Cover fertilized flowers with plastic bags. Label them and leave them alone to develop seeds. Then save all the seeds from the seed parent. Plant them next year and see what happens.

## Water Drowns Pollen

Pollen will not work after it gets wet. It must stay dry. The pistils of the female flower also must be dry, or the plant will not be pollinated.

Use a hose wisely. Don't water flowers when pollen is falling. And whenever you start to cross-pollinate anything, check to be sure your hands, brush, bowl, and bags are dry.

## How to Cross-Pollinate Corn

### Pollen Parent

1. Wait for tassels to open and pollen sacks to hang down. Tap pollen into bowl. Keep pollen in dry place until seed parent's silks are ready.

### Seed Parent

2. Cut off tassels before they open and drop pollen. So it can't pollinate itself.

3. When corn silks show on seed parent, brush pollen onto silks. Not too much. One grain of pollen makes one kernel of corn.

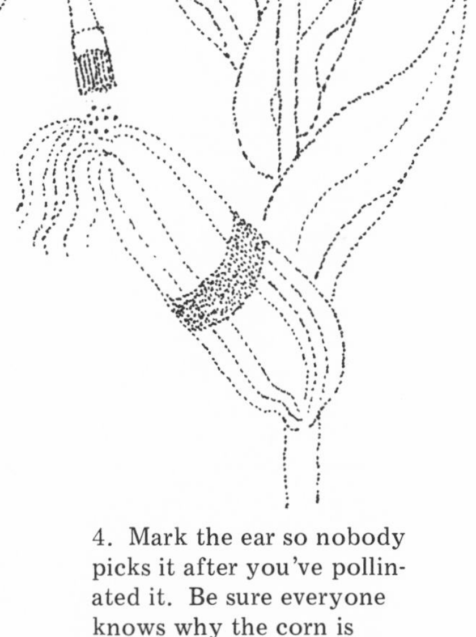

4. Mark the ear so nobody picks it after you've pollinated it. Be sure everyone knows why the corn is marked.

# Selection: Another Kind of Picking

Luther Burbank was considered a "wizard" and "genius" mostly because he was a good picker. He could select the strongest, sweetest, rarest plant out of thousands. And he did it so quickly that people could not believe it.

A big part of Burbank's secret wasn't really a secret. He always planted very large amounts of one kind of plant. Then after they had grown long enough to show him what they could do, he would pull up all but a few of them. Hundreds of plants would be destroyed, all at once. And only one or two would breed the next generation.

This way he copied nature and what happens when weeds plant themselves. Thousands of seeds are planted but only the strongest weeds survive and carry in the strongest seeds for the next generation.

## Mutation and Other "Sports"

Any time you plant any seed, there is a chance for an oddball. The seed could grow into something like nothing anyone has ever seen before. A strange new kind of plant. One that has never grown anywhere else. Gardeners call these plants "sports." Scientists call them "mutations." A few scientists believe that mutations are the main way a life form evolves.

The chances for a mutation or sport are better in a garden than in the wilds. Because garden plants are more hybridized and crossbred. Garden seeds don't have to fight for space as much as wild seeds. Only the strongest survive in the wild. Weird plants can come out of any regular seed pack. When a sport grows in your garden, you have something no one else has. Maybe it's the beginning of a whole new genus.

How can you find a sport in your garden? Almost the same way you crossbreed and select for a new variety. First you learn how the plant usually grows. Then you look for the most unusual ones.

## Plant Breeder's Checklist

What should you look for when you crossbreed and select plants to create a new one? When you're with any plant you think is special, find the answers to these questions.

### For Flowers

*Colors* — What are the normal colors for this kind of flower? Does this flower's color seem new?

*Sizes* — How big is the flower supposed to get? Is this larger or smaller than usual?

*Shape* — How does the flower normally look? Is this one really different?

*Smell* — Nothing can tell you this but your own nose. Do you know how the plant usually smells? Is this aroma different?

*Bloom time* — How long do flowers normally last on the plant? How long do they last when cut?

*Anything else* — Do you want something else in the flower? Curled petals or double blossoms? Does this flower have it?

## For Fruit

*Season* — How long does the plant normally take for the first fruit to mature? How long does this one take?

*Size* — How big is this variety supposed to get? Is the new fruit larger, smaller, or what?

*Flavor* — Do you know how the fruit usually tastes when it's really ripe? How does this one taste?

*Shape* — What is the normal shape of the fruit? How is this one different?

*Diseases* — What diseases usually bother the plant? How well does this one grow? Does anything make it sick?

*Anything else* — Do you want seedless fruits? Or thin-skinned ones? Or what? Does this plant have it?

## For Whole Plants

*Growth* — How long and how fast does the plant normally take to grow? Is this plant faster?

*Size* — Is the variety normally a vine, dwarf, or giant? How is this new plant different?

*Pests* — What usually bothers the plant? Does it bug this new plant?

*Attractions* — What do you normally like about the leaves and shape of the plant? How is this one different?

*Anything else* — Does it transplant well? Or stand up against a stiff wind? Or what?

Do you have the new plant you want? Save the seeds from it.

## Burbank's Advice

When gardeners and others asked Luther Burbank about the best way to breed plants he gave this good advice.

Picture clearly in your mind the new kind of plant you want to create. It might be a certain color, a certain shape, a certain size. Whatever you want. Just have a clear picture.

Crossbreed and select plants for many seasons. As long as it takes. Until you get the plant to match the picture in your mind.

Keep trying. Selection and breeding take time and patience.

## Forgotten Secrets

Scientists have one big complaint about Luther Burbank. He did not take good notes. Many plants he created no longer exist because he did not write down how he did it. This is important to scientists who want to try the same experiments.

Many of Burbank's super cereal grains are lost. Grains that were four times more productive than any known today. Many fruits, flowers, and vegetables that he invented are also lost. Because no one knows how he created the plants.

Certainly, much of what Burbank did cannot be written down. He relied on instincts and senses that cannot be put into words. He kept most of it in his head, or on napkins and scribbled notes. They are all his secrets.

## Plant Breeders Journal

When you experiment with crossbreeding, keep a journal. Make it look something like this:

| Type | Seed Parent | Pollen Parent | Date Crossed | Remarks |
|---|---|---|---|---|
| CORN | | | | |
| | Black Aztec | Illini Xtra Sweet | Aug. 8 | hot + dry |
| | Six-Shooter | " " " | Aug. 8 | small silks |
| | Black Aztec | " " " | Aug. 16 | second try |
| MELON | | | | |
| | Sugar Baby | Yellow Baby | Aug. 10 | hot |
| | Honey Dew | " " | Aug. 12 | windy |
| | | | | |

Chapter 10

# Being a Bee and Being a Burbank

Bees have been crossbreeding plants longer than anyone can tell. People have been crossbreeding plants for only 200 years. The busiest and best plant breeder was Luther Burbank. He was so active. He invented an average of one new variety of plant every three weeks of his career.

Any gardener can be like a bee or be like a Burbank. Anybody can be a plant breeder and invent new plants. It's easy. As long as you pay attention to what you do. And as long as you realize it takes a few seasons to get exactly what you want.

## Bees: Those Bugs You Can't Do Without

Most people think the scariest thing in any garden is bees. Buzzing bees with big stingers. Stingers that hurt worse than any shot the doctor gives. Scare stories and wild rumors float around about "killer bees." These make matters worse. Scared people don't know a good thing when they see it.

Bees are the best bugs in your garden. It can't do without them. Bees pollinate most of the vegetables and fruits we eat. They also crossbreed plants and help make vigorous seeds for the next generation. They've been doing this all quite by accident for thousands of years without even bragging about it.

## The Powers of Pollen

Bees go after it. Some people sneeze at it. A few people think it's more valuable than gold. But without it, no one would eat. And all life on earth as we know it would end. What is it?

Pollen. The magic dust. The stuff that falls from male flowers. And makes its way somehow to the female flowers, where the seed for the next generation of the plant is born. Pollen seems to be an almost indestructible form of life. Botanists and scientists using high-powered microscopes have found pollen grains many thousands of years old.

## More Than Enough

The first plants grew in the oceans. As they slowly evolved to grow on land, plants developed pollen and seeds — parts that needed to be dry and exposed to air instead of water. Pollen and seeds allowed plants to grow and spread all across the earth.

As pollen develops in the stamens of male flowers, it is sticky. It won't fall until it's ready. Pollen is dry and powdery when it's ready. Like dust. When it falls, it is sent by wind or buzzed by bees to fertilize female flowers.

There's always more pollen than needed. Lots of it gets blown away, or used by insects. Unless it's refrigerated in dry air-tight containers, the life-giving quality of pollen lasts about a week. But the pollen grains are never destroyed.

### Breezes and Beeses

Bees use pollen for food. Mostly to feed larval bees. Older bees eat nectar, but sometimes they eat pollen. Bees know when flowers are ready to drop pollen. They even know when the plant is going to flower, days before any buds show. When bees go after pollen both bees and plants benefit.

Some plants don't need to be pollinated by bees and other insects. They are pollinated by the wind, or by gravity, or by themselves. These plants include grains like oats, rice, wheat, barley, or weeds like nettle and dock. You might find bees around a few wind-pollinated plants, especially corn. But the bees aren't there to pollinate flowers. They're just after the pollen.

### Who Can See What a Bee Sees?

Different gardeners and different insects are lured to different flowers. But bugs and bees don't see the same colors you do. A bee can't see red, but it can see blue, green, and yellow. A bee also sees ultraviolet — a color humans can't see. Because it sees ultraviolet, a bee probably sees stripes, spots and designs on twice as many flowers as people can see. You don't know the same garden the bees know.

# Do You See a Difference?

Imagine you are a bee for a minute. Look at the two different flowers below. Which would attract you? Why?

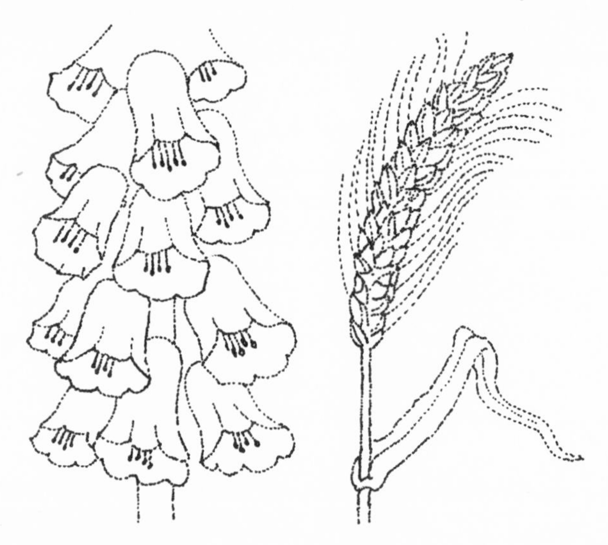

The flower on the left is a foxglove. Who could miss a flower like this? It has an interesting shape, nice patterns, bright colors. Foxgloves can be purple, yellow, red, and pastels. Flowers like foxglove need bugs to pollinate them. So they always look attractive when pollen begins to fall.

The flower on the right is simple and uncolorful. Some people would not call it a flower. It doesn't attract bees or bugs either. It doesn't need to attract anything because it is pollinated by wind. But this dull flower does attract farmers and plant breeders. They have been interested in its seeds throughout history. What is it? Wheat. The flower that makes flour, and becomes the daily bread of many people.

# Plant Breeding

Gardeners are always looking for something special to plant in next year's garden. They always want something new. Something different. Plant breeders try to give gardeners what they want: bigger berries, brighter flowers, or whatever. Breeders invent new plants by selecting and cross-pollinating old ones. The plants they know well.

This is how gardeners got seedless oranges, stringless beans, and fuzzless peaches. Plant breeding is a big business. Each year seed catalogs brag about their new varieties. New ones always cost more than old ones. Most people don't mind paying more, as long as it's new.

## What Can One Little Daisy Do?

Oxeye daisies grow wild just about everywhere. Farmers call them "pernicious weeds." This means evil, destructive, harmful to other plants around it.

When he was a boy, Luther Burbank transplanted some oxeye daisies into his family's vegetable garden in Lancaster, Massachusetts. His dad got mad. Wild daisies don't belong in the garden. They grow wild everywhere else. Besides, they're pernicious. No good. But young Burbank thought otherwise. He wanted to improve the daisies by cross-pollinating them with other daisies. He wanted a perennial white daisy with longer stems and bigger flowers.

Burbank grew to become a famous plant breeder. And he kept growing oxeye daisies in his own garden. He was still hoping to create that better daisy. For many years Burbank crossbred and re-crossed Japanese, European, and American wild daisies. From these he selected the few plants that seemed most like the one he wanted. Then he crossed them again. And again.

Finally, in 1901 Burbank gave the world a new flower. A flower he had been working on two-thirds of his life. Since the days his father caught him transplanting weeds into the garden. What's the flower? The Shasta daisy. A perennial white daisy with big flowers, long stems. A glorious offspring of common weeds.

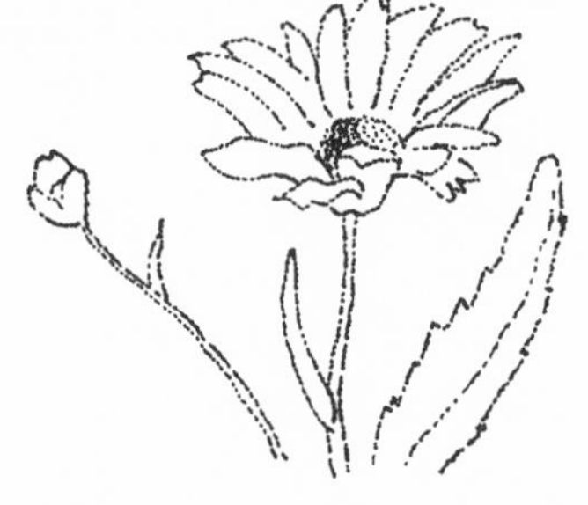

The Shasta daisy is one of the most popular garden flowers of all time. Most new flowers last only ten years before gardeners get tired of growing them. Gardeners have grown the Shasta daisy for more than 75 years. And it's still popular. Do you know it?

## The Experimental Garden

A plant breeder needs an experimental garden. An experimental garden is a magic garden. A special place where new plants are invented. Plants the world has never known before.

You can have an experimental garden anywhere you have a regular garden. Indoors or outdoors. North or south. But it's always best if you have lots of room. With lots of room, you can plant lots of seeds. Even three or four whole packages of seeds! All at once. Then as they grow you can select the few plants you want to save or crossbreed. The more plants you have to pick from, the better chance you have of finding something unique.

A good plant breeder must be a good selector as well as a good picker. Because anything might grow in his garden.

### Plant Breeder's Tools

You won't need any fancy tools to crossbreed plants. You'll probably find most everything you need at home. Besides, your most important tool is always your own sense of selection.

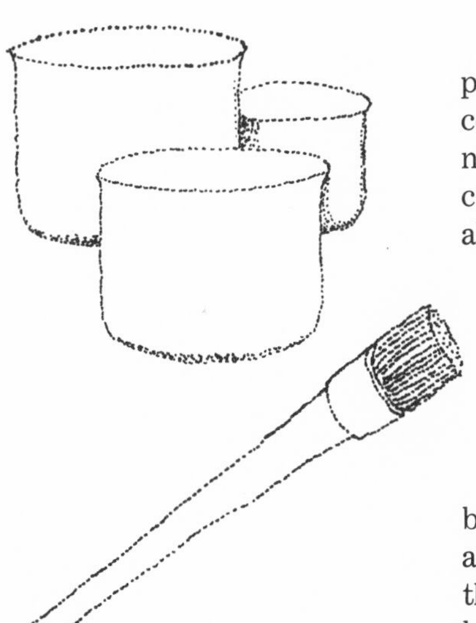

*Dry bowls* — Metal or plastic are best. Wood or ceramic bowls have too many small holes where pollen can get stuck. Bowls must always be dry.

*Brush* — A camel's-hair brush is good. But any good art brush will do. Sometimes this tool is unnecessary. Burbank used his finger instead of a brush.

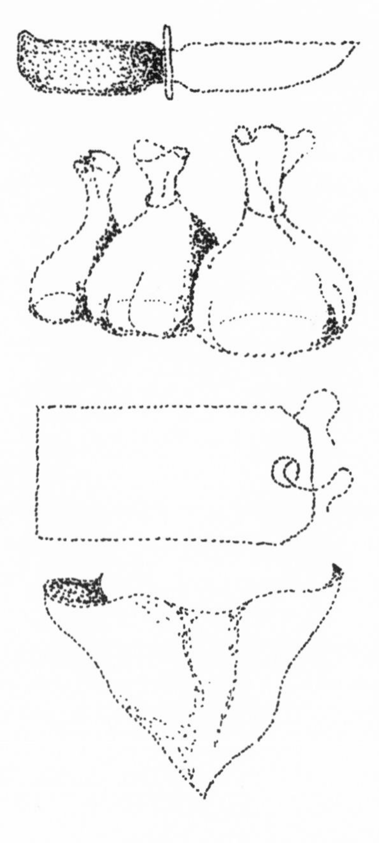

*Knife* — Same as pruning knife — clean and sharp like a steak knife. Used to cut into flowers.

*Plastic bags* — To wrap around a flower after it has been pollinated.

*Tags or Labels* — To record the names of plants and the dates they were cross-pollinated.

*Handkerchief* — Or something else to cover your nose and mouth if the pollen is too thick, so you don't breathe it. This is important if you have hay fever.

## Can You Invent a New Plant?

If bees and other beings can invent new plants, so can you. But plant breeding isn't something you do one day and forget the next. It takes many seasons to create a new plant. Decide which kinds of plants you want to cross. Any two plants can be easily crossed, as long as they're in the same family. Sometimes unrelated plants can also be crossed.

thing to save it, replace it with something else. Only the strongest and healthiest plants should live in your garden — for the good of the whole garden.

### Keep Out of Reach of Children

You've probably seen those words on many containers. They mean that grownups think whatever's inside the container is dangerous to children. It doesn't say exactly what children. And it doesn't say that whatever's inside should sometimes be kept away from certain grownups as well.

"Keep out of reach of children" is an odd but important phrase. It is printed on *Bacillus thuringiensis* containers. *Bacillus* is not harmful to kids, grownups, or anything else but the bugs it attacks. But it will make a big mess if you spill it. A better phrase for the container might be "Careful! Don't spill!" or "Keep out of reach of fumblers."

However, "Keep out of reach of children" is a very important warning when it's printed on packages of poisons, chemicals, and things that can hurt you and others. You must always know what's in the box before you use it. Read the whole label and understand it. Then answer this question: Are you certain you aren't handling a poison or some other substance that's dangerous to you, your family, pets, or your garden? If it's not dangerous, then you can read "Keep out of reach of children" to mean "Handle with caution" or "Don't be clumsy!" or whatever. But when you're not sure what's in the container, ask someone who really knows.

Chapter 9

# All the Trimmings

People clip their fingernails, trim their toenails, have their hair cut. Why do we do this? To get rid of old, unwanted, decaying cells. To clean up, look better, and feel better. To be healthy and stay healthy. So we can grow more fingernails, toenails, and hair.

Plants need to be trimmed too. They need to be pinched, pruned, and picked. Not just to look nice, keep clean,and grow healthy. But for other reasons as well.

## Pinching and Pruning

Plants are made to change. If they lose a limb, they can grow another one. People and animals can't. Trimming, pinching, pruning, and picking are necessary acts of gardening. Don't be afraid to trim or cut a plant. Just remember: Prune, pinch and pick in the right season for a good reason.

| PINCH | WHEN | USE |
| --- | --- | --- |
| herbs<br>vines<br>annuals<br>biennials<br>soft-stem plants | During growing season (usually summer).<br><br>Figure out where plant will grow after it's pinched. | fingers<br>scissors |

| PRUNE | WHEN | USE |
| --- | --- | --- |
| roses<br>berry bushes<br>fruit trees<br>other trees<br>perennials<br>hardwood shrubs | During dormant season (usually winter but not always).<br><br>Learn what each plant needs, get help for hard pruning jobs. | knife<br>other pruning tools |

| PICK | WHEN | USE |
| --- | --- | --- |
| vegetables<br>fruits<br>berries<br>cut flowers | Harvest when ready (Know growing season for each variety you plant).<br><br>Special case: Pick flowers after they open but before bugs pollinate them. | fingers<br>knife |

## The Good Reasons

The main reason gardeners prune or pinch plants is to keep them healthy by removing sick, injured, weak, dead parts. But there are other reasons to trim plants: to help roots adjust when transplanting, to coax plants into making more flowers and fruit, to train plants to grow where you want them, to force tall plants to branch out, to open up the middle of the plant so more light and air can get in, to keep trees out of telephone lines and other trouble, to shape up the plant and make it look nice, and to make the garden look better by removing dead leaves and faded flowers.

## Powers of Picking: Forcing Flowers

When I was a kid (even a college kid) I thought that picking flowers was stupid. "Killing" seemed to be a better word for it. "Picking" is too nice a word for what really happens. The flower is dead after it's picked. It can't finish its job of making seeds or fruit or whatever it makes. At least that's the way I felt about it when I was a kid. Later in my life, after I had been gardening a couple years, I realized something. Gardeners pick flowers for a very good reason. Besides wanting to bring cut flowers indoors, or give them away.

Picking flowers forces the plant to make new flowers because cutting a flower interrupts the plant's vital seed-making process. The plant must make seeds, so it makes more flowers. Picking lengthens the life and flowering time of the plant, which is what most gardeners want. I still don't feel great about cutting flowers. But I know that the plant will make more.

# How to Cut Flowers

Cut flowers will wilt unless you put them in fresh water right after you cut them. Here's how to cut flowers so they will last longer in a vase of water:

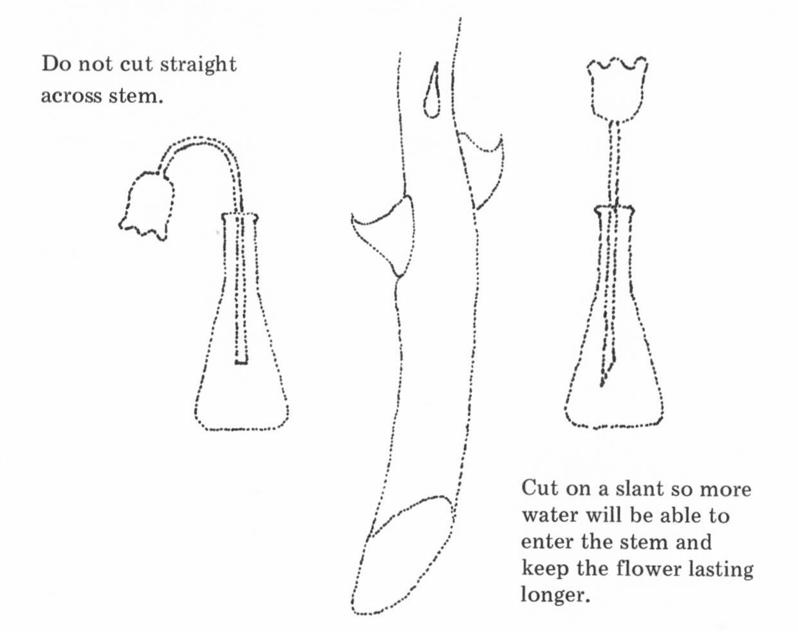


# Pruning Tools and Rules

Pruning tools should be sharp and clean so they can make a clean cut. After pruning season, these tools should be oiled and stored in a dry place. Before you actually start to prune a tree or plant, test the tool by practicing cuts on a long stick. Be sure the tool is cutting cleanly. Get it sharpened if it isn't. Pruning tools are hard to make for yourself. If you get used tools for pruning, they will probably need to be sharpened.

**Pruning Tools**

*Ladder*

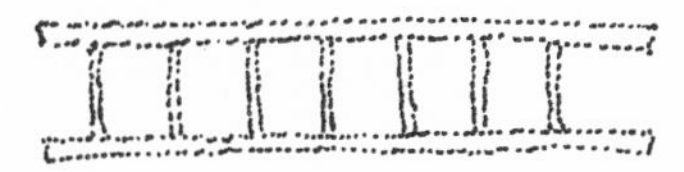

For getting up there! Be sure it is steady and secure each time you use it. Don't lean or cut in an uncomfortable position.

*Knife*

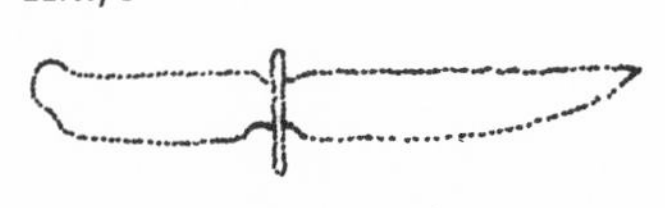

For cutting leaves, small stems. Removing diseased or dead parts. Be sure it is sharp, not rusty.

*Hand Shears*

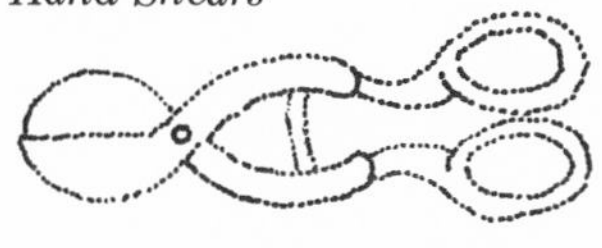

For small twigs, stems, and branches. Cut only with one hand. If shears won't cut easily, use loppers.

*Branch Lopper*

For bigger branches, stems, and limbs. Use two hands. Make a clean, sharp cut. If lopper won't cut easily, use saw.

*Pruning Saw*

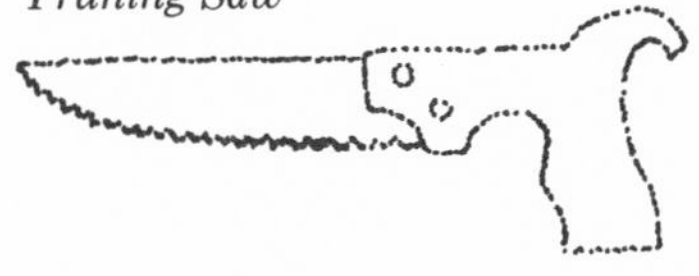

For branches and limbs that can't be cut with hand shears. Know how to cut so rest of plant won't be hurt. Get help with bigger branches. Be careful!

## Pruning Rules

## Don't

Decide where you want the plant to grow.

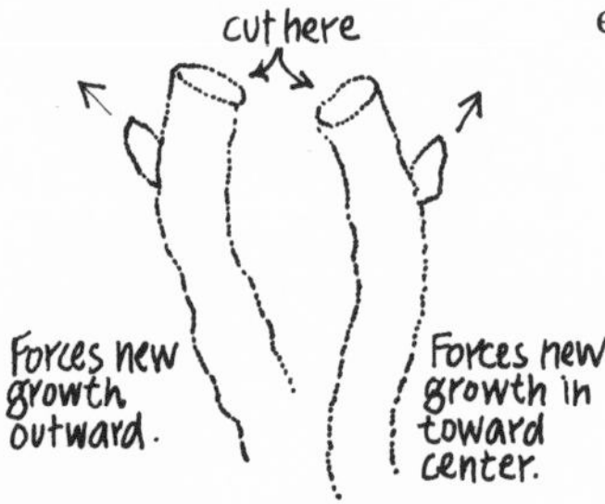


Cut without seeing where new branch will go. Cut all branches so buds grow inward.

Cut unwanted stem to nearest bud or leaf axis.

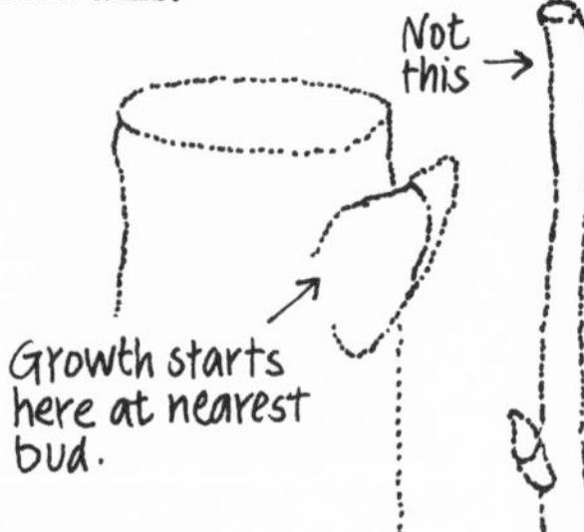


Leave long stem going nowhere so it will rot and be easy for bugs to enter.

Make clean, straight cuts.

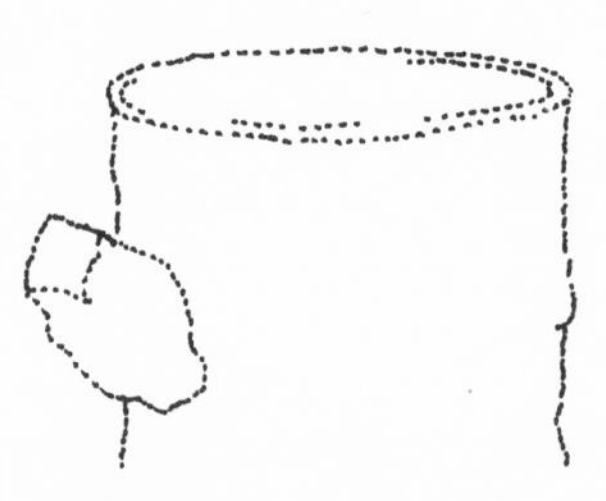

Leave jagged, torn, broken stubs because bad cuts are easy for insects to enter.

### Know When to Stop

Pinching and pruning plants can be difficult in the beginning. It's hard to know just how much to trim and how much to leave on the plant.

Every expert on pruning seems to give the same advice for beginners: Don't prune too much, too fast. Prune a little at one time. Then wait and see what happens. Ask a neighborhood gardener if you can watch when they prune their trees and bushes this winter. If you feel unsure about what you're doing, let the plant tell you when to stop.

### Know When to Call a Tree Surgeon

Sometimes a tree is so sick, tangled, and neglected that it's unwise for a gardener to prune it, especially a beginning gardener. Tree limbs look lighter than they really are. When you least expect it, heavy branches can fall and break things like other limbs. Including people's limbs. When you see a heavy pruning problem somewhere in your garden, tell someone about it. A landscape gardener or tree surgeon should be called to handle the problem.

## Picker's Advice

You can pick most herbs and cut flowers almost anytime in your garden. The same is true for fast-growing vegetables, like radishes, lettuce, carrots, beans, peas.

Slower-growing fruits and vegetables (corn, peanuts, pumpkins, popcorn, soybeans, watermelon) need more time. They are usually ready in the fall. Although some can be picked in late summer — if you start early and grow fast varieties. Seed catalogs usually tell how fast or slow a plant will grow. But how do you know exactly when something in your garden will be ready to pick?

# How to Tell When Fruits or Vegetables Are Ready to Pick

It is hard to say exactly when the fruits of your garden should be picked. Every plant is different. Every single one. You must get to know each plant's timing. Pay closer attention to the plant when it starts to produce the part you want. The plant will tell you when it's ready. It takes a few seasons. I'm still learning. Here are some hints. Remember, only you and the plant knows when it's ready.

Carrots, cucumbers, and squash can be picked young and small. Or you can wait until they get bigger.

Watermelon has its "thump" to tell when it's right. Other melons have a particular smell. Some break off the vine by themselves when they're ready.

Corn has a firm feeling when it's ready and waiting. Some people pull down the corn husks to see if the kernels are full.

Lettuce, root vegetables, and the cabbage family members should be picked before they bolt, or form flower stalks.

## Thanking the Plant Before You Pull It

Any plant that grows in your garden is a blessing. From a seed of almost nothing, it has grown its best and filled you with its delights. Maybe the plant has helped you see forces of life that you don't totally understand. Maybe it has helped keep you alive and healthy. In a very short time you and the plant certainly have changed a lot. How will you thank the plant for what it has given you? You won't have to say much. The plant will know.

I am always saddened when I pull up a plant that has lived its course in my garden. But I don't stay sad long. Because I know I have seeds for the same plant. I will see it again next year.

# Celebrations of the Harvest Season

Throughout history, fall has been a time of holidays and festive events in every culture. Basic traditions and rituals seem to center around autumn. Harvest Moon in September. Hunter's Moon in October. The Autumn Equinox. Halloween. Thanksgiving. Family reunions. People celebrate this time of year to thank nature for its gifts.

Today the connection between the season and the celebration is hard for us to see. People live in too many paved places and not enough green ones. But in the garden this connection is clear. As the days get shorter and another growing season slows down, you can feel it. Things in the garden and in the wilds outside it are becoming dormant again. You look at your wise old plants and remember them when they were little specks of nothing called seeds.

What should you do to celebrate?

## Garden Parties

Anybody with a garden can have a harvest celebration. It's easy. When you feel the time is right, have a party in your garden. If you plan ahead you can have fresh garden treats — sweet corn, watermelon, pumpkin pie, peanuts, fresh-cut flowers, anything — waiting for everyone when they arrive. Who knows? You might start your own holiday!

Around our house, we celebrate Maize Days. Maize is the Indian word for corn. Each fall we invite city folk out to have a taste of real sweet corn. We've done it for the last four years. It's becoming a tradition among friends of our family. Nobody ever gets enough garden sweet corn!

Part Three

# Anyhow You Garden

Chapter 10

# Being a Bee and Being a Burbank

Bees have been crossbreeding plants longer than anyone can tell. People have been crossbreeding plants for only 200 years. The busiest and best plant breeder was Luther Burbank. He was so active. He invented an average of one new variety of plant every three weeks of his career.

Any gardener can be like a bee or be like a Burbank. Anybody can be a plant breeder and invent new plants. It's easy. As long as you pay attention to what you do. And as long as you realize it takes a few seasons to get exactly what you want.

## Bees: Those Bugs You Can't Do Without

Most people think the scariest thing in any garden is bees. Buzzing bees with big stingers. Stingers that hurt worse than any shot the doctor gives. Scare stories and wild rumors float around about "killer bees." These make matters worse. Scared people don't know a good thing when they see it.

Bees are the best bugs in your garden. It can't do without them. Bees pollinate most of the vegetables and fruits we eat. They also crossbreed plants and help make vigorous seeds for the next generation. They've been doing this all quite by accident for thousands of years without even bragging about it.

## The Powers of Pollen

Bees go after it. Some people sneeze at it. A few people think it's more valuable than gold. But without it, no one would eat. And all life on earth as we know it would end. What is it?

Pollen. The magic dust. The stuff that falls from male flowers. And makes its way somehow to the female flowers, where the seed for the next generation of the plant is born. Pollen seems to be an almost indestructible form of life. Botanists and scientists using high-powered microscopes have found pollen grains many thousands of years old.

## More Than Enough

The first plants grew in the oceans. As they slowly evolved to grow on land, plants developed pollen and seeds — parts that needed to be dry and exposed to air instead of water. Pollen and seeds allowed plants to grow and spread all across the earth.

As pollen develops in the stamens of male flowers, it is sticky. It won't fall until it's ready. Pollen is dry and powdery when it's ready. Like dust. When it falls, it is sent by wind or buzzed by bees to fertilize female flowers.

There's always more pollen than needed. Lots of it gets blown away, or used by insects. Unless it's refrigerated in dry air-tight containers, the life-giving quality of pollen lasts about a week. But the pollen grains are never destroyed.

### Breezes and Beeses

Bees use pollen for food. Mostly to feed larval bees. Older bees eat nectar, but sometimes they eat pollen. Bees know when flowers are ready to drop pollen. They even know when the plant is going to flower, days before any buds show. When bees go after pollen both bees and plants benefit.

Some plants don't need to be pollinated by bees and other insects. They are pollinated by the wind, or by gravity, or by themselves. These plants include grains like oats, rice, wheat, barley, or weeds like nettle and dock. You might find bees around a few wind-pollinated plants, especially corn. But the bees aren't there to pollinate flowers. They're just after the pollen.

### Who Can See What a Bee Sees?

Different gardeners and different insects are lured to different flowers. But bugs and bees don't see the same colors you do. A bee can't see red, but it can see blue, green, and yellow. A bee also sees ultraviolet — a color humans can't see. Because it sees ultraviolet, a bee probably sees stripes, spots and designs on twice as many flowers as people can see. You don't know the same garden the bees know.

# Do You See a Difference?

Imagine you are a bee for a minute. Look at the two different flowers below. Which would attract you? Why?

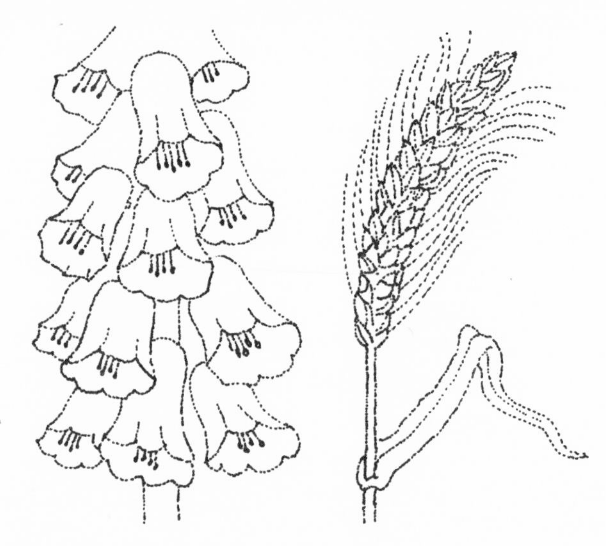

The flower on the left is a foxglove. Who could miss a flower like this? It has an interesting shape, nice patterns, bright colors. Foxgloves can be purple, yellow, red, and pastels. Flowers like foxglove need bugs to pollinate them. So they always look attractive when pollen begins to fall.

The flower on the right is simple and uncolorful. Some people would not call it a flower. It doesn't attract bees or bugs either. It doesn't need to attract anything because it is pollinated by wind. But this dull flower does attract farmers and plant breeders. They have been interested in its seeds throughout history. What is it? Wheat. The flower that makes flour, and becomes the daily bread of many people.

# Plant Breeding

Gardeners are always looking for something special to plant in next year's garden. They always want something new. Something different. Plant breeders try to give gardeners what they want: bigger berries, brighter flowers, or whatever. Breeders invent new plants by selecting and cross-pollinating old ones. The plants they know well.

This is how gardeners got seedless oranges, stringless beans, and fuzzless peaches. Plant breeding is a big business. Each year seed catalogs brag about their new varieties. New ones always cost more than old ones. Most people don't mind paying more, as long as it's new.

### What Can One Little Daisy Do?

Oxeye daisies grow wild just about everywhere. Farmers call them "pernicious weeds." This means evil, destructive, harmful to other plants around it.

When he was a boy, Luther Burbank transplanted some oxeye daisies into his family's vegetable garden in Lancaster, Massachusetts. His dad got mad. Wild daisies don't belong in the garden. They grow wild everywhere else. Besides, they're pernicious. No good. But young Burbank thought otherwise. He wanted to improve the daisies by cross-pollinating them with other daisies. He wanted a perennial white daisy with longer stems and bigger flowers.

Burbank grew to become a famous plant breeder. And he kept growing oxeye daisies in his own garden. He was still hoping to create that better daisy. For many years Burbank crossbred and re-crossed Japanese, European, and American wild daisies. From these he selected the few plants that seemed most like the one he wanted. Then he crossed them again. And again.

Finally, in 1901 Burbank gave the world a new flower. A flower he had been working on two-thirds of his life. Since the days his father caught him transplanting weeds into the garden. What's the flower? The Shasta daisy. A perennial white daisy with big flowers, long stems. A glorious offspring of common weeds.

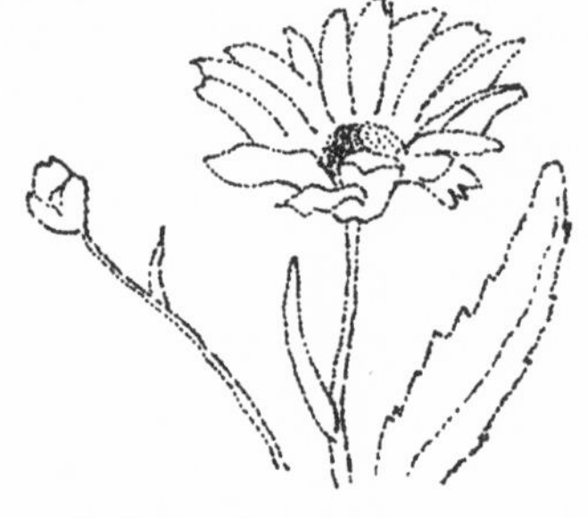

The Shasta daisy is one of the most popular garden flowers of all time. Most new flowers last only ten years before gardeners get tired of growing them. Gardeners have grown the Shasta daisy for more than 75 years. And it's still popular. Do you know it?

## The Experimental Garden

A plant breeder needs an experimental garden. An experimental garden is a magic garden. A special place where new plants are invented. Plants the world has never known before.

You can have an experimental garden anywhere you have a regular garden. Indoors or outdoors. North or south. But it's always best if you have lots of room. With lots of room, you can plant lots of seeds. Even three or four whole packages of seeds! All at once. Then as they grow you can select the few plants you want to save or crossbreed. The more plants you have to pick from, the better chance you have of finding something unique.

A good plant breeder must be a good selector as well as a good picker. Because anything might grow in his garden.

### Plant Breeder's Tools

You won't need any fancy tools to crossbreed plants. You'll probably find most everything you need at home. Besides, your most important tool is always your own sense of selection.

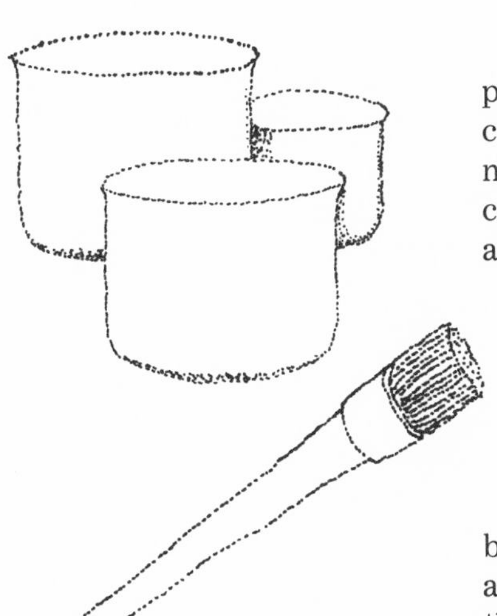

*Dry bowls* — Metal or plastic are best. Wood or ceramic bowls have too many small holes where pollen can get stuck. Bowls must always be dry.

*Brush* — A camel's-hair brush is good. But any good art brush will do. Sometimes this tool is unnecessary. Burbank used his finger instead of a brush.

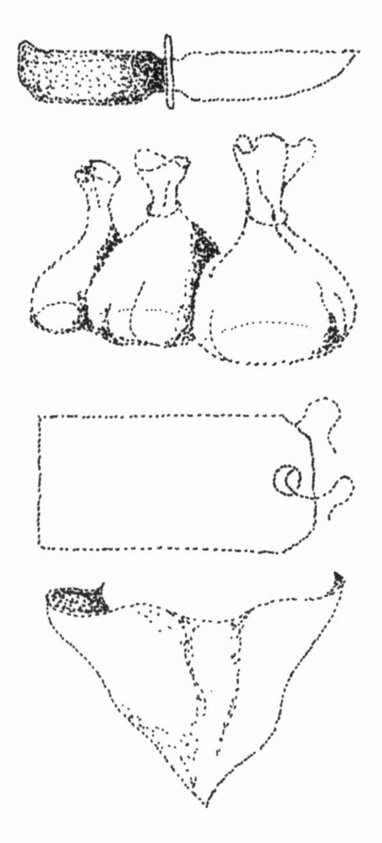

*Knife* — Same as pruning knife — clean and sharp like a steak knife. Used to cut into flowers.

*Plastic bags* — To wrap around a flower after it has been pollinated.

*Tags or Labels* — To record the names of plants and the dates they were cross-pollinated.

*Handkerchief* — Or something else to cover your nose and mouth if the pollen is too thick, so you don't breathe it. This is important if you have hay fever.

## Can You Invent a New Plant?

If bees and other beings can invent new plants, so can you. But plant breeding isn't something you do one day and forget the next. It takes many seasons to create a new plant. Decide which kinds of plants you want to cross. Any two plants can be easily crossed, as long as they're in the same family. Sometimes unrelated plants can also be crossed.

It's best to begin with plants that have big flowers because they're easier to work with. Cucumbers, squash, gourds, pumpkins, chayote, and melons all have big flowers and belong to the same family, Cucurbitaceae. All of them can be cross-pollinated. But before you try to cross anything you should get to know what you want to grow.

## Good Inventors Don't Always Know What They're Doing

Plant breeders work two ways. Both ways are mysterious. They involve forces of life outside anyone's control.

*Cross-pollination* — Taking pollen from the male flowers of one plant and putting it onto the female flowers of another plant. Usually the plants are in the same family. Often they are different varieties of the same plant like corn.

*Selection* — Seeds from the cross-pollinated plants are sown next season. As the seedlings grow, the breeder selects the best of them according to the type of plant he has in mind. If none of the selected plants are exactly what he wants, he might cross them again. Or he might not. Anyway, he selects the best plants and plants the seeds from them each year until he finds what he wants. Sort of on purpose and sort of by accident. He doesn't always know what he's doing. He'll just do what feels right until he gets the plant he wants.

## But How Do You Actually Cross the Plants?

Have you decided which plants you want to cross? Then get a lot of good seeds for those plants and plant all of them at once. Thin out all but the best-growing seedlings. When these mature, you will select the two parents. The plants you want to cross.

The "pollen parent" is the father. The "seed parent" is the mother. Collect pollen from the pollen parent any time before the seed parent's flowers open.

Then watch those unopened flowers of the seed parent. And watch the bees. Be there with a knife when the flowers first open. Carefully cut away the petals and any anthers.

All that should remain are the seed parent's pistils, which are now ready to receive pollen.

Be sure to get to the seed parent's flowers before the bees do. Otherwise they'll pollinate them first. But once the petals and anthers have been cut away, bugs won't be attracted to the flower.

Brush, sprinkle, or dust the collected pollen onto the pistils. Once this happens, the flower is pollinated. It is fertilized.

## After Pollination

Cover fertilized flowers with plastic bags. Label them and leave them alone to develop seeds. Then save all the seeds from the seed parent. Plant them next year and see what happens.

## Water Drowns Pollen

Pollen will not work after it gets wet. It must stay dry. The pistils of the female flower also must be dry, or the plant will not be pollinated.

Use a hose wisely. Don't water flowers when pollen is falling. And whenever you start to cross-pollinate anything, check to be sure your hands, brush, bowl, and bags are dry.

## How to Cross-Pollinate Corn

### Pollen Parent

1. Wait for tassels to open and pollen sacks to hang down. Tap pollen into bowl. Keep pollen in dry place until seed parent's silks are ready.

### Seed Parent

2. Cut off tassels before they open and drop pollen. So it can't pollinate itself.

3. When corn silks show on seed parent, brush pollen onto silks. Not too much. One grain of pollen makes one kernel of corn.

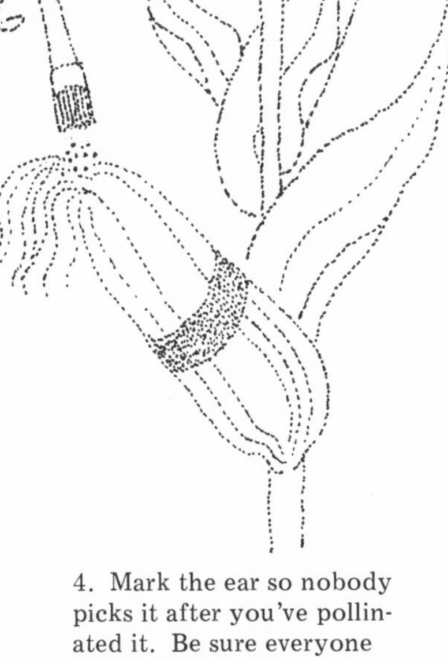

4. Mark the ear so nobody picks it after you've pollinated it. Be sure everyone knows why the corn is marked.

# Selection:
# Another Kind of Picking

Luther Burbank was considered a "wizard" and "genius" mostly because he was a good picker. He could select the strongest, sweetest, rarest plant out of thousands. And he did it so quickly that people could not believe it.

A big part of Burbank's secret wasn't really a secret. He always planted very large amounts of one kind of plant. Then after they had grown long enough to show him what they could do, he would pull up all but a few of them. Hundreds of plants would be destroyed, all at once. And only one or two would breed the next generation.

This way he copied nature and what happens when weeds plant themselves. Thousands of seeds are planted but only the strongest weeds survive and carry in the strongest seeds for the next generation.

### Mutation and Other "Sports"

Any time you plant any seed, there is a chance for an oddball. The seed could grow into something like nothing anyone has ever seen before. A strange new kind of plant. One that has never grown anywhere else. Gardeners call these plants "sports." Scientists call them "mutations." A few scientists believe that mutations are the main way a life form evolves.

The chances for a mutation or sport are better in a garden than in the wilds. Because garden plants are more hybridized and crossbred. Garden seeds don't have to fight for space as much as wild seeds. Only the strongest survive in the wild. Weird plants can come out of any regular seed pack. When a sport grows in your garden, you have something no one else has. Maybe it's the beginning of a whole new genus.

How can you find a sport in your garden? Almost the same way you crossbreed and select for a new variety. First you learn how the plant usually grows. Then you look for the most unusual ones.

## Plant Breeder's Checklist

What should you look for when you crossbreed and select plants to create a new one? When you're with any plant you think is special, find the answers to these questions.

### For Flowers

*Colors* — What are the normal colors for this kind of flower? Does this flower's color seem new?

*Sizes* — How big is the flower supposed to get? Is this larger or smaller than usual?

*Shape* — How does the flower normally look? Is this one really different?

*Smell* — Nothing can tell you this but your own nose. Do you know how the plant usually smells? Is this aroma different?

*Bloom time* — How long do flowers normally last on the plant? How long do they last when cut?

*Anything else* — Do you want something else in the flower? Curled petals or double blossoms? Does this flower have it?

## For Fruit

*Season* — How long does the plant normally take for the first fruit to mature? How long does this one take?

*Size* — How big is this variety supposed to get? Is the new fruit larger, smaller, or what?

*Flavor* — Do you know how the fruit usually tastes when it's really ripe? How does this one taste?

*Shape* — What is the normal shape of the fruit? How is this one different?

*Diseases* — What diseases usually bother the plant? How well does this one grow? Does anything make it sick?

*Anything else* — Do you want seedless fruits? Or thin-skinned ones? Or what? Does this plant have it?

## For Whole Plants

*Growth* — How long and how fast does the plant normally take to grow? Is this plant faster?

*Size* — Is the variety normally a vine, dwarf, or giant? How is this new plant different?

*Pests* — What usually bothers the plant? Does it bug this new plant?

*Attractions* — What do you normally like about the leaves and shape of the plant? How is this one different?

*Anything else* — Does it transplant well? Or stand up against a stiff wind? Or what?

Do you have the new plant you want? Save the seeds from it.

## Burbank's Advice

When gardeners and others asked Luther Burbank about the best way to breed plants he gave this good advice.

Picture clearly in your mind the new kind of plant you want to create. It might be a certain color, a certain shape, a certain size. Whatever you want. Just have a clear picture.

Crossbreed and select plants for many seasons. As long as it takes. Until you get the plant to match the picture in your mind.

Keep trying. Selection and breeding take time and patience.

## Forgotten Secrets

Scientists have one big complaint about Luther Burbank. He did not take good notes. Many plants he created no longer exist because he did not write down how he did it. This is important to scientists who want to try the same experiments.

Many of Burbank's super cereal grains are lost. Grains that were four times more productive than any known today. Many fruits, flowers, and vegetables that he invented are also lost. Because no one knows how he created the plants.

Certainly, much of what Burbank did cannot be written down. He relied on instincts and senses that cannot be put into words. He kept most of it in his head, or on napkins and scribbled notes. They are all his secrets.

## Plant Breeders Journal

When you experiment with crossbreeding, keep a journal. Make it look something like this:

| Type | Seed Parent | Pollen Parent | Date Crossed | Remarks |
|---|---|---|---|---|
| CORN | | | | |
| | Black Aztec | Illini Xtra Sweet | Aug. 8 | hot + dry |
| | Six-Shooter | " " " | Aug. 8 | small silks |
| | Black Aztec | " " " | Aug. 16 | second try |
| MELON | | | | |
| | Sugar Baby | Yellow Baby | Aug. 10 | hot |
| | Honey Dew | " " | Aug. 12 | windy |
| | | | | |

## Impossible Possibilities

Plants have always helped people become more civilized. Every great civilization has great gardens where plants help people slow down and relax.

Plant breeders know more about plants than most people. In the last quarter of the 20th century, plant breeders will be looking into the following possibilities.

Taking gasoline and other oil products directly from new varieties of "mole plant" or *Euphorbia*, instead of drilling messy wells.

Crossbreeding members of the Gramineae family to find supergrains. New kinds of rice, wheat, oats, corn, as well as entirely new grains.

Selecting and crossbreeding heirloom varieties of all kinds of garden plants. Hardy new species and stronger old one will be developed from old Indian and family seed collections.

Breeding and selecting vegetables and fruits suited for gardens rather than mechanical cultivation.

Creating more vital varieties of global plant life. Not just the standard farm and garden favorites, but more useful plants as well.

Chapter 11

# Seasons Under the Wonder of the Sun and Moon

China. Egypt. Greece. Rome. Peru. Central America. In every early civilization people worshipped the sun and moon as gods. People planned their daily lives around the rhythmic movements of these two brightest of heavenly bodies.

Old-time farmers and gardeners also know how the moon, sun, and other celestial bodies move people and plants on earth. Around the world, people still plant, transplant, cultivate, and harvest according to moon phases.

There is much mystery in this. A lot that cannot be explained. Many people believe "moon planting" is stupid. Others do not. If it works for you, fine. If it doesn't, don't worry about it.

# Journey to the Barycenter of the Earth

The moon is so huge that some scientists consider it a planet. They say the earth and moon make a "double-planet" system. Certainly the moon is the closest celestial body to the earth. The moon's pull is among the strongest forces we feel. Although the moon is large for a satellite, the earth is 81 times more massive than the moon. If both globes could be put on a teeter-totter, the moon could never budge the earth. The teeter-totter couldn't move unless the earth rolled over a bit onto the moon's side.

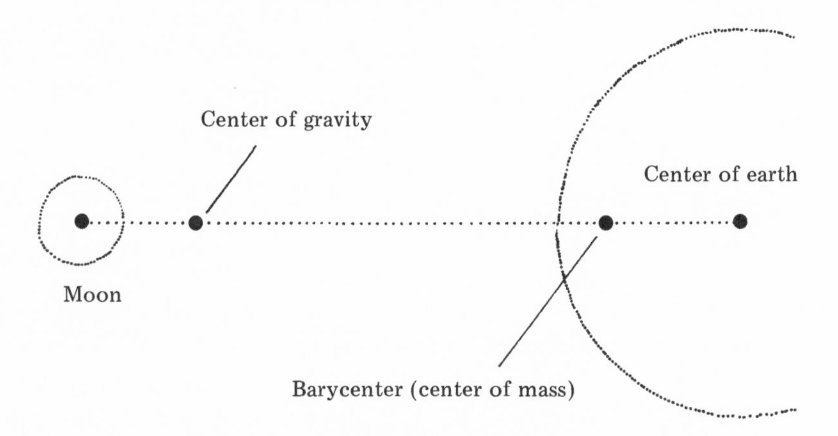


The center of mass between earth and moon is called the "barycenter." It is an imaginary balance point between the mass of earth and the mass of the moon. It is located inside the earth. It is not a fixed point. It is always moving. It changes as the earth spins. It changes as the moon moves closer or farther from the earth.

## Barycentric Circles

Life on earth is always teetering on the moon's side of the barycenter. This is one reason the moon has such a big influence on our lives. As the earth and moon move, so moves the barycenter. As these regular movements change we feel it. Plants feel it too.

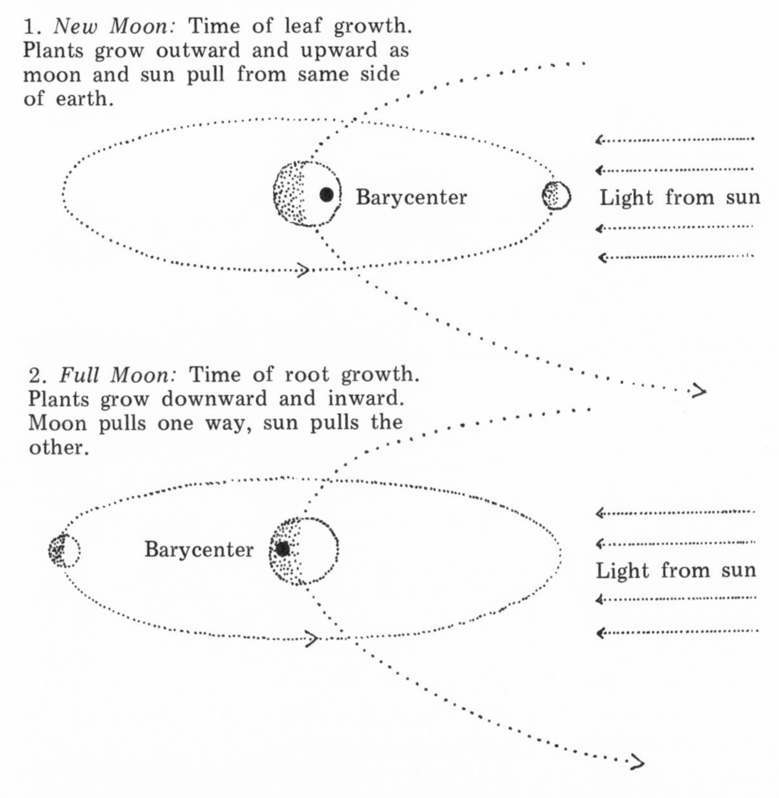


The Barycenter always moves as earth rotates on axis and as moon revolves around the earth.

# The Tides in the Trees and the Tides in Your Toes

Everyone knows the moon causes tides in the sea. But some scientists now realize the moon causes other tides as well. One of these is the earth tide. All lands on earth rise and fall each day, just like sea tides. The average difference between high and low earth tides is 12 inches. The moon makes the ground move! Up and down! Two times every day!

The earth's atmosphere also has tidal bulges. These are called "lunar winds." They are very slight, but measurable, about 1/20 mph.

High and low water tides are also felt in lakes, ponds, rivers, streams, creeks, cups of coffee, and in all other liquids and bodies of water, including your body and everybody's body. People are made mostly of fluids. And no fluid escapes the tidal pull of the moon. This includes the fluids moving in plants too.

# Moon Pull

Many people think the moon has no influence on the growth of plants and gardens. These people say any gardener who cultivates, plants, and harvests according to the moon is superstitious. And a little crazy. But a lot of gardeners believe the moon moves their garden. It's common sense to them. They can see the moon's effects. Planting by the moon makes their gardens grow better, they say.

### A One-Month Observation

Does the moon really have an effect on the growth of plants? You can find out for yourself. Do this little experiment. It's similar to one Francis Bacon tried when he wanted to answer the same question in the 16th century.

Select a blank spot in your garden for the experiment. It should be at least five feet long and one foot wide. Be sure the soil is freshly dug and throughly mixed. Plant two seeds a day in that spot for the next month. Plant in two long rows, four inches between rows, and two inches between each day's new planting.

If it is summer, plant beans. If it is spring or fall, plant peas. Pick seeds that all seem to have the same vitality. Don't plant any dry ones or monster seeds. Also try to plant all the seeds at the same time each day. And keep track of when you planted them. Make a chart something like this:

| Day Planted | Time | Weather | Day Sprouted |
|---|---|---|---|
| May 2 | 8:10 A.M. | hot and dry | |
| May 3 | 8:20 | hot and dry | |
| May 4 | 8:15 | warm and wet | |
| May 5 | 8:40 | hot and dry | |
| | | | |
| | | | |
| | | | |

After all the plants have sprouted and you've completed the chart, find the date of the last full moon and the last new moon. Check a farmer's almanac, calendar, your local newspaper, or the local weather bureau. Mark these dates on your chart.

Did the seeds sprout one day at a time? Or was there one time during the month when more seeds sprouted at once? If so, did it happen near full moon, new moon or when?

**The Sun Cycle**
**(365 days in one year)**

*Spring* (Vernal Equinox around March 21) — Wait for soil to warm and open up. Dig as soil warms, add compost and manures. Plant cool season vegetables (lettuce, peas, carrots . . .). Plant early annual flowers (sweet pea, snapdragon, cosmos). Start warm season tomatoes, melons, or peppers indoors. Keep compost heaps full and moist.

*Summer* (Summer Solstice around June 21) — Plant, plant, plant until you run out of room. Plant successively short-season vegetables (carrots, lettuce, beets). Pick first flowers to make more blooms. Keep vines and pole beans staked up. Remove dead leaves. Watch for pests and diseases, remove damaged plants. Don't let compost dry out.

*Autumn* (Autumnal Equinox around September 23) — Harvest moon appears in September. Plant cool season vegetables where you have room. Plant cover crops (clover, rye, vetch) in vegetable beds. Clean up, fill compost heaps. Keep fallen leaves in separate piles for leaf mold. Watch for first frost of winter. Cover tender plants during light frosts.

*Winter* (Winter Solstice around December 22) — Time of slow growth. Sort and store seeds. Mail seed order before January rush. Prune back fruit trees and shrubs. Clean, oil, and store tools. Start a few spring seeds indoors in February.

## The Earth Cycle
## (one day in 24 hours)

*Morning* (dawn until day heats up) — Best time to water, before heat speeds evaporation. Bad time to transplant, except on dark cloudy days. Cut flowers for arrangements. Good time to catch slow pests: snails, earwigs. OK to plant seeds that need warm season. Welcome the day, find out what plants need today.

*Noon* (time of fullest hottest sun) — Worst time to water, unless very cloudy. Worst time to transplant. Usually too hot to dig, wastes your energy. OK for weeding, but why bother? Do hobbies or chores. Go swimming if it's too hot!

*Evening* (day begins to cool) — good time to pick fruits, vegetables and flowers. Good time to dig and cultivate. Best time to transplant. OK to water but will cause bug and mildew problems. Good time to find evening-eating pests.

*Night* (no sunlight in garden) — Maybe catch a few snails and slugs. Poor time to plant or dig. Bad time to garden. Plants need sleep too!

**The Moon Cycle**
**(29½ days in one phase)**

*First quarter* (new moon to waxing crescent) — Time of most leaf growth. Good time to plant leafy greens (spinach, lettuce, chard). Plant, plant, plant as moon is waxing.

*Second quarter* (waxing half to full moon) — Best planting time of month. Good time to plant vines (tomatoes, pumpkins, beans). Saps run high, things hold more moisture. People, seeds, and things, hold more fluids.

*Third quarter* (full moon to waning crescent) — Time of most root growth. Good time to plant bulbs (onions, tulips), corms (gladiolus). Also plant rhizomes (lily) and tubers (potatoes). Transplant perennials, biennials, berries at full moon.

*Fourth quarter* (waning half to new moon) — Saps fall, things dry out. Don't plant, time of slowest growth. Dig, hoe, or otherwise cultivate. Put weeds and dead plants in compost. Best time to prune and cut wood.

## Cycles of the Sun, Earth, and Moon

Time spins with the sun, the moon, the planet earth. All turn together in the dance of life. The best gardeners follow the rhythms of the sun, the earth, and the moon. These gardeners know there are favorable times and unfavorable times to do everything in the garden.

## Planting Signs

Planting "by the moon" actually means planting by the moon and stars. But not just any stars — the stars in the signs of the zodiac. The zodiac is a belt around the sky where the sun, moon, and planets always travel. Throughout history, people have known this is a special part of the sky.

The zodiac is divided into twelve parts or "signs" — Aries, Taurus, Gemini, Cancer, Leo, Virgo, Libra, Scorpio, Sagittarius, Capricorn, Aquarius, Pisces. Each night the moon is seen against the backdrop of stars in one of these signs. Every two or three days, the moon moves into another sign. Some people plan their gardens according to the signs of the zodiac. What signs are best for planting? No one really agrees.

Most gardeners who plant by the moon say Pisces, Cancer and Scorpio are the best planting signs. Capricorn, Taurus, and Libra are OK for planting. But the other six signs

(Gemini, Leo, Virgo, Sagittarius, Aquarius, Aries) are "barren." These are favorable signs for digging and cultivation, but not for planting.

### No Sign Is a Bad Sign

Other gardeners and farmers believe that no zodiac sign is a bad sign for planting. Each sign has a good influence, based on what part of the plant is being cultivated.

| Plants Grown For: | Quarter: | Moon Sign: |
|---|---|---|
| *Roots* | | |
| potatoes, beets, turnips, carrots, celeriac, radish, Jerusalem artichoke | third | Taurus<br>Virgo<br>Capricorn |
| *Flowers* | | |
| all annuals, perennials, grown for flowers, also buckwheat and flax. | second<br>and<br>third | Gemini<br>Libra<br>Aquarius |
| *Leaves* | | |
| lettuce, spinach, chard, salad bitters, kohlrabi, cauliflower, and leeks. | first<br>and<br>second | Cancer<br>Scorpio<br>Pisces |
| *Fruits* | | |
| tomatoes, cucumbers, melons, beans, corn, peppers, other grains. | second | Leo<br>Sagittarius<br>Aries |

Chapter 12

# What Else Will You Find in the Garden?

Something new grows every day in a garden. It may be a weed. A new leaf. A flower. A hiding surprise of any size. Life creates life in a garden. You start things but you never finish them. Everything takes care of itself. And nothing seems impossible. Everything you need to know about the garden is in the garden. Waiting for you to find it. What will you grow in your next garden? And the one after that? And the . . .

## "All Flowers Talk to Me"

After the War Between the States, the world became concerned with machines. This was the time of the Industrial Revolution.

During this time there lived a genius of a boy in the Ozark hill country of southwestern Missouri. He lived on the frontier between the growing mechanized cities and the Wild West. The boy was blessed with a unique understanding of plants.

By himself, he turned a forgotten piece of river bottom land into a lush secret garden full of rare flowers and vegetables. He also built his own hidden greenhouse, mixed his own special soil, and earned a reputation among the farming people in the area. People thought the boy was a magician who knew every trick of the plant world.

Neighbors and farmers brought ailing animals and potted plants to the boy. They expected him to know how to heal these sick creatures. He usually did. People often asked him how he performed such magic. "All the flowers talk to me," he would say, "and so do hundreds of little living things in the woods. I learn what I know by watching and loving everything."

Of course, the flowers didn't talk out loud. They talked to him silently, in his mind. From gardening and backwoods country healing, the boy went on to become a famous teacher in Alabama. Much of his fame came after he showed the world how to transform the lowly sweet potato and peanut into cosmetics, grease, ink, coffee, and many other products. The world remembers him as George Washington Carver.

Who knows when another kid will show the world a plant as useful as the sweet potato or the peanut? Certainly it will be someone special. Someone who will listen when the flowers talk silently.

## Living with Creatures That Don't Walk to Dinner

Sometimes plant life seems to be the most intelligent life form on earth. Certainly plants are not destructive, violent beings. They don't go around biting people, making war, or spraying poisons on other creatures.

Scientists have been amused and confused by recent news about plants. Plants have been wired to a machine. The machine is similar to a lie detector. It shows that plants seem to know when someone is thinking of hurting them!

Electronics wizards have wired up computers and motors to plants. They report the plants have sent signals that opened garage doors, started cars, and taped telephone messages. However, some scientists have tried many of the same experiments and found conflicting results. The plants couldn't do what other scientists said they could. Many of the unsuccessful scientists said they always had doubts about the magic abilities of plants.

"That's their whole problem," said the first group of scientists, "plants won't cooperate with skeptical scientists." "Hogwash," said the skeptical scientists. The argument is still going on.

## Garden Creatures Who Don't Have Roots and Don't Have Eyes

The difference between a rose bush and a greyhound dog is obvious, right? One is a plant and one is an animal. That's simple enough. But the difference between plants and animals gets blurry the farther you go down the ladder of life. Protozoa, algae, bacteria, viruses, molds, rusts, smut. Things you can't see with unaided eyes.

Under a microscope it's hard to tell plants from animals. Scientists aren't always sure what to call many of the weird creatures they see, creatures in the soil, air, and water.

Today's plants and animals probably had common ancestors among the many microscopic forms that lived millions of years ago. Back in the soupy seas where the first life on earth was born. And in the first soils.

Then and now there is no straight line dividing plants from animals. Biologists have created a third kingdom of life. It is called *Protista.* Creatures that are somewhere between plants and animals. These creatures are under your feet every time you walk in your garden.

## Conversations with Plants

Some people talk to their garden and house plants. The plants don't talk back. So it seems a little ridiculous. Many people tease talking gardeners. "You're only talking to yourself," they say. But the gardeners go right on talking. It probably doesn't make much difference whether people talk to their plants or not. Plants don't need words to understand people's thoughts and feelings. Plants are intelligent beings. They can converse in other ways. They carry on silent conversations.

### Silent Conversations

There is no easy way for a book to tell you how to mentally converse with plants. But here are some hints.

Have a good feeling toward the plants you want to "talk" to. A bad attitude will affect the plants and they won't want to hear you. Who wants to talk to a grump anyway?

Pick one plant you like and want to get to know. Look at it a while. Get to know it. Then close your eyes and find a quiet spot in your mind.

Concentrate on the plant. Say hello, in your mind. Let the plant know you are ready to hear its secrets.

## Drawing and Photographing Your Garden

Do you like to draw? Do you have a camera? Your garden might grow better if you draw or take pictures of it. Try this experiment to find out how much your plants like to have their pictures made.

Plant popcorn, peanuts, or something else you really like. Make a big enough planting so several plants will grow in one spot. After you have thinned out the plants to their normal spacings, select one of the plants to be your model. Don't pick the fastest-growing plant. Pick one that is like most of the others.

Each day for the next month make a picture of the special plant. Don't pay attention to the other plants. Try not even think about them. Just concentrate on the one plant. Try to take or make pictures that show how much you appreciate the plant.

At the end of the month, look at the pictures and see how the plant has changed. Maybe it grew better. Maybe not. Some plants could be shy.

## Bringing Music into the Garden

Do you take your radio into the garden? What stations do you listen to? Are they loud with fast-talking jive commercials? Have you ever wondered how music sounds to plants, bugs, and other animals in your garden? Can plants even hear sounds? They don't have ears. Maybe they feel it some other way. Maybe it tickles their leaves.

A few scientists and college students have tested plants to see how they grow with different kinds of music playing around them. In one test at Temple Buell College in Denver, cucumber plants were grown in separate rooms. The plants grew under the same conditions of light, heat, and humidity. But each environment was different. In one room the music of Brahms, Mozart, and Beethoven was played all day. In the other room, loud rock-and-roll music was played. In the room with classical music, the plants grew toward the speakers. In the rock-and-roll room, the plants grew away from the speakers.

Other plants have been tested at other colleges. Some of them lean to the music of Bach, Ravi Shankar, and Louis Armstrong. One record company has released an album of music especially recorded for plants.

## Muzak Makers

It's easy enough to find out what kind of music your plants like. You can even set up your own tests with house plants. Maybe asparagus ferns like the Beatles better than Bach, or spider plants like Lester Flatt better than The Who. But what difference does it make, really?

Tests like these get pointless after a while. After all, the plants aren't deciding what music they "hear." People are. How would you like it if someone made you listen to Lawrence Welk bubble music all day? Maybe the plants would just like a little peace and quiet. Why not let them listen to the music inside themselves?

## A Garden Is a Quiet Place

Things usually move slowly in a garden. Unless people or bugs are chasing after something. Garden life goes on simply, surely, and quietly. A garden is a special place where people can get away from radio barkers and screaming TV hyenas. A garden is a place where your ears can relax along with the rest of you.

### Sports You Don't Need in Your Garden

Certainly a garden isn't a playground, ball field, or race track. Don't let people treat it like one. Make sure your friends understand this. Nothing hurts a gardener more than to see a plant suddenly injured by a careless friend after it has grown hardily for five months. Put signs up if you have to.

## Careers in the Garden

If you really enjoy gardening, you might want to make a career of it. There are many jobs you can teach yourself. Many plant breeders, landscape gardeners, grounds keepers, market gardeners, "plant doctors," seedmen, botanists, farmers, growers, and others have started their careers at home, in their own gardens.

Some of these jobs you might be able to do now. For some you'll have to wait until you're older. But you can start learning any one of them today.

### Grounds Keepers

Many public buildings, civic parks, and other large estates have grounds keepers. Their job is to keep everything pinched, pruned, and looking nice, including the lawns. Most of the plants are perennials. Trees and flowering shrubs. But sometimes a grounds keeper will keep beds of annuals.

Garden Fresh
VEGETABLES
AND FRUIT

## Landscape Gardeners

When some people have a new home built, they hire a landscape gardener to design and plant the entire lot around the home. Landscaping is expensive but it's worth it. Especially for people with homes on hills that would wash away if they weren't planted with trees, shrubs, and ground covers.

## Market Gardeners

People with big food gardens near a town, suburb, or city often sell vegetables and fruits. This fresh produce is sold off a cart, from a stand on a nearby road with lots of traffic, or sometimes it is sold through small food stores. A 15-year-old who lives near my home made $1,500 last year in his roadside food stand.

## Seedmen

All it takes to start a seed company is seeds. Of course, you know that. The trick is finding enough seeds of everything that everyone wants to grow. And that is often the job of the plant breeder, not the seedmen.

## Collegiate Gardening

In college, gardeners can study their craft in three different departments — Botany, Horticulture, and Agriculture.

## Botany

Botanists are concerned with naming and classifying plants and observing how they grow. They're interested in new plants and the histories of old ones. Botanists are more concerned with grouping plants than with growing them.

### Horticulture

This is the study of gardening. Horticulture involves actually growing plants. Often the plants are ornamentals Often they are grown in greenhouses.

### Agriculture

Agriculture is big business and many schools are noted for their agricultural programs. The concern of agriculture is feeding everyone. This is usually done with big machines. But the plants are the same ones growing in your vegetable garden.

### "Plant Doctors"

In some parts of New York, Los Angeles, and other cities, people pay up to $50 an hour for a "plant doctor" to make a house call. A plant doctor is little more than someone who can figure out if a plant needs watering or drying out. If it needs more light or less light. If it's being bugged by something.

## Every Gardener's Goal: The Year-Round Garden

After a few years a gardener begins to understand how certain plants grow only at certain times. Different flowers bloom in each season and at different times during the day. Vegetables and fruits are ripe at certain seasons. And they taste different when picked at different times of the day. Herbs also have their own seasons. So do all other plants. Slowly a gardener gets to know them.

The common goal of most gardeners usually becomes to have something blooming and ripe all year long — annuals, vegetables, herbs, perennials. That way the plant life is most attractive to the other kinds of life that are drawn to the garden.

### Gifts from the Garden

The best things that can come out of any garden are presents. Birthday presents, Christmas presents, anniversary, and other holiday gifts. If you have a big garden, it can provide an endless supply of gifts.

Most people appreciate the taste of fresh garden food. Anytime you have extra vegetables or fruits, you can give them away to neighbors. Invent a holiday if you need one.

## An Indian Attitude: Don't Waste It

Any part of a plant is valuable, if you know how to use it. Indians and early people tried using all parts of plants for all kinds of things. Roots for soap. Stems for rope. Stalks for building houses. Fibers for clothing. Leaves for eating and healing. Flowers for pleasure. Seeds for the future and fruits for dessert. Anything that wasn't used was composted back into the soil. Indians knew a very basic law of life: Nothing is "waste."

## Variety Is the Paradise of Life

"Garden." Say the word and a different picture will come to everybody's mind. Completely different pictures. To some people, a garden means vegetables or fresher, healthier food. To other folks, a garden means flowers or a place full of color or maybe roses. Other people may have only herbs in mind.

Some people think of gardens as jungles. Places to grow all the flowers, vegetables, fruits, herbs, shrubs, trees, bees, frogs, birds, worms, bugs, and unseen living things that will possibly fit. Everybody has a different idea of what a garden is, or what a garden should be. Thank goodness! This gives you a lot more freedom to decide what your garden can be.

You may have a garden of only strawberries. Or your garden might have every growing thing you can imagine, plus exotic dog-eating tropical plants that aren't supposed to grow in your area. I don't know what kind of garden you should have. Neither does anyone else. But you know. You can have any kind of garden you want.

# Your Next Gardens

SEEDS

# The Planter's and Picker's Pages

The next pages are for all planters and pickers. And any other gardeners ready to breathe life into their gardens. The pages are written like a baseball box score. The plants are in alphabetical order, so you can read them quickly and find things fast. Like where the plant comes from. Who its friends are. What family it belongs to. How it grows.

Come back to the pages when you need to remember anything about a plant you're growing. Here they are: 50 plants to plant and pick.

aloe vera
alyssum
balm
bamboo
barley
basil
beans
carrots
celtuce
chayote
chervil
comfrey
compass plant
corn
cosmos
cotton
crocus
cucumbers
daffodil
dill
flax
gladiolus
iris
kohlrabi
lettuce
luffa
marigold
mint
nasturtium
onions
parsley
peas
peanuts
popcorn
potatoes
pumpkin
purslane
radishes
rye
sage
soybeans
strawberries
summer savory
sunflower
thyme
tomatoes
tulip
watermelon
yucca
and
zinnia

# How to Use the Planter's and Picker's Pages

There are millions of plants on earth. On these pages, there are 50 plants. Some of them are very popular. Others are known only to a few. Not every plant on these pages is easy to grow. But many of them are almost weeds. They grow that fast.

Seeds for most of the plants can be found through mail-order seed houses, garden supply centers, and local nurseries. But if seeds are hard to find, the page will tell you where to get them.

The Planter's and Picker's Pages are written in garden language. Use the Dictionary of Garden Language that begins on page 305 to help if you don't understand something you read in this section.

Here's what you will find on the pages:

**The Plant's Origin, History, and Relatives**

*proper name:* The plant's full scientific name. A name known worldwide. Based on Swedish botanist Carolus Linnaeus' classifications.

*common names:* Some of the many names the plant has in different cultures and different countries.

*family:* Plants have families too. Usually based on the shape and process of the plant's flowers.

*relatives:* Some other members of the family.

*native land:* Where scientists think the plant was first grown by natives who selected it from native wild plants.

*history:* How the plant spread from its native land to other places around the world, and into our gardens.

## How to Grow the Plant

*generation:* hardy annual, perennial vine, whatever
*growing season:* time of year it grows
*time to plant:* when to start plants in garden or flats
*time to pick:* when flowers, fruits, etc. are ready
*needs:* what kind of soil is best for the plant
*location:* where the plant grows best
*distance apart:* how much space between each plant
*height:* how tall the plant can grow
*propagation:* starting the plant by seed, bulb, cuttings
*germination:* how many days seeds need to sprout
*seed life:* how long seed will last in storage
*companions:* other plants it likes to grow with (when known)
*types and colors:* different varieties you can grow (when available)
*where to get it:* if it's hard to get
*cultivation:* anything special you need to know about growing it.
*water:* how much moisture the plant needs
*parts and uses:* how each part of the plant has been used
*picking:* how to cut flowers or harvest vegetables

# Aloe Vera

This ancient plant looks like a cactus but it belongs to the lily family. Aloe has a jelly inside its leaves. This jelly can be a very useful skin care salve. The plant also looks healthy and happy, anywhere you plant it.

*proper name:* *Aloe vera*
*common name:* aloe, aloe vera, true aloe, Barbados aloe
*family:* lily (Liliceae)
*relatives:* onions, lily tulip, butterfly lily, garlic, chives, hyacinth, asparagus, lily of the valley, yucca
*native land:* southern Africa
*history:* An old plant known in many lands for its healing properties. Prized during Roman empire and in other countries around the Mediterranean. The Spanish brought it to the New World. Many gardeners grow aloes just because they look good. Now widely "naturalized."

**How to Grow Aloe Vera**

*generation:* hardy perennial succulent in frost-free places
*growing season:* hot dry summer days
*time to plant:* anytime, but best in early spring
*time to pick:* anytime leaf is big enough
*needs:* not particular
*location:* open full sun, also in the kitchen
*distance apart:* 18 to 24 inches
*height:* 12 to 48 inches
*propagation:* stolons from parent plant
*companions:* cactus and succulents
*color:* yellow flowers
*cultivation:* easy to grow
*water:* don't overwater, likes dry soil and climate
*parts and uses:* as a salve for skin burns, sunburn, bruises, heals wounds on tree and plant trunks, also as a kitchen plant
*picking:* pinch off part of leaf, healing gel is inside

# Alyssum

Many gardeners like to grow alyssum because it grows fast and its flowers last a long time. They look best along pathways and borders.

*proper name: Lobularia maritima*
*common name:* alyssum, sweet alyssum, madwort, gold dust, basket of gold
*family:* cabbage (Cruciferae)
*relatives:* cabbage, cauliflower, turnip, mustard, cress, wallflower, stocks, lunaria
*native land:* probably Mediterranean
*history:* The name "alyssum" comes from the Greek word meaning "not enraged." Plant was fabled to quiet angry tempers. This seaside plant spread from the Mediterranean to Europe, then to other coastal areas where it became naturalized.

Alyssum

**How to Grow Alyssum**

*generation:* hardy annual, perennial in mild coastal areas
*growing season:* summer
*time to plant:* very early spring
*time to pick:* six weeks after seed is sown! until frost
*needs:* almost any garden loam, well-drained
*location:* full sun
*distance apart:* 6 inches for annuals, 12 inches for perennials
*height:* 6 to 18 inches
*propagation:* seeds, cuttings, division
*germination:* 4 to 11 days
*seed life:* three to four years
*companions:* purple aubrietas, cabbage family members
*colors:* flowers white, pink, yellow, blue
*cultivation:* when early plants die back in summer, trim off the dead parts and they will grow back
*water:* needs adequate moisture
*parts and uses:* border, edging; rock garden, dry wall; long lasting blooms

# Balm

This lemony smelling herb is a favorite hangout of bees after a hard day's work. Bees like the aroma of the balm leaves. If you like the taste of lemonade, you might like iced lemon balm tea. The drink is supposed to soothe overworked minds.

*proper name:* *Melissa officinalis*
*common name:* balm, lemon balm, sweet balm, Melissa
*family:* mint (Labiatae)
*relatives:* thyme, rosemary, lavender, hyssop, catnip, oregano
*native land:* Asia
*history:* From Asia, balm spread to the Mediterranean where it became a popular herb in a place where herbs were important to everyday life. Old herbalists believed that balm soothed the brain. Europeans brought balm to the New World. Many gardeners know the importance of balm in attracting bees.

Balm

**How to Grow Balm**

*generation:* hardy perennial
*growing season:* balmy summers
*time to plant:* spring
*time to pick:* anytime leaves and stems are available
*needs:* average soil
*location:* sun or shade
*distance apart:* 8 to 12 inches
*height:* 24 inches
*propagation:* seed and root division
*germination:* 7 to 21 days
*seed life:* two to three years
*companions:* anywhere around garden, near flowers where bees work the most
*cultivation:* conserve moisture, mulch during dry season
*water:* needs lots, don't let it get dry!
*parts and uses:* leaves attract bees; make tea; flavor salads, soups, and sandwiches; also used as mouthwash and healing herb
*picking:* cut off a bunch of stems anytime, use fresh for best tea

# Bamboo

Scientists may be confused about what to call it, but people around the world know bamboo is one of the most useful plants. Bamboo has been used for food, clothing, shelter, plumbing, containers, fences, bridges, and on and on. If you know how to use it, bamboo can help provide many of life's necessities.

Bamboo

*proper name:* *Phyllostachys*, many species also *Bambusa*, *Sinocalamus* and *Dendrocalamus* many species
*common name:* bamboo, leaf-spike
*family:* grass (Gramineae)
*relatives:* corn, oats, wheat, rice, zoysia and other grasses
*native land:* China and elsewhere around Orient
*history:* Very old and well known plant in the East. Bamboo forests still grow there, sometimes as tall as 80 feet! Bamboo grows two inches an hour sometimes. So fast you can almost see it. Only recently has the usefulness of bamboo been realized in the USA. A few gardeners have begun to grow it as a vegetable.

**How to Grow Bamboo**

*generation:* hardy perennial
*growing season:* summer
*time to plant:* anytime
*time to pick:* harvest shoots after plants are established
*needs:* fertile loam, well-drained
*location:* full sun with room to spread, but watch out that it doesn't take over more than you want it to
*distance apart:* 36 to 180 inches
*height:* 72 to 960 inches
*propagation:* rhizome, divide in spring
*companions:* other bamboo
*types:* get edible kinds: moso *(Phyllostachys edulis)*, green sulpher *(P. sulfurea viridis)*, pak-koh-poo-chi (*P. dulcis)*
*where to get it:* Fruitland Nurseries, Agusta, Georgia 30904 George M. Darrow, Glenn Dale, Maryland 20769; McIlhenny Nursery, Avery Island, Louisiana 70513
*cultivation:* plant in boxes to confine roots and limit growth
*water:* medium
*parts and uses:* stalks used for building bridges, houses, fences, pipe, food, clothes, containers, musical instruments
*picking:* pick shoots before long bamboo cane begins to develop

# Barley

At most meals we try to have steamed rice or another grain. Grains are an important protein source in our diet. We like how they taste underneath our peas, beans, corn, and other garden vegetables. Lately we've been trying barley as a table grain. Barley is meatier than rice. It also tastes great in soup. I'm thinking about growing it just to see how it grows.

*proper name: Hordeum vulgare*
*common name:* barley, common barley
*family:* grass (Gramineae)
*relatives:* wheat, oats, rye, corn, rice, other grasses and grains
*native land:* Southeast Asia or Abyssinia
*history:* Some scientists believe barley is the oldest grain grown. The early farmers grew barley 7,000 years ago in Africa and Southeast Asia. Barley was the main source of bread and flour for the Greeks, Romans, and Hebrews. The grain also has been grown in China and Europe for over 4,000 years. Now many forms of wild and domestic barley can be found in the milder regions of the earth, as well as subtropic and subarctic areas.

**How to Grow Barley**

*generation:* hardy annual
*growing season:* cool and moist (60 to 90 days)
*time to plant:* early spring or late summer through fall
*time to pick:* summer, fall through spring
*needs:* fertile loam, well-drained

Barley

*location:* full sun
*distance apart:* one inch
*height:* 36 to 60 inches
*propagation:* seed, broadcast sow
*germination:* 14 to 21 days
*seed life:* unknown
*companions:* use to follow other grains, crop rotation
*where to get it:* as a whole "unpearled" grain from health food stores or check local farm suppliers
*cultivation:* grow barley on time, it doesn't like hot weather
*water:* keep well-watered, but don't overdo

# Carrots

Garden carrots taste so juicy and sweet that you'll think market carrots are only good for animal food. The best thing about carrots — they fit anywhere in the garden.

*proper name: Daucus carota, sativa*
*common name:* carrots, carotte Mediterranean carrot, carota
*family:* parsley (Umbelliferae)
*relatives:* parsnip, parsley, celery, dill
*native land:* probably Afghanistan
*history:* Originally people were interested in the medicinal qualities of carrots and not concerned with food value. But by the 13th century, carrots began to be grown in Europe for human and animal food, and in China also. European explorers brought carrot seeds to the New World and Indians in America learned of carrots this way. In the USA carrots have been popular in the last half century.

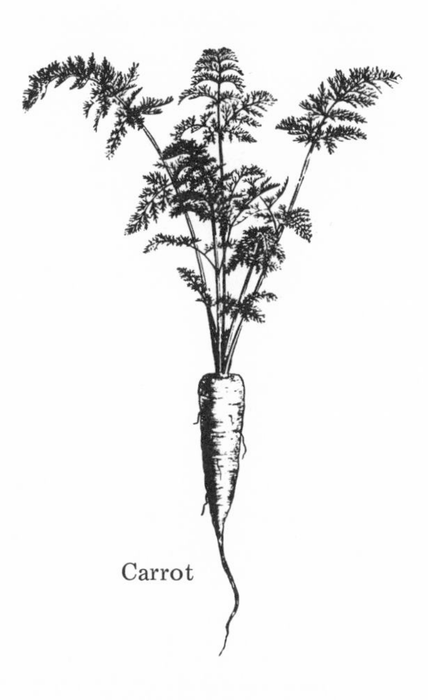

Carrot

## How to Grow Carrots

*generation:* hardy biennial
*growing season:* year round in mild climates, 50 to 70 days
*time to plant:* anytime soil can be worked in spring until fall
*time to pick:* late spring through fall
*needs:* fertile sandy loam, well-worked, no big rocks, well-drained, avoid fresh manures
*location:* anywhere they fit, like sunlight
*distance apart:* one to two inches
*height:* 12 inches
*propagation:* mix tiny seed with sand to better control sowing, rake into topsoil where they are to grow; don't transplant
*germination:* 12 to 18 days, be patient
*seed life:* three years
*companions:* peas, leaf lettuce, leeks, chives, tomatoes, rosemary, sage

*types:* Parisian or Rondo varieties are good for clay soil
*cultivation:* keep weeded and thinned so taproot can develop
*water:* lots, don't let them dry out
*parts and uses:* taproot as food, young green leaves as seasoning
*picking:* know the variety maturity dates, pull carrot out anytime before flower stalk appears

# Celtuce

A few vegetables are so handy that more than one part of them can be eaten. These vegetables are very useful in small gardens where more food needs to be grown in less space. Turnips, beets, and carrots are three common double-use vegetables. The roots and the leafy green parts of these plants can be eaten. Celtuce is not so common. The leaves of celtuce are picked like leaf lettuce. Later the thick celtuce stalk is harvested for soups and salads.

*proper name: Lactuca sativa, asparagina*
*common name:* celtuce, stalk lettuce, palm tree lettuce
*family:* daisy (Compositae)
*relatives:* lettuce, dandelion, girasol, chicory
*native land:* western China
*history:* Rather new vegetable in the West. Introduced to American gardeners in the late 1930s. Difficult to find in supermarkets.

*generation:* hardy annual
*growing season:* cool season (90 days)
*time to plant:* early spring and late summer
*time to pick:* anytime leaves are big enough; stalk ready two to three months after planting
*needs:* fertile loam, well-drained
*location:* partial shade, cool spots
*distance apart:* 10 to 15 inches
*height:* 10 to 18 inches

Celtuce

*propagation:* easily started from seed, sow thinly
*germination:* two to seven days
*seed life:* two to four years
*companions:* leeks, carrots, cabbage, corn
*where to get it:* Burpee Seeds, Warminster, Pennsylvania 18974
*cultivation:* weed frequently
*water:* thirsty, enjoys daily watering
*parts and uses:* leaves go well in salads like leaf lettuce; stalks can be used like celery in soup and salad
*picking:* pinch back leaves until stalk starts to swell cut stalk after it grows taller than 12 inches

## Chayote

Chayote is a spiny member of the gourd family. It is unknown to many Americans, but chayote is a big part of many people's daily diet in the tropics of North and South America. It is the oddball among members of its family. It produces only one seed per fruit, instead of many seeds like melons and squash.

*proper name: Sechium edule*
*common name:* chayote, Christophine, vegetable pear, chayotli, tayote, chocho, chuchu, chayota
*family:* gourd (Cucurbitaceae)
*relatives:* melons, cucumbers, squash, watermelon, gourds, pumpkins
*native land:* Central American tropics
*history:* An important and well-known plant among natives in Mexico, Guatemala and elsewhere in the North and South American tropics: Brazil, Puerto Rico, Louisiana, Haiti, Trinidad, British West Indies. An Aztec King, Montezuma, valued chayote.

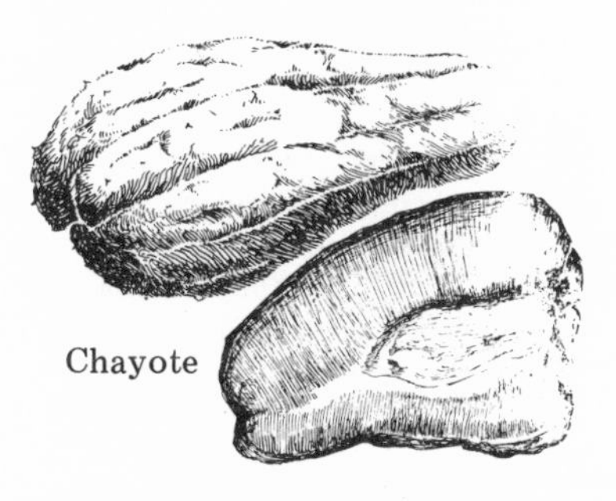
Chayote

**How to Grow Chayote**

*generation:* annual vine, perennial in mild regions
*growing season:* warm summer days
*time to plant:* early spring
*time to pick:* late summer, fall
*needs:* fertile sandy loam, well-drained
*location:* sunny, lots of room to climb or run along ground, some shade from afternoon sun
*distance apart:* two plants per hill, ten feet between hills
*height:* low-growing vines — sometimes up to 50 feet in length

*propagation:* plant entire fruit with seed inside
*germination:* usually fast, sometimes seed germinates inside fruit
*seed life:* unknown
*companions:* other chayotes
*where to get it:* Mexican markets, some supermarkets
*cultivation:* chayote likes steady conditions; quick changes in moisture or temperature bother its growth
*water:* steady moisture, don't overwater
*parts and uses:* fruits eaten boiled, baked, or fried; tubers can be eaten; also young leaves and blooms attract bees; vines make animal food or can be woven into hats and mats
*picking:* bloom starts when days get shorter in fall, chayotes are ready to pick one month after blooming

# Chervil

A cheerful but forgotten herb, chervil was a favorite among old-time gardeners. Now it isn't grown very often. Maybe you might want to grow it and see if the leaves make you happy as they dangle and dance in the wind.

*proper name: Anthriscus cerefolium*
*common name:* chervil, fence flower, salad chervil
*family:* parsley (Umbelliferae)

Chervil

*relatives:* dill, parsley, carrot, celery
*native land:* Caucasus, southern Russia and western Asia
*history:* An old plant. Proper name means "leaves bring gladness." The scent of chervil reminded people of the holy spice myrrh. Some Christians still use chervil as an Easter season herb. It is much prized in Europe but unknown to most American gardeners.

## How to Grow Chervil

*generation:* hardy annual
*growing season:* likes cool days (30 to 40 days)

*time to plant:* March
*time to pick:* anytime for leaves
*needs:* rich loam, well-drained
*location:* likes shade
*distance apart:* 6 to 12 inches
*height:* 12 to 24 inches
*propagation:* grows easily from seed
*germination:* 10 to 14 days
*seed life:* three to four years
*companions:* radishes or taller plants to provide shade
*cultivation:* transplanting usually causes chervil to bolt
*water:* needs adequate moisture
*uses:* flavoring for salad, soup, meat, and candy
*picking:* pick leaves anytime for spices

# Comfrey

Gurney Seed Company's catalog says comfrey is "Grandma's most useful plant." Grandma used it for tea, boiled greens, soap, and secret ingredient in compost. You don't have to be as smart as Grandma to grow comfrey. It's easy.

*proper name:* *Symphytum*, many species
*common name:* comfrey, knitbone, healing herb, Quaker comfrey, Russian comfrey
*family:* borage (Boraginaceae)
*relatives:* forget-me-not, borage, anchusa, heliotrope
*native land:* Mediterranean
*history:* An ancient and important garden plant from the Old World. The Greek word for comfrey is "to grow together," pointing to its importance as a general garden companion plant

**How to Grow Comfrey**

*generation:* hardy perennial
*growing season:* does best in cool weather
*time to plant:* spring and fall

Comfrey

*time to pick:* leaves in early summer, roots in fall
*needs:* average soil
*location:* sunny airy spot
*distance apart:* 36 inches
*height:* 30 to 60 inches
*propagation:* rootstock, division
*companions:* everyone!
*where to get it:* Gurney Seed and Nursery, Yankton, S. D. 57078
*cultivation:* cut plants two inches above ground and they will grow back
*water:* needs good supply of moisture, although it has deep roots
*parts and uses:* boiled greens and tea made from leaves; soap from roots; poultice; good addition to compost for balance
*picking:* pinch off early leaves for boiled greens, older leaves of late summer aren't so tasty

# Compass Plant

You can grow your own chewing gum?!! Especially if you live in high, dry, and hot prairie regions. Compass plant is not commonly grown in gardens, but I grew it in mine last year. I wanted to find out if the story about compass plant is true. The story: It is called "compass plant" because its flat leaves line up with the edges pointing north and south. That way it gets direct sunlight in the morning and evening, but avoids it during the midday heat.

*proper name: Silphium laciniatum*
*common name:* compass plant, rosinweed, pilotweed
*family:* daisy (Compositae)
*relatives:* lettuce, daisy, zinnia, sunflower, corn flower, cup-rosinweed, dandelion
*native land:* tall grass regions of North American prairies
*history:* Prairie native; still grows wild. Considered cattle feed in some areas, a weed in others. Not sold by seed companies nor listed in most garden books. This plant is said to have helped many lost pioneers as they traveled westward across the great prairies.

## How to Grow a Compass Plant

*generation:* hardy annual
*growing season:* warm summer
*time to plant:* early spring
*time to pick:* fall
*needs:* well-drained and somewhat fertile soil
*location:* open full sun
*distance apart:* 12 inches
*height:* 36 to 144 inches
*propagation:* seed
*germination:* 7 to 21 days
*seed life:* unknown
*companions:* grasses
*where to get it:* Windrift Prairie Seeds, RD 2, Oregon, Illinois 61061. If you live on the tall-grass prairies, ask local gardeners if it still grows wild along some railroad tracks.
*cultivation:* hot and dry, more

chance for north-south leaves
*water:* can tolerate dry conditions
*parts and uses:* milky resin of plants used by Indians and pioneer kids for chewing gum; cut flowers
*picking:* cut flowers in fall before they fade; get chewing gum anytime plant is big enough to pinch

# Corn

Farmers know four kinds of corn: popcorn, Indian corn, dent corn, and sweet corn. Gardeners usually care about one kind: sweet corn. Of course you know corn-on-the-cob. But you can't really say you've eaten sweet corn until you've tasted garden sweet corn cooked just after it was picked. You won't ask for dessert!

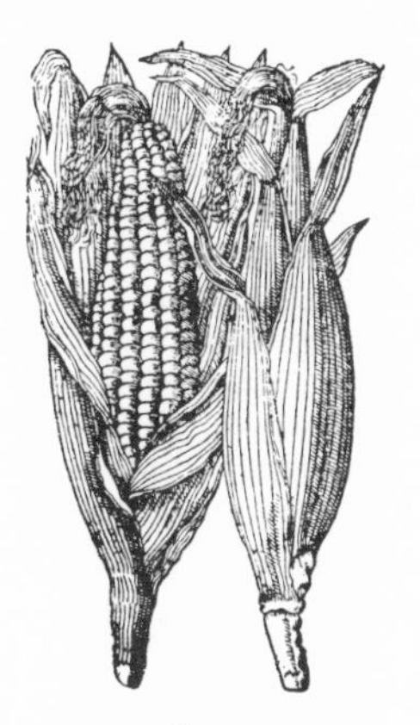

Corn

*proper name: Zea mays, saccharata*
*common names:* sweet corn, sugar corn, Turkie wheat, Indian wheat, maize, corn-on-the-cob
*family:* grass (Gramineae)
*relatives:* bamboo, rye, barley, oats, wheat, rice, other cereals and grasses
*native land:* somewhere in Central America
*history:* A very holy food plant. Origins mysterious. Mexican Indians may have grown corn 7,000 years ago. Prehistoric Indians in Peru also grew primitive corn. Inca, Maya, and Aztec civilizations could not have flourished without corn. In the New World, Columbus found luxurious corn fields, some 18 miles long! Sweet corn — developed through selection by Indians and others — is a recent invention, around 1800 AD. Sweet corn is the only vegetable member of the big Gramineae family. It has been extensively studied and hybridized.

### How to Grow Sweet Corn

*generation:* hardy annual
*growing season:* hot summers, 60 to 100 days
*time to plant:* early spring to mid-July
*time to pick:* late summer through fall
*needs:* fertile, well-dug medium loam, well-drained

*location:* full sun on north side, plant in blocks instead of long rows
*distance apart:* 9 to 12 inches
*height:* 60 to 90 inches
*propagation:* grows quickly from seed after soil warms
*germination:* 4 to 11 days
*seed life:* one to two years
*companions:* pole beans growing up stalks, cucumbers, pumpkin, potatoes, onions, lettuce, beets, carrots, peas
*types:* Illini Xtra Sweet is sweeter than a good dessert! Shumway Six Shooter is good for small spaces
*cultivation:* hand pollinate, especially if you are only growing a few plants
*water:* deep soak when tassels and silks appear but don't water flower parts during pollination
*parts and uses:* ears for eating fresh or as cornmeal; stalks for building things; husks and silks for weaving
*picking:* gently pull back husks and pinch one seed of the ear; if liquid is milky, it's ready; if liquid is clear or there is no liquid, it's too early or too late.

## Cosmos

These flowers are as bright as the sun and as happy as the stars. They can withstand drought. They come from Mexico — one of the world's great garden centers.

*proper name: Cosmos bipinnatus; Cosmos sulphureus*
*common name:* cosmos
*family:* daisy (Compositae)
*relatives:* lettuce, zinnia, sunflower, compass plant
*native land:* Mexico
*history:* Cosmos have long been prized in their native land. Traders and travelers brought them from Mexico to Europe, but flowers were not extensively hybridized until 1900s when they gained in popularity in Europe and Asia

### How to Grow Cosmos

*generation:* annual
*growing season:* warm summer
*time to plant:* May onward
*time to pick:* July through fall

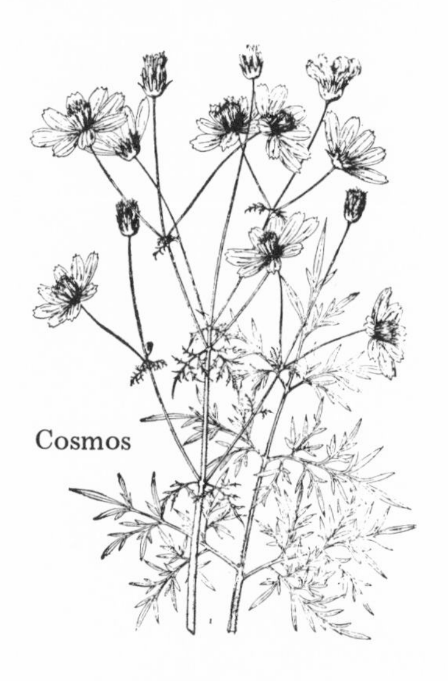
Cosmos

*needs:* not too rich, sandy loam, well-drained
*location:* full sun
*distance apart:* 18 to 36 inches, depending on variety
*height:* 48 to 120 inches
*propagation:* seed, started indoors or in soil
*germination:* 4 to 21 days
*seed life:* unknown
*companions:* other cosmos, evergreens, shrubs
*types and colors:* white, pink, red, lavender, purple, yellow, orange
*cultivation:* tall varieties may need stakes
*water:* drought-resistant, likes it dry
*parts and uses:* cut flowers, background in border, filler over bulbs and spring flowering things
*picking:* cut on stem to point of next blooms; cut dead flowers to force more blooms

# Cotton

Unless everything you wear is made of synthetic fibers, some of your clothes were grown from plants. Cotton plants. You could grow your own cotton and try to spin it into thread. If you could figure out how to make a spinning wheel! But you could also grow it just to see how it grows. Cotton isn't often grown in gardens, so you may have trouble finding seed for it. But you can find it.

*proper name:* *Gossypium*, many species
*common name:* cotton, tree cotton, sea-island cotton, Jamaican cotton, Mexican cotton, Peruvian cotton, Levant cotton
*family:* mallow (Malvaceae)
*relatives:* rose of China, rose mallow
*native land:* somewhere in tropics of Old and New World

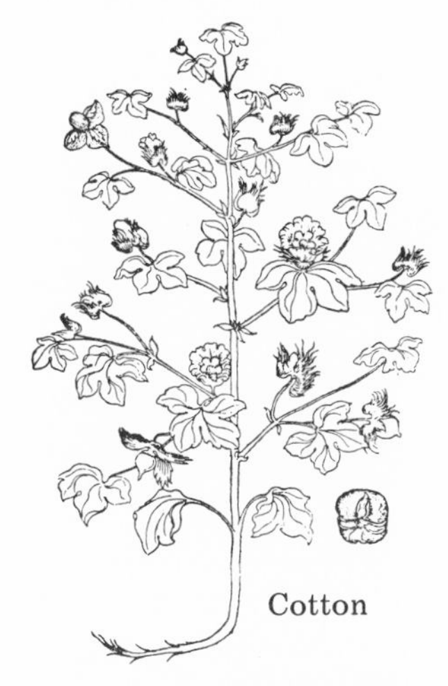

Cotton

*history:* A true mystery plant. No one knows where it came from. Cotton was spun into fabric in many prehistoric cultures. Columbus found Indians using native cotton in the New World. Three hundred years after Columbus sailed west, the cotton gin began to change the world. Cotton industry improved life for many people. And made it difficult for others.

**How to Grow Cotton**

*generation:* annual or perennial (check variety)
*growing season:* hot summer
*time to plant:* spring, when soil warms
*time to pick:* fall
*needs:* fertile loam, well-drained
*location:* full sun
*distance apart:* eight to ten inches
*height:* 24 to 36 inches
*propagation:* seed
*germination:* unknown
*seed life:* unknown
*companions:* alfalfa, more cotton
*where to get it:* Gurney Seed Co., Yankton, South Dakota 57078 or ask local Soil Conservation Service.
*cultivation:* inspect for bugs
*water:* steady moisture and humidity
*uses:* cotton fiber spun into textile products; meal from cotton seed used for fertilizer
*picking:* pull off fibers after seed boll ripens and splits

# Crocus

Crocus originates in high mountain meadows — the land called the tundra. In the tundra, seasons are short and the weather is harsh. Tundra plants know how to grow very fast in cool weather. This explains why crocus is among the first flowers of spring and the last flowers of fall in most gardens.

Crocus

*proper name:* *Crocus vernus* (spring) and *C. sativus* (fall)
*common name:* crocus, Dutch crocus, cloth-of-gold, saffron
*family:* iris (Iridaceae)
*relatives:* iris, gladiolus, tiger flower, African corn lily
*native land:* southern and central Europe, alpine meadows
*history:* Greeks cultivated fall crocus for the spice, saffron. Arabs also used the flower for the same purpose. From the Mediterranean, crocuses spread throughout the world via Rome and China.

**How to Grow Crocus**

*generation:* perennial
*growing season:* cool or cold
*time to plant:* fall
*time to pick:* spring and fall
*needs:* light rich loam, well-drained
*location:* sunny but will tolerate light shade

*distance apart:* two to three inches
*height:* 6 to 12 inches
*propagation:* corms
*companions:* other crocus, lawns, daffodils, crown imperial, tulips
*types and colors:* many, try fall and spring varieties
*cultivation:* wild crocus can spread everywhere and bloom fall and spring
*water:* needs plenty during early growth
*parts and uses:* edging, naturalized, forced in pots, rock gardens, borders, around shrubs; also as a dye; salad herb and medicine plant; dried stigmas of fall crocus make the rare spice, saffron

# Cucumber

Cucumbers are hard to grow. They need lots of good soil, moisture, and attention. Sometimes they need lots of pruning and hand-pollination. So you will really have to care for them, if cucumbers tickle your taste.

*proper name: Cucumis sativus*
*common name:* cucumber, cowcumbers, concombre, gherkin
*family:* gourd (Cucurbitaceae)
*relatives:* melons, squash, pumpkin
*native land:* southern Asia, probably India
*history:* Cucumbers spread from India into Greek, Arabic, Armenian, and Latin gardens before recorded history. By the Christian era, cucumbers had spread to China, Africa, Italy, and Asia Minor. Columbus brought them to the New World along with other vegetables. Cucumbers quickly gained popularity among Indians and spread throughout the Americas.

**How to Grow Cucumbers**

*generation:* very tender annual vine
*growing season:* long hot summers (50 to 80 days)
*time to plant:* early spring, indoors
*time to pick:* summer, fall
*needs:* warm fertile well-dug loam, well-drained
*location:* full sun with room for vines to spread

Cucumber

*distance apart:* 12 inches
*height:* grows low to ground or can be trained to run up poles
*propagation:* plant seeds indoors for early start or in soil after it warms up
*germination:* six to ten days
*seed life:* five years
*companions:* dill, beans, corn, peas, onions, radish, sunflower, marigold, lettuce
*types and colors:* check if you want pickle types or salad types
*cultivation:* dig in fresh manure two feet deep to warm up soil
*water:* thirsty plant, needs lots of moisture, mulch
*parts and uses:* fruits to pickle or use in salads
*picking:* any time, any size

# Daffodil

Older gardeners call daffodils "poets" and "trumpets." Daffodil poetry and daffodil music fill gardens in early spring. The flowers are hardy. They can take cold and hot days. Plant daffodils once and you'll hear them every spring.

*proper name: Narcissus pseudonarcissus*
*common name:* daffodil, trumpet, poet, daffadown dillies
*family:* amaryllis (Amaryllidaceae)
*relatives:* amaryllis, jonquil, narcissus
*native land:* Mediterranean
*history:* Grown and respected since early times around the Mediterranean, western Europe, North Africa and Asia. Prolific growers in groups near forests. Spread from Mediterranean and became naturalized in Scandinavia and central Europe. Most new varieties bred by the English, Dutch, and Americans within last 300 years.

Daffodil

**How to Grow Daffodils**

*generation:* bulbous perennial
*growing season:* cool
*time to plant:* fall
*time to pick:* spring
*needs:* well-drained sandy loam, add bone meal when planting
*location:* almost anywhere, sun or shade
*distance apart:* four to five inches
*height:* 12 to 18 inches
*propagation:* bulb
*companions:* other bulbs, corms, marigolds, other daffodils.

*cultivation:* be careful not to disturb bulbs when digging
*water:* good drainage, reliable spring rains
*parts and uses:* bedding plant, cut flowers, naturalized, forced in pots
*picking:* when flower first opens before pollination

## Dill

Pickles and salads wouldn't be the same without dill. The stems, leaves, and seeds of the plant can be used for seasoning. Bees love dill and so do members of the cabbage family.

*proper name:* *Anethum graveolens*
*common name:* dill
*family:* parsley (Umbelliferae)
*relatives:* parsley, carrot, celery, celeriac, parsnip
*native land:* unknown
*history:* known and grown since ancient times. The ancients believe dill was a magic plant. It affected the mind as well as the mouth and the nose. Now dill is grown as a major farm side crop, mostly for the large pickle demand in the USA.

### How to Grow Dill

*generation:* hardy annual or biennial
*growing season:* summer, 70 days

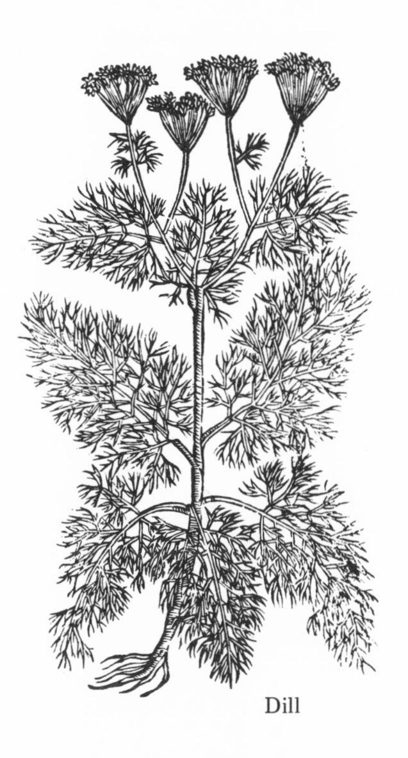

Dill

*time to plant:* early spring
*time to pick:* late summer for seed, leaves anytime
*needs:* average light loam, well-drained
*location:* anywhere they can fit
*distance apart:* 6 to 12 inches
*height:* 24 to 36 inches
*propagation:* grows well from seed, succession plant through the season, may resow itself the next season
*germination:* 10 to 28 days
*seed life:* two to three years

*companions:* cabbage, lettuce, cucumber, onions, beets
*cultivation:* plants get bushy, so give them room to grow
*water:* needs lots
*parts and uses:* leaves and seeds used for flavoring in salad, pickles, meat, fish, cheese, soup, stew; considered a medicine in some cultures
*picking:* pick leaves anytime for seasoning and salad; pick seeds when they start to turn brown and fall out

# Flax

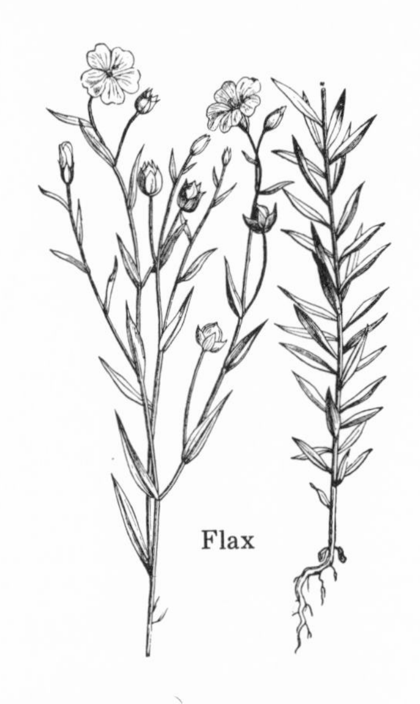
Flax

Flax is the forgotten fiber plant that once clothed the world. Now cotton and synthetic fibers have replaced flax as a major source of commercial linen. Many home weavers say flax fiber is easier to handle and weave than cotton. Flaxseed is still grown for its oil, used in paint. Species of flax have been developed for ornamental flowers.

*proper name: Linum usitatissimum*
*common name:* flax, common flax, linseed
*family:* flax (Linaceae)
*relatives:* none familiar
*native land:* probably Asia
*history:* An ancient and well-known plant. The word "linen" comes from the Greek word for flax. For centuries people everywhere have woven flax into linen. In the New World colonists grew flax to provide family clothing. After the invention of the cotton gin the use of flax fiber was greatly reduced. Now farmers grow flax mostly for linseed oil and its products.

### How to Grow Flax

*generation:* annual
*growing season:* early cool days before summer heat
*time to plant:* as early in spring as possible
*time to pick:* late summer, fall
*needs:* fertile heavy loam
*location:* full sun
*distance apart:* one inch
*height:* 24 to 48 inches

*propagation:* seed, broadcast sow
*germination:* 14 to 21 days
*seed life:* unknown
*companions:* flax is a good companion for most everything because it doesn't shade other plants
*colors:* white, yellow, red, blue flowers
*where to get it:* See Selected Seed Traders (page 322)
*cultivation:* keep weeded
*water:* don't let the plant dry out, needs abundant moisture
*parts and uses:* seeds used for oil and seed-remains used for fertilizer; linseed oil used for paint, varnish, and lacquer; flax straw used for weaving linen, rugs, insulating material, book paper, cigarette paper, fiberboard
*picking:* for fiber wait until the stems turn yellow, then crack open the stems and the flax straw will pop out

# Gladiolus

Gladiolus remind many people of gladiators and swords. The word gladiolus comes from the Latin word for sword. Gladiolus leaves look like swords or sharp blades. But they're green. They bend. And they don't cut.

*proper name:* *Gladiolus*, many species
*common name:* gladiolus, glads glad-to-know-ya, corn flag, sword lily, maid of the mist
*family:* iris (Iridaceae)
*relatives:* crocus, iris, tiger flower, African corn lily
*native land:* Mediterranean
*history:* Gladiolus grew extensively throughout the Mediterranean area and southward. But original flowers were not as impressive. In Europe, the gladiolus were hybridized into the many current colorful forms. In some corn fields, "glads" become a "weed" called corn flags.

**How to Grow Gladiolus**

*generation:* tender perennial
*growing season:* warm summers
*time to plant:* mid-May until two months before frost
*time to pick:* July to fall
*needs:* medium-sandy loam
*location:* full sun
*distance apart:* four to six inches

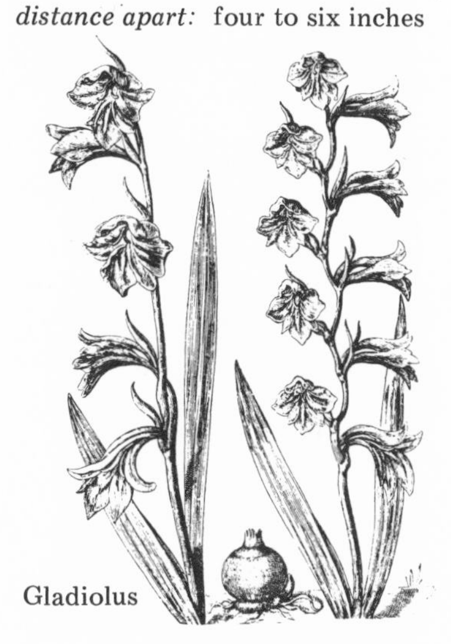
Gladiolus

*height:* 30 to 60 inches
*propagation:* corm planted in fall or early spring
*companions:* nasturtium, marigold, alyssum, other gladiolus
*colors:* white, cream, yellow, orange, pink, red, blue, purple, violet, mixed colors
*cultivation:* remember where you plant them so you don't dig them up next spring!
*water:* don't overwater, but they don't like drought either
*uses:* cut flowers, tall background, borders
*picking:* when bottom flowers open, cut on diagonal so plant can take up enough water

## Iris

Do you know anyone named Iris? You'll give her a great present anytime you give her the flower she is named for. If you don't know anyone named Iris, find someone. Then grow this flower for her. And everyone else.

*proper name:* *Iris,* many species
*common name:* Iris, flag, flagge, fleur-de-lis, flower-de-luce
*family:* iris (Iridaceae)
*relatives:* crocus, gladiolus, tiger flower, African corn lily
*native land:* uncertain
*history:* Named after the Greek goddess Iris, keeper of the rainbow, messenger of the gods. A true world-wide plant. Over a hundred varieties of wild iris exist, and countless hybrids are sold. Most breeding and development of new iris types is done in Holland, England, Spain, Japan, and Russia

**How to Grow Iris**

*generation:* hardy perennial
*growing season:* cool
*time to plant:* fall
*time to pick:* spring
*needs:* average, well-drained

Iris

*location:* full sun
*distance apart:* 12 inches
*height:* 6 to 48 inches
*propagation:* rhizome, plant so top is exposed to warmth of sun
*companions:* nasturtium, morning glory, alyssum, other irises
*colors:* blue, lavender, purple, violet, red, white, yellow
*cultivation:* every other year, dig up crowded clumps of rhizomes and cut back to six inches, replant elsewhere
*water:* don't dry out, but don't overwater
*uses:* delicate cut flower, outdoor spectacle
*picking:* cut when first flower opens

# Kohlrabi

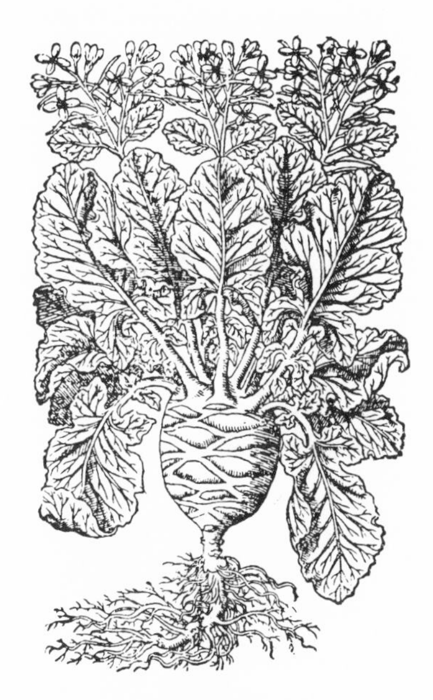

Kohlrabi

Kohlrabi is a strange-looking plant. In the market, it looks like a big round root like turnips, beets, rutabagas, and some types of carrots. But kohlrabi is not a root vegetable. The part we eat grows above the soil.

*proper name: Brassica oleracea, Caulo-Rapa*
*common name:* kohlrabi, turnip-rooted cabbage
*family:* cabbage (Cruciferae)
*relatives:* cabbage, turnips, broccoli, cauliflower, Brussels sprouts
*native land:* northern Europe
*history:* It is truly a recent vegetable, less than 500 years old. Kohlrabi means cabbage-turnip in German. Also known in England, Italy, Spain and eastern Mediterranean areas in 17th century. First grown in USA after 1800s. Still an unknown vegetable to many people.

*generation:* hardy annual
*growing season:* cool days, 55 to 60 days
*time to plant:* early spring, late summer to fall
*time to pick:* late spring, early summer, fall
*needs:* fertile well-drained loam, lots of compost and manure worked in

*location:* shade from late-day heat, filtered sunlight
*distance apart:* four to six inches
*height:* 12 to 8 inches
*propagation:* start in flats, transplant when plants have first six true leaves
*germination:* five to ten days
*seed life:* five years
*companions:* onions, beets, cucumbers, broccoli, cabbage, cauliflowers
*types and colors:* white or purple-leafed kinds
*cultivation:* needs rich soil, mulch helpful
*water:* steady moisture for steady growth
*parts and uses:* eat large, aboveground, swollen stem in soups or salads
*picking:* before the skin of the stem gets too thick and certainly before the flower stalk appears

## Lettuce

Lettuce is so basic to our diet that we often forget it's there. You should grow lettuce in the cool spots of your garden. But remember, lettuce goes fast on the table. Replant lettuce every other week throughout the growing season.

*proper name:* *Lactuca sativa*
*common name:* lettuce, laitue, salad
*family:* daisy (Compositae)
*relatives:* sunflowers, dandelion, endive, chicory, girasol, zinnia, cosmos, marigold, compass plant

Lettuce

*native land:* southwest Asia and Asia Minor
*history:* Persian, Greek, Roman, and Chinese empires had lettuce. Big-headed types of lettuce did not become popular until the 16th century. Columbus and later explorers brought lettuce seeds to the New World. Lettuce was among the first seeds sown in the Colonies.

### How to Grow Lettuce

*generation:* hardy annual
*growing season:* cool moist shady days (40 to 94 days)
*time to plant:* as soon as soil can be worked in spring, replant throughout season for continuous supply
*time to pick:* depends on variety, leaf lettuce can be picked after

three or four weeks, pick before they bolt
*needs:* slightly rich loose loam, well-drained
*location:* partial shade is best, doesn't like hot spots
*distance apart:* head types 12 inches, leaf types 8 inches
*height:* 9 to 18 inches
*propagation:* sow thinly! grows quickly from seed; best planted in ground or salad bed
*germination:* four to ten days
*seed life:* five years
*companions:* carrots, radishes, strawberry, cucumber, onions, chervil, Brussels sprouts, cabbage, broccoli, shallots, corn, and other tall plants for shade
*types:* butterhead, bibb or cabbage types have soft rounded heads; cos or romaine can stand some heat; Christ heart and curl-leaf types take longer to head up; loose-leaf types are picked before heading up
*cultivation:* don't waste seed, plant thinly
*water:* water early in day, needs ample moisture
*picking:* know the variety, cut heading types at ground level when heads are full

# Luffa

Do you think you could grow a shoe, a sponge, and a meal on the same plant? You can on a luffa plant. Not many people grow luffa, so you'll have to look hard for seeds. Many old-time gardeners call it "dish-cloth gourd."

*proper name: Luffa cylindrica*
*common name:* luffa sponge, dish-cloth gourd, rag gourd, vegetable sponge
*family:* gourd (Cucurbitaceae)
*relatives:* cucumber, squash, melon, gourds, pumpkin
*native land:* Old World tropics
*history:* An old and well-known tropical plant. Many cultures in the East and West use luffa as a food and as a cleaning sponge. The army and navy used them in World War II.

**How to Grow Luffa**

*generation:* annual vine
*growing season:* hot summers
*time to plant:* start indoors

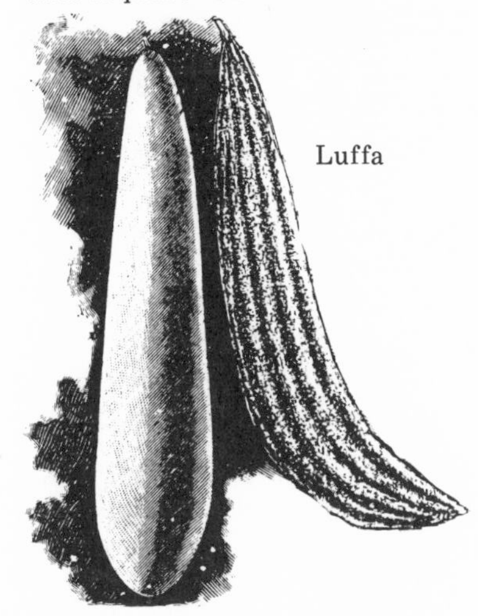
Luffa

early in spring and transplant to garden when soil warms
*time to pick:* fall
*needs:* fertile sandy loam, well-drained
*location:* full sun with room for vines to spread
*distance apart:* two plants per hill
*height:* long vines can be trained up poles as high as you want
*propagation:* big seeds, sprout easily
*germination:* 5 to 12 days
*seed life:* unknown
*companions:* other luffa
*where to get it:* Grace's Gardens, Autumn Lane, Hackettstown, New Jersey 07840; Gurney Seed Co., Yankton, South Dakota 57078
*cultivation:* mulch to save moisture
*uses:* young fruits may be eaten; old fruits when peeled are used as scrubbing sponges, and when not peeled as shoes
*picking:* for food pick before fruits become six inches long; for sponges and shoes wait until plants die and fruits dry

# Marigold

Marigold is one of the best flowers for summer gardens. I even plant them in my vegetable beds. They improve the soil and discourage nematodes. They also have a scent you can never forget. And they bring good luck!

*proper name:* *Tagetes patula*
*common name:* marigold, French marigold, Mexican marigold, African marigold, pot marigold
*family:* daisy (Compositae)
*relatives:* lettuce, artichokes, sunflowers, compass plant
*native land:* Mexico
*history:* "French" and "African" varieties grew originally in Mexico. When Spain conquered the country, traders took marigold seeds back to Europe where they spread and were developed into many varieties.

Marigold

### How to Grow Marigolds

*generation:* hardy annual
*growing season:* summer
*time to plant:* early spring until late summer
*time to pick:* mid-spring through fall
*needs:* any average garden loam
*location:* full sun, plant dwarf types throughout the beds
*distance apart:* 6 to 36 inches
*height:* 8 to 36 inches
*propagation:* grows well from seed
*germination:* seven to ten days
*seed life:* unknown
*colors:* many, see seed catalogs
*cultivation:* pick flowers after they fade, picking forces more blooms
*water:* don't let them dry out
*uses:* cut flowers, edging, friendly companion, bedding plants
*picking:* for seeds wait until the flower fades and dries out

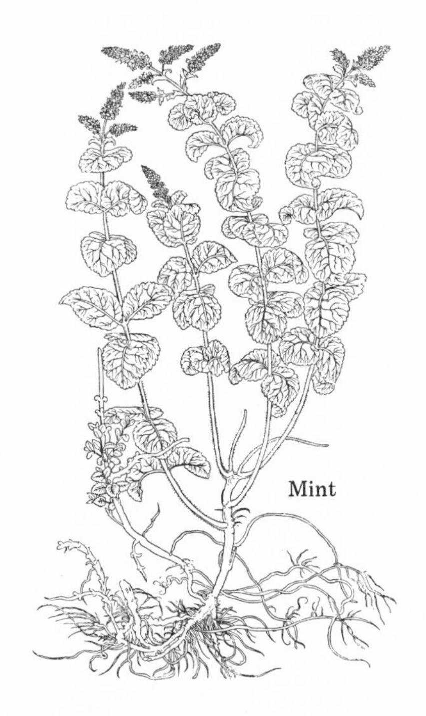
Mint

# Mint

Mint is an old and well-traveled plant. It grows just about everywhere but the hottest places. Like parsley, it is the grandparent plant of a whole family. Labiatae or the mint family. You may find mint already growing in your garden, as a "weed."

*proper and common names:* *Mentha canadensis* (common mint), *M. piperita* (peppermint), *M. spicata, viridis* (spearmint)
*family:* mint (Labiatae)
*relatives:* thyme, lavender, catnip, rosemary, oregano, dragon's head, hyssop
*native land:* Asia
*history:* An important herb used in religious and festive occasions. Many types of mint grow wild throughout the milder regions of the world. There is a name for mint in most cultures. But many herbalists think the best mint grows in England. Half of the 30 *Mentha* species are native or naturalized in North America.

**How to Grow Mint**

*generation:* hardy perennial
*growing season:* most growth in summer
*time to plant:* anytime
*time to pick:* anytime leaves and stalks are ready
*needs:* average loam
*location:* open airy spot with room to spread
*distance apart:* 6 to 12 inches
*height:* 12 to 36 inches
*propagation:* runner or stolons; can become a weed
*companions:* cabbage, tomato, cauliflower, Brussels sprouts, broccoli
*where to get it:* mint (especially spearmint) grows wild in many places, but to be sure you get the kind you want, ask for it at a nursery or garden supply
*cultivation:* mulch if soil is sandy and tends to dry out
*water:* needs lots of moisture
*uses:* tea, aromatic oil for seasoning
*picking:* pick leaves and stems before flowers show

# Nasturtium

Have you ever looked inside a nasturtium flower? Do it and you won't need a reason to grow it.
*proper name: Tropaeolum majus*
*common name:* nasturtium, Indian cress, great Indian cress
*family:* tropaeolum (Tropaeolaceae)
*relatives:* flame flower
*native land:* Central American tropics
*history:* Many varieties of wild nasturtiums range from southern Mexico to Chile. However nasturtiums adapt well to other climates outside the jungle. They were popularized in Spain and France and are now grown throughout the world. Nasturtiums are hardy, and will do well just about anywhere.

**How to Grow Nasturtiums**

*generation:* hardy annual vine
*growing season:* long and cool, doesn't like hot weather or frost

Nasturtium

*time to plant:* from early spring on
*time to pick:* when flowers show
*needs:* average soil, well-drained
*location:* sun, shade, or anywhere vines can roam or climb, needs protection from wind, heat, harsh weather
*distance apart:* 6 inches for dwarfs, 12 to 15 inches for climbers
*height:* as tall as they can climb
*propagation:* grows easily from seed, sows itself
*germination:* four to seven days
*seed life:* unknown
*companions:* squash, cucumbers, melons, potatoes, broccoli, cabbage, cauliflower, kohlrabi, turnips, radishes, apple trees, as ground cover for other tall plants
*colors:* white, pink, red, orange, yellow
*cultivation:* once started it will replant itself next year
*water:* not a lot, but don't dry out
*parts and uses:* cut flowers; flowers and young leaves as salad bitters (cut up well!)
*picking:* pick small leaves as needed for salad; pick flowers before they fade

## Onions

The best thing about onions is they fit anywhere. Use onions, like radishes, to fill in the blank spots in your garden.

*proper name: Allium cepa, (Allium fistulosum* is the green onion)
*common name:* onion, green onion, Spanish onion, white onion, red onion, tree onion, potato onion, everything onion, oignon, unyun, unio, cepa

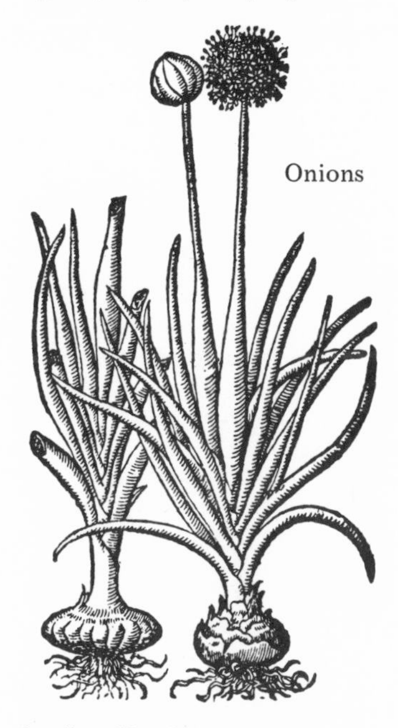

Onions

*family:* lily (Liliaceae)
*relatives:* garlic, leeks, shallots, chives
*native land:* probably Persia
*history:* The word for onion can be found in many early languages. Workers on the Great Pyramids ate onions and garlic 4,800 years ago. Druids used

them in Great Britain. Spaniards introduced them to the New World after 1500 A. D. Colonial settlers brought onions with them.

### How to Grow Onions

*generation:* hardy biennial
*growing season:* does best in cool weather, year-round in places with mild winters
*time to plant:* anytime for green onions, bulb onions in late summer and early spring
*time to pick:* before the flowers start to show on top; pick green onions as needed
*needs:* loose sandy loam, well-drained
*location:* just about any place they fit
*distance apart:* three to five inches
*height:* 12 to 24 inches
*propagation:* big onions usually grown from sets (little bulbs); green onions usually started from seed
*germination:* 7 to 14 days
*seed life:* one to two years
*companions:* tomatoes, lettuce, strawberry, beets, chamomile
*types:* red, yellow, and white-skinned
*cultivation:* mulch in hot weather
*water:* lots, don't let them dry out
*picking:* pull green onions as you need them; pull big onions before they flower

# Parsley

You may not even notice it on your plate next to that juicy sandwich. It's only a "garnish" anyway. But this ancient creature is the grandparent plant of a whole family of herbs and vegetables, the Umbelliferae, or parsley family. Many forms of parsley exist and have been grown in gardens for centuries. Pick one. Or let one pick you.

*proper name: Petroselinum hortense* and *Petroselinum crispum*
*common name:* parsley, moss parsley, root parsley, Italian parsley, plant of the rock
*family:* parsley (Umbelliferae)
*relatives:* carrot, celery, dill, chervil
*native land:* unknown
*history:* One of the oldest known garden plants. Parsley is mentioned in early Greek myths and stories. Romans also prized parsley and carried it throughout their empire. Christians knew parsley as the sacred herb of St. Peter. Parsley now grows in gardens throughout the world.

### How to Grow Parsley

*generation:* hardy biennial herb, annual vegetable
*growing season:* summer
*time to plant:* spring
*time to pick:* anytime leaves are big enough

*needs:* fertile loam, well-drained
*location:* full sun or partial shade, all around the garden
*distance apart:* six to ten inches
*height:* 6 to 12 inches
*propagation:* soak seed overnight in water
*germination:* very long, 28 to 42 days — seeds are said to "go to the Devil and come back" before they sprout

Parsley

*seed life:* five years
*companions:* roses, potatoes, asparagus, celery, leeks, tomatoes, dwarf peas
*types:* plain-leaved, curled-leaved, flat-leaved, and Hamburg types all look different
*cultivation:* add nitrogen to improve leaf growth
*water:* needs steady moisture, don't let plants wilt
*uses:* leaves used in salads, and as garnish, and to flavor potatoes, sauces, soups, stews, and stuffings
*picking:* pick leaves as needed but use plant before it flowers

## Peas

When it's just not warm enough to grow beans, grow peas. Peas enrich the soil with nitrogen, like beans. But they need cool weather. Plant them early in the spring and late in the summer so you have enough. We never have enough garden peas.

*proper name: Posum sativum*
*common name:* green peas, English peas, pease, petits pois, snow peas, pisos, pisu
*family:* legume (Leguminosae)
*relatives:* beans, lima beans, soybeans, mung beans, wisteria
*native land:* Asia Minor
*history:* Peas have a long history in many lands of Asia and Mediterranean regions. First peas were grown mostly for dry seed for use in soup. But green peas did not appear until the 16th century. The most development of green peas happened in England. Gregor Mendel studied peas while forming the scientific principles of genetics. European explorers and traders brought peas to America.

Peas

**How to Grow Peas**

*generation:* hardy annual vine
*growing season:* cool days of early spring, late summer
*time to plant:* early as possible in spring, late summer
*time to pick:* late spring, early summer, fall
*needs:* light rich loam
*location:* shade much of day, especially in early summer
*distance apart:* one to three inches
*height:* as tall as vines will grow, except dwarf varieties
*propagation:* grow fast from seed; peas don't like transplanting
*germination:* 7 to 11 days
*seed life:* three years
*companions:* carrots, potatoes, turnips, radishes, cucumbers, corn, herbs
*types:* snow peas or sugar peas have good tasting pods, soup peas should dry out
*cultivation:* mulch early to keep plants cool
*water:* keep soil moist and cool
*picking:* know the variety; some pods can be eaten, some can't; feel how big peas are inside pod before picking; keep picking to force more flowers

# Peanuts

The peanut plant is an amazing creature. Most nuts grow on trees, but peanuts grow underground. A relative of beans and peas, the peanut plant is short and bushy. After it flowers, the plant is pollinated. The flowers dig themselves into the ground where they swell up and become peanuts. Each peanut is a seed for a new plant.

Peanuts

*proper name: Arachis hypogaea*
*common name:* peanuts, goober, pindar, ground nut, earth nut
*family:* legume (Leguminosae)
*relatives:* chickpeas, lentils, peas, and beans
*native land:* prehistoric Brazil, Peru
*history:* Domesticated in South American highlands 2,400 to 3,000 years ago. Peanuts spread to the Amazon River delta. From there explorers and traders carried nuts to Mexico and the West Indies. On return voyages from the New World, European explorers took them to Europe and Africa. They became common in the USA after the 1860s. By the turn of the century, George Washington Carver had proved their commercial worth. Peanuts are now widely grown in India, China, West Africa, and the USA.

### How to Grow Peanuts

*generation:* annual
*growing season:* long hot humid summers (120 days to set seed)
*time to plant:* early spring when soil warms
*time to pick:* late fall after plants die
*needs:* sandy loam, slightly acid; add potash, phosphorous and magnesium limestone for best nuts
*location:* full sun, room for plants to spread, avoid shadows
*distance apart:* six inches
*height:* 12 to 18 inches
*propagation:* plant raw, untreated, unsalted peanut seeds in the ground where they are to grow
*germination:* two to seven days

*seed life:* two to three years
*companions:* likes dill and marigolds, good as second crop following beets, carrots, lettuce, or ground cover under orchard
*types and colors:* Spanish varieties are small and red, sweet Virginia varieties are large and tan
*cultivation:* soil must be well worked so nuts can bury themselves
*water:* water well, especially before hot days but don't overwater when nuts are setting
*parts and uses:* nuts to eat, shells for mulch; plants return nitrogen to soil
*picking:* wait until the plants die back, then pull them out and pick peanut shells away from roots; nuts should dry out inside shells for a couple of days.

# Popcorn

Not many gardeners grow popcorn because they would rather have sweet corn. Pollen from popcorn will mess up the taste of sweet corn. Unless you live on a farm with lots of room to put between popcorn and sweet corn, you should choose one or the other. Or you can be brave and try this trick: plant an early variety of sweet corn and a late variety of popcorn that matures at least a month later.

*proper name:* *Zea mays, everta*
*common name:* popcorn
*family:* grass (Gramineae)
*relatives:* barley, oats, wheat, sorghum, other kinds of corn
*native land:* Central or South tropics
*history:* The oldest kind of corn. Some historians think Indians realized the food value of corn when an ear of popcorn on the stalk was accidentally heated, perhaps by lightning or fire. And the corn popped! Some Indians ate popcorn for breakfast but nobody is certain when popcorn became a food crop. European traders found popcorn and field corn growing throughout the Americas. These traders spread the seeds across the world.

**How to Grow Popcorn**

*generation:* tall half-hardy annual
*growing season:* long warm dry summers, around 110 days to set seed
*time to plant:* plant in hills or beds as soon as soil warms
*time to pick:* late fall after plants die
*needs:* fertile, sandy loam, well-drained, don't overload with nutrients
*location:* full sun, north side
*distance apart:* 9 to 12 inches
*height:* 96 to 144 inches
*propagation:* grows easily from seed; in cold climates soak seed overnight for faster start

*germination:* 7 to 21 days
*companions:* pole beans growing up corn stalks, also potatoes, peas, pumpkins, trailing squash, melons, cucumbers, onions, lettuce
*types:* strawberry, hull-less, Japanese hull-less
*cultivation:* hand pollinate when silks show
*water:* deep soak when tassels and silks appear, don't water flowering parts during pollination
*parts and uses:* ears dry into popcorn seeds; stalks make fences and building material; silks and husks can be used to make cornhusk dolls
*picking:* plants should die and dry completely in ground, then remove seeds from cob

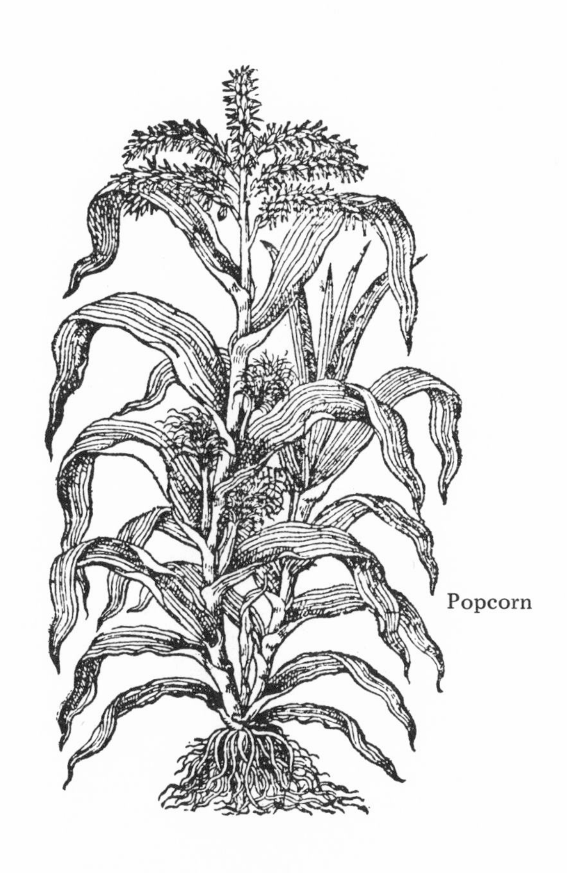

Popcorn

# A Story of Wild and Wooly Popcorn

My son and his friends were playing and eating popcorn in our backyard one spring day. I was in the vegetable garden, hoeing the soil and preparing it for squash. The kids finished the popcorn. Without thinking, one of them tossed the burnt and unpopped corn into the freshly dug soil. When I noticed what had happened, I worried about salt in the soil. Salt isn't good for gardens. But there wasn't much salt, only a few seeds and some burnt crumbs. It won't matter, I thought as I covered the mess with some soil.

I thought the salt would wash out quickly and the popcorn would decay and break down into the soil. After all, the corn had been stranded at the bottom of a red-hot skillet. It certainly couldn't grow. But it did! Two weeks later, the first cape-like leaves of corn cracked the soil near the squash. Somehow the unpopped seeds had germinated! It seemed impossible, but true. I knew no other corn seeds had been planted there.

Four of these wild popcorn plants survived the summer and a few ears managed to become pollinated. But cold weather and greenfly aphids came before the ears could finish growing.

The seeds of the wild popcorn were small, but many of them popped. We were grateful just to have seen such magical corn.

I tried to repeat the popcorn miracle last year with a bunch of popcorn bowl discards. But the seeds didn't germinate. Nothing came up. Must have been another sort of seed.

# Potato

Grow potatoes in a "patch" away from the main garden. Potatoes take up a lot of room and tend to become a "weed." Unless you love French fries, mashed potatoes, potato pancakes, baked potatoes, hash browns.

Potato

*proper name: Solamum tuberosum*
*common name:* potato, spuds, Irish potato, white potato
*family:* nightshade (Solanaceae)
*relatives:* tomato, eggplant, pepper, tobacco, petunia
*native land:* highlands of Chile and Argentina
*history:* South American Indians were cultivating potatoes over 6,000 years ago. Potatoes were important in their diets because they could be baked in the sun or stored for cooking later. Invading Europeans were afraid to eat potatoes because they belong to the nightshade family. Europeans grew potatoes mostly for hog food until the 1770 grain famine forced people to use them. Europeans also brought potatoes back to the New World with them. The Chinese and Japanese have never been interested in potatoes for their diet.

## How to Grow Potatoes

*generation:* half-hardy annual
*growing season:* cool days
*time to plant:* early spring to midsummer
*time to pick:* late summer through fall
*needs:* rich loose loam, well-worked and well-drained
*location:* sunny patch by themselves, cool soil, afternoon shade
*distance apart:* 12 inches
*height:* 18 inches
*propagation:* order "seed potatoes" from seed companies or just plant a potato from the kitchen.
*companions:* parsley, peas, beans, horseradish, corn, cabbage, celery, marigold, eggplant, summer savory, strawberries, nasturtiums
*types:* In the South get heat-tolerant varieties, Chippewa is one
*cultivation:* grows well under a six-inch deep mulch of lawn trimmings

*water:* needs abundant moisture and good drainage
*uses:* underground tubers are eaten
*picking:* wait until plants die down, then dig up as many potatoes as you find; if you use a thick mulch, you will be able to pull out potatoes early without hurting plants

# Pumpkin

Pumpkin vines need a lot of space. Gardeners with small gardens don't grow pumpkins very often. But then, they don't have fresh pumpkin pie very often either!
*proper name: Cucurbita pepo*
*common name:* pumpkin, pompion
*family;* gourd (Cucurbitaceae)
*relatives:* squash, melon, cucumber, watermelon
*native land:* Central America, probably Mexico
*history:* Mexican Indians were the first to recognize the food value of pumpkins. Indians carried the seeds to North America where they were grown before Europeans discovered them. The word "pumpkin" comes from the French word "pompion — cooked by the sun." The best pumpkins are left to ripen in the sun.

**How to Grow Pumpkins**

*generation:* very tender annual
*growing season:* warm summers
*time to plant:* as soon as the soil warms in spring

Pumpkin

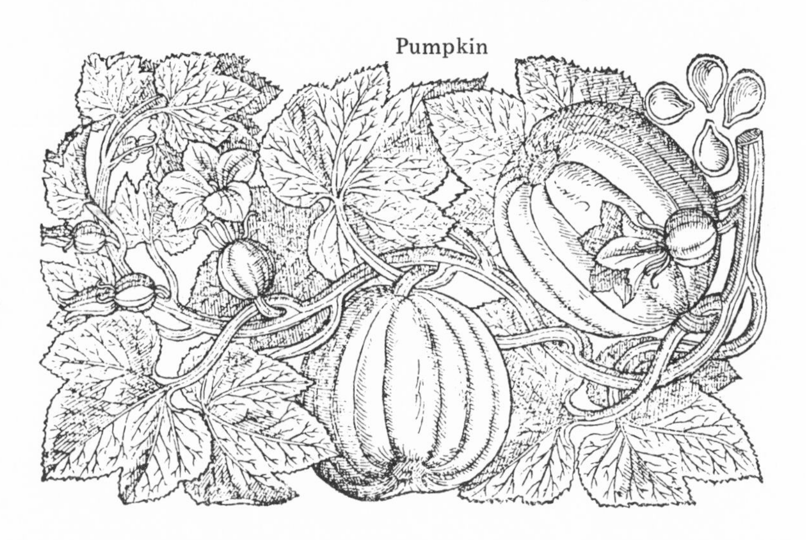

*time to pick:* just before the first frost
*needs:* fertile, loose sandy loam, well-drained and well-worked
*location:* full sun with lots of room for vines to run
*distance apart:* two plants per hill, 25 feet between hills
*height:* low growing vines, too heavy to climb poles
*propagation:* seed planted directly in warm soil
*germination:* seven to ten days
*seed life:* four years
*companions:* corn, radishes
*types:* Tricky Jack variety (Farmer Seed Co.) is a bush type that needs less room and has seeds without hulls for easy eating
*cultivation:* work in lots of compost and manure before planting
*water:* keep well-watered, don't let leaves wilt
*parts and uses:* fruits used for Thanksgiving and Christmas pies and dried seeds used for snacks
*picking:* gather vines with pumpkins still attached; cure in sun for a week; store in a cool dry place

# Purslane

Most Americans think purslane is a weed. But it's really a gift. It grows very well everywhere in the United States. It plants itself mostly in gardens and cultivated fields, where it grows fast and low. It has a mild taste.

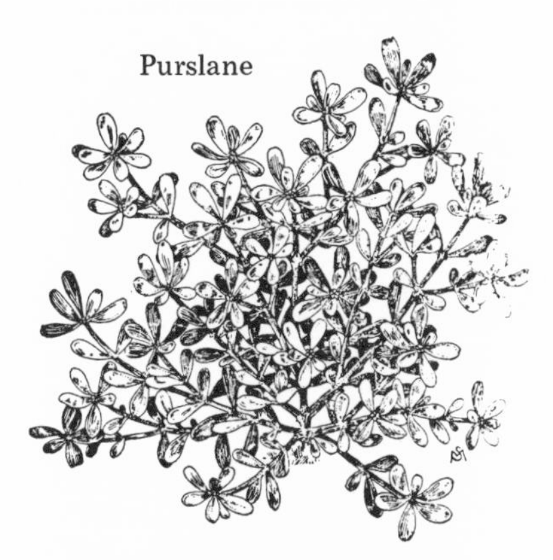
Purslane

Some people like it better than spinach as a boiled green. It can be cooked many ways, pickled, or eaten raw in salads.

*proper name:* *Portulaca oleracea*
*common name:* purslane, common purslane, false pigweed, pusley, postelein
*family:* purslane (Portulacaceae)
*relatives:* Portulaca, Lewisia, spring beauty
*native land:* probably India
*history:* Purslane is a well-known and valued food in many parts of Europe and Asia. It has been used in India and Persia for more than 2,000 years. Early Colonial gardeners brought purslane to America from southern Europe. Now it is a common weed that grows throughout the USA. Most people don't know about its food value, although it tries to grow in everyone's garden.

**How to Grow Purslane**

*generation:* annual herb
*growing season:* all but hottest season
*time to plant:* it plants itself, usually spring and fall
*time to pick:* leaves and stems anytime
*needs:* fertile garden loam
*location:* anywhere
*distance apart:* 12 to 24 inches
*height:* one to two inches
*propagation:* seed, it will plant itself
*germination:* very fast
*seed life:* unknown
*companions:* corn; ground cover for other tall plants
*where to get it:* look for it
*cultivation:* keep picking stems and leaves to force more to grow, wash well before eating
*water:* don't let it dry out
*parts and uses:* leaves and stems can be cooked, frozen, pickled, eaten raw in salads; some Indians use seeds to make bread
*picking:* pick before flowers appear

# Radishes

No garden vegetable grows as fast as the radish. Some mature in three weeks. This is good for many gardeners. They plant and pick radishes all during the growing season. And they plant radishes to fill in the blank spots around the garden.

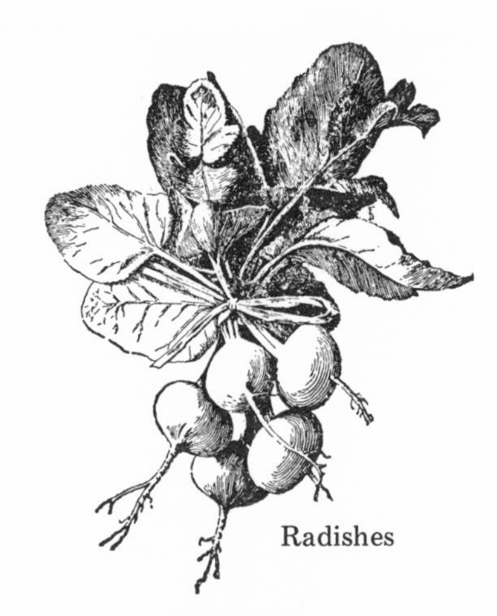

Radishes

*proper name:* *Raphanus sativus*
*common name:* radish, winter radish, radis, radix, rave
*family:* cabbage (Cruciferae)
*relatives:* cabbage, broccoli, cauliflower, collards, kale, kohlrabi,
*native land:* probably China
*history:* many forms of radishes have been grown and respected for centuries in China and Japan. Egyptians and Greeks also valued radishes. At one time, large radishes (up to 100 pounds each!) grew in Europe. Spanish and other explorers brought radish cultivation to the New World.

**How to Grow Radishes**

*generation:* hardy annual, also biennial
*growing season:* cool days, short (20 to 60 days)
*time to plant:* early spring until fall

*time to pick:* know how long the variety takes, pick before they get old and pulpy
*needs:* loose fertile loam, well-drained
*location:* any place they fit but avoid hot dry spots
*distance apart:* one to two inches
*height:* 12 inches
*propagation:* grow fast from seed, succession plant for continuous supply
*germination:* two to five days
*seed life:* five years
*companions:* carrots, cucumber, lettuce, peas, pole beans, (chervil makes hot radishes!)
*types:* French breakfast and icicle varieties are mild
*cultivation:* mulch to keep moist; old dry slow-growing radishes taste bitter
*water:* lots, don't let them dry out
*parts and uses:* bulbs and leafy tops of some varieties are eaten when young and tender
*picking:* depends on variety; don't let them get too old; pick before flower stalk begins to show

# Rye

Some farmers use rye to improve their soil during the winter when nothing else grows. Rye grass has powerful roots that can grow as much as three miles in one day! Rye roots may stretch out as much as 380 miles during one growing season. When rye grass is cut, these deep-digging roots decompose and add humus to the soil. Some people call rye the "underground compost" maker.

*proper name: Secale cereale*
*common name:* rye
*family:* grass (Gramineae)
*relatives:* corn, oats, barley, bamboo, wheat, rice, other grasses and grains
*native land:* southwestern Asia
*history:* One of the "minor" grains. Rye has been widely grown for the last 2,000 years in cooler areas of Europe and Asia. Rye feeds both humans and animals. Wise farmers have known about the soil building powers of rye. Not many gardeners know about rye. But you do.

## How to Grow Rye

*generation:* hardy annual grass
*growing season:* cool
*time to plant:* fall
*time to pick:* spring or earlier
*needs:* any soil well-drained
*location:* full sun, areas with poor soil
*distance apart:* one inch
*height:* 36 to 60 inches
*propagation:* seed, broadcast sow
*germination:* 14 to 21 days
*seed life:* unknown
*companions:* more rye, cornflowers, pansies

*where to get it:* L. L. Olds Seeds, Madison, Wisconsin 53701 Joseph Harris Co., Rochester, New York 14624; DeGiorgi Co. Seeds, Council Bluffs, Iowa 51501; Burnett Bros., 92 Chambers St., New York, New York 10007
*cultivation:* cut rye when you are ready to dig in spring
*water:* don't worry about it, let roots dig for water
*parts and uses:* roots deep dig soil; seeds make flour and flavor bread; straw used for packing, bedding material, and paper
*picking:* dig rye into the soil before planting in the spring

# Sage

Sage has a strong aroma you won't forget. The smell of sage reminds many folks of the American West, where big sagebrush grows across miles of dry open range. But garden sage is not the same plant as big sagebrush. They are from entirely different families. But they both have that sage smell.

*proper name:* *Salvia officinalis*
*common name:* sage, perennial garden sage, common sage
*family:* mint (Labiatae)
*relatives:* mint, thyme, oregano, rosemary, basil
*native land:* Mediterranean
*history:* Sage, a very popular garden herb, was valued by early Mediterranean cultures. It spread throughout Europe where it was widely used in cooking and home medicine. Europeans brought sage to the New World. They found Brazilian "scarlet sage" and American sagebrush growing wild with that familiar sage aroma.

**How to Grow Sage**

*generation:* hardy perennial
*growing season:* brisk dry summers

Sage

*time to plant:* anytime after soil warms
*time to pick:* anytime leaves and stems are big enough
*needs:* dry, not too fertile soil, well-drained
*location:* full sun, in a spot that dries out faster than most
*distance apart:* 14 to 16 inches
*height:* 6 to 18 inches
*propagation:* seed, crown division (after first year), layering, cuttings
*germination:* 10 to 21 days
*seed life:* two to three years
*companions:* cabbage, cauliflower, broccoli, kohlrabi, carrots, rosemary
*cultivation:* mulch sage before northern winters
*water:* likes it dry, don't overwater
*uses:* cough syrup, tea, seasoning for sausage, dressings, sauces
*picking:* pick leaves anytime, dry

## Soybeans

Some people say soybeans are the "meat without the bone." Soybeans are becoming more popular in American farms and gardens. Soybeans are a great source of protein. Have you ever had a soyburger?

*proper name: Glycine max,* also *Soja max*
*common name:* soybeans, soya, soya bean
*family:* legume (Leguminosae)
*relatives:* peas, beans, broad beans
*native land:* China
*history:* May be the oldest cultivated food plant. Soybeans did not become known in the West until missionaries brought seeds to Europe in the 18th century. Ben Franklin and Admiral Perry brought soybean seeds to America, but only recently has the value of soybeans been acknowledged.

Soybeans

### How to Grow Soybeans

*generation:* tender annual
*growing season:* long and warm, 100 days
*time to plant:* as soon as ground is completely warmed up
*time to pick:* fall
*needs:* average soil with a little compost

*location:* full sun with plenty of room
*distance apart:* 15 inches
*height:* 36 to 48 inches
*propagation:* the soybean is the seed, sow thinly in ground where it will grow
*germination:* four to eight days
*seed life:* two to three years
*companions:* corn, black-eyed peas
*types:* get "edible" types, such as Kanrich, Verde
*where to get it:* Burpee Seeds, Warminster, Pennsylvania 18974
*cultivation:* do not walk among wet soybeans
*water:* needs steady moisture
*parts and uses:* beans are eaten when young or when mature, also eaten as sprouts; also makes soap, paint, plastics
*picking:* anytime beans feel big enough inside shell; pods are hard to shell, steam them seven minutes, then shell

## Strawberries

Just about everybody's favorite berry. Grows in gardens everywhere, north and south. It adapts well to most gardens due to world-wide crossbreeding. It grows by runners, making new plants as it grows.

*proper name:* *Fragaria virginiana*
*common name:* strawberry
*family:* rose (Rosaceae)
*relatives:* apples, pears, peaches, apricots, bramble berries, roses

Strawberries

*native land:* Europe, North and South America
*history:* Although wild strawberries grew in most continents, the major efforts of crossbreeding happened in Europe. Colonists found wild North American strawberries that tasted better and carried more fruit than European kinds. Later, strawberries native to Chile which were larger and pulpier were crossed with wild Virginia and European kinds by chance in European gardens.

### How to Grow Strawberries

*generation:* perennial
*growing season:* cool moist spring and early summer

*time to plant:* set plants in early spring, fall for some varieties
*time to pick:* mid-May to mid-July for common types, all summer and fall for everbearing types
*needs:* fertile sandy loam, well-drained, don't overdo nitrogen
*location:* pick a permanent spot for the bed with morning sun and afternoon shade and room enough for runners
*distance apart:* 12 to 18 inches
*height:* grows low to the ground
*propagation:* set out new plants in spring; new plants grow on stolons or runners (strawberries are rarely grown from seed although some alpine varieties are)
*companions:* bush beans, spinach, borage, lettuce, marigolds
*types and colors:* check garden supply for best local variety
*cultivation:* give plants enough room to spread
*water:* needs lots of moisture, does well under mulch
*picking:* pull off berries between first two fingers, wait until they're red and ripe

## Summer Savory

Tomatoes and basil go together in the garden and on the dinner table. Beans and summer savory are another friendly garden combination. If you grow beans, grow savory with them.

*proper name:* *Satureia hortensis*
*common name:* summer savory common savory
*family:* mint (Labiatae)
*relatives:* mint, thyme, basil, oregano, rosemary, catnip, yerba buena
*native land:* Mediterranean
*history:* Summer savory was well-known in early cultures around the Mediterranean, especially in southern Europe. It became a standard herb in European castle, monastery, and cottage gardens. Colonists brought savory to the New World, where it "escaped from cultivation." Savory now grows wild in most warm areas of the earth.

Summer Savory

**How to Grow Summer Savory**

*generation:* hardy annual
*growing season:* warm summers
*time to plant:* when spring warms
*time to pick:* anytime
*needs:* average garden loam
*location:* sunny, airy spot
*distance apart:* six inches
*height:* 6 to 18 inches
*propagation:* seed, start indoors early
*germination:* 14 to 21 days
*seed life:* two years
*companions:* beans! onions
*cultivation:* put savory on south side of the bean patch
*water:* needs adequate moisture
*uses:* flavoring soup, meat, salad; relieves pain of bee stings; border or edging plant
*picking:* cut stems before flowers show; dry in cool place

# Sunflower

Sunflowers are more American than apple pie. They are native to North America. All the best gardens always seem to have a sunflower standing guard over everything. Certainly we must all look up to sunflowers.

*proper name: Helianthus annus*
*common name:* sunflower, helianthus, Texas corn
*family:* daisy (Compositae)
*relatives:* lettuce, cosmos, zinnias, marigolds, Jerusalem artichoke
*native land:* North America
*history:* Indians throughout North America grew sunflowers. Large-headed varieties were developed through plant selection by Indians. Indians wanted fat seeds for oil and meal. Another variety of sunflower has been grown for centuries in Russia

Sunflower

### How to Grow Sunflowers

*generation:* hardy annual
*growing season:* summer
*time to plant:* in spring when soil warms to midsummer
*time to pick:* late summer, fall
*needs:* fertile sandy loam, well-drained
*location:* full sun on north side of garden
*distance apart:* 12 to 18 inches
*height:* 48 to 231 inches
*propagation:* grows as fast as Jack's beanstalk
*germination:* three to six days
*seed life:* two to three years
*companions:* peas growing up them, kohlrabi, corn, cucumber
*types and colors:* mammoth is tallest; yellow, orange, and mahogany colors
*cultivation:* give them lots of room
*water:* needs steady supply
*parts and uses:* seeds for snacks and oil; stalks could be used for poles; cut flowers
*picking:* after seeds form and dry out

# Thyme

There are so many kinds of thyme that you can always find space for some in your garden. Some types of thyme creep along the ground and across walls. Others stretch their stems toward the sun. Any thyme is the right thyme.

*proper name:* *Thymus vulgaris* and *T. serpyllum*
*common names:* thyme, creeping thyme, mother-of-thyme
*family:* mint (Labiatae)
*relatives:* rosemary, mint, lavender, hyssop, catnip, oregano
*native land:* Mediterranean
*history:* Thyme is an ancient seasoning and a favorite garden plant from the time of the Greeks until today. Also an important medicine plant for many old cultures. Not all types of thyme are used in cooking. The French and the English developed better-tasting thymes. Although it is grown in many gardens in America, thyme has never become naturalized here.

### How to Grow Thyme

*generation:* aromatic perennial
*growing season:* brisk days of summer
*time to plant:* early spring onward

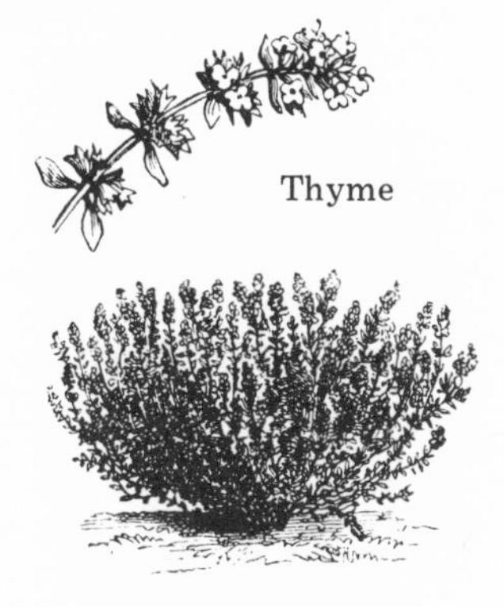
Thyme

*time to pick:* anytime for leaves
*needs:* average garden loam, well-drained
*location:* sunny airy spot, spread throughout garden
*distance apart:* six inches
*height:* six to ten inches
*propagation:* start seeds indoors in pots and transplant when soil warms, or start new plants from cuttings
*germination:* 14 to 28 days
*seed life:* two to three years
*companions:* everybody! but especially cabbage, cauliflower, broccoli, kohlrabi, turnips, radishes
*types:* creeping, wooly, lemon, silver, common thyme
*cultivation:* grow in masses to protect tender stems
*water:* keep fairly dry, don't overwater
*uses:* seasoning for soup, stew, meat, poultry; various medicinal uses: mouthwash, gargle, decongestant, essential oil
*picking:* cut stems before flowers show, dry out in cool dry place

# Tomatoes

Every summer garden always seems to have tomatoes somehow. The awful taste of store-bought tomatoes isn't the only reason people grow tomatoes. Smell your fingers after you've tied up the tomato vines. That smell is the reason I grow tomatoes. (Besides, they taste fantastic!)

*proper name: Lycopersicum esculentùm*
*common name:* tomato, love apple, gold apple, rage apple, wolf peach, tomate, tomati, tomata, tomatle
*family:* nightshade (Solanaceae)
*relatives:* potato, eggplant, pepper, tobacco, petunia, salpiglossis
*native land:* northern Andes (Peru, Ecuador, Bolivia)
*history:* Tomatoes grew wild in South America, but the Indians didn't value them as much as other vegetables. Becaues they didn't know how to dry and store them. Andes Indians ate wild tomatoes and the seeds were easily spread. Europeans were slow to eat tomatoes, and early American colonists were even slower. They considered tomatoes poisonous. Tomatoes became popular in the USA only after the Civil War.

**How to Grow Tomatoes**

*generation:* annual vine
*growing season:* long hot humid summers (50 to 80 days)
*time to plant:* start indoors in early spring and set out when nights start to warm
*time to pick:* summer to frost
*needs:* deep-dug loam, well-drained and fertilized
*location:* full sun with room to climb poles or fences

*distance apart:* 24 inches
*height:* as tall as poles allow
*propagation:* grows fast from seed, transplant deeply
*germination:* 7 to 14 days
*seed life:* one to two years for hybrids, four years for standard types
*companions:* asparagus, basil, onions, chives, carrots, parsley, marigolds
*types:* get early varieties if you have short summers, Tiny Tim is earliest
*cultivation:* tomatoes like heat, warm nights, and high humidity; pinch sucker shoots to force more fruiting

Tomatoes

*water:* deep soak occasionally, don't water leaves in hot weather
*picking:* feel them; sweeter before they turn completely red and lose firmness

# Tulip

Holland is the land where the tulips were made famous. But tulips did not originally come from Holland. No matter where they originated, many gardens are incomplete without tulips blooming in spring.

*proper name:* *Tulipa gesneriana*
*common name:* tulip, tulipase, toliban
*family:* lily (Liliaceae)
*relatives:* onions, garlic, leeks
*native land:* origin uncertain, perhaps Turkey
*history:* Wild tulips were probably included in Persian gardens. The Turks grew tulips. In Columbus' time, tulips were taken from Turkey to Austria where they later spread throughout Europe. Most recent hybrids are a result of intensive breeding by the Dutch.

### How to Grow Tulips

*generation:* perennial
*growing season:* cool
*time to plant:* October and November
*time to pick:* spring
*needs:* not too rich, well-worked, well-drained soil

Tulip

*location:* sunny airy spot
*distance apart:* eight to nine inches
*height:* 24 to 36 inches
*propagation:* bulbs
*companions:* other tulips and bulbs; follow with summer flowering annuals: cosmos, zinnias, marigolds
*types and colors:* many, see catalogs before deciding
*cultivation:* when planting put wire around bulbs under the soil so gophers, moles, and mice won't get them
*water:* regular water during spring growth
*parts and uses:* borders, bedding, cut flowers, forcing in pots
*picking:* as soon as flower begins to open

## Watermelon

You could plant a watermelon seed from the refrigerator and it might grow a watermelon plant. But you couldn't be sure what variety it is. Or when it would be ready to pick. Or if it would be ready to pick. What if you want to grow a watermelon that you can eat? Start with seeds suitable for your area.

*proper name: Citrullus vulgaris*
*common name:* watermelon, Turkie melon, melon citrall
*family:* gourd (Cucurbitaceae)
*relatives:* cucumbers, squash, pumpkin, other melons
*native land:* dry regions of Central Africa
*history:* Gardeners grew watermelons before history was recorded. Ancient Egyptians grew watermelons and drew pictures telling about it. In semi-deserts, native Africans still grow watermelons to ease drought conditions. From Africa, watermelon spread throughout the Mediterranean regions into the warmer parts of Europe and Asia.

**How to Grow Watermelon**

*generation:* very tender annual
*growing season:* long hot summers (110 to 140 days are best) for big varieties (75 to 90 days for smaller)
*time to plant:* early spring in warm soil
*time to pick:* late summer and fall
*needs:* fertile sandy loam, well-drained; too much nitrogen leads to thick vines and no fruit
*location:* full sun, room for vines to run, avoid tall plant shadows
*distance apart:* two or three best plants in hills
*height:* vines stay low to ground

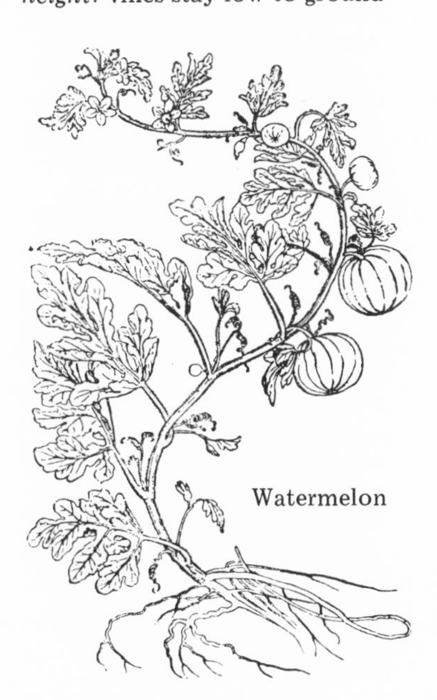
Watermelon

*propagation:* grows quickly from seed, can be started indoors
*germination:* 4 to 11 days
*seed life:* four to five years
*companions:* lettuce, radishes, and other salad plants which mature in spaces where the vines will later run, also good with potatoes
*types and colors:* icebox types are best for small gardens, try Yellow Baby, icebox type with yellow meat!
*cultivation:* pinch back vines to force fruiting
*water:* deep soak frequently, especially during fruiting stages
*picking:* find out how to "thump" a watermelon; people in the produce section of a supermarket might know, or a neighborhood gardener; watermelon picked too early or too late tastes awful

# Yucca

It may seem strange but some gardeners can find soap hidden in their soil. This soap is "packaged" in the root of some yucca plants. The roots of century plant and saponaria can also be used to make soap.

*proper name: Yucca glauca*
*common name:* yucca, soapweed, small soapweed
*family:* lily (Liliaceae)
*relatives:* onion, leeks, garlic,

shallots, asparagus, tulip, aloe, hyacinth
*native land:* North America
*history:* This type of yucca soapweed still grows wild from Montana to South Dakota to New Mexico to Texas. American Indians have known and used yucca for centuries. Early pioneers in the West also used yucca for soap. But nowadays few people know how to grow their own soap.

Yucca

*growing season:* long hot summers
*time to plant:* anytime
*time to pick:* two to three years after plants are established
*needs:* average, well-drained soil
*location:* full sun
*distance apart:* 60 inches
*height:* 72 inches
*propagation:* seed
*germination:* unknown
*companions:* tulip, daffodil, cactus, other succulents
*where to get it:* J. L. Hudson's World Seed Service, Redwood City, California 94064
*cultivation:* don't plant near walkways; the sharp leaves hurt
*water:* likes dry desert-type conditions; don't overwater
*uses:* soap made by pounding roots; fruits of this variety are edible; attractive as rock garden ornamental
*picking:* to make soap: peel and slice roots, pound them into pulp, add a little water and churn until soapy enough

## Zinnia

Usually the last plant on everyone's list, but the first flower in many gardeners' hearts. Shop a seed catalog before deciding on a variety of zinnia. There are lots of choices.

*proper name: Zinnia elegans*
*common name:* zinnia, youth-and-old-age
*family:* daisy (Compositae)
*relatives:* cosmos, sunflower, lettuce, compass plant, dahlia, daisy, dandelion
*native land:* Mexico
*history:* Indians cultivated zinnias for a long time in Mexico. Aztecs prized the flower and it was a major element in Montezuma's gardens. But Europeans did not become interested in the flower until the 1750s. From there it became hybridized and changed in both annual and perennial varieties.

### How to Grow Zinnias

*generation:* half-hardy annual
*growing season:* warm summers
*time to plant:* early spring, or start early indoors
*time to pick:* summer through fall
*needs:* nothing special but well-drained soil
*location:* full sun
*distance apart:* nine inches
*height:* 8 to 36 inches depending on variety
*propagation:* grows easily from seed
*germination:* 7 to 14 days
*seed life:* unknown
*companions:* other zinnias, spring bulbs
*colors:* many, see catalog
*cultivation:* pinch out dead flowers
*water:* medium
*uses:* long-lasting as cut flowers, border, bedding
*picking:* frequent cutting of blooms forces more

Zinnia

## A Plant Is Not a Sofa

All these neat groups of numbers and facts may make it seem that plants are very exact things like a chair or a brick wall. Or other things that don't move around and don't change much. Things that all seem the same and stay the same.

But any gardener knows that plants change all the time. They move and grow every day. No two plants are alike. Ever. No single plant ever stays the same.

Don't be surprised if you grow a plant that disobeys all the rules and sinks all the facts in this book. Plants are living things. They grow and change just like you do.

## Finding Out about Other Plants You Want to Grow

Do you want to grow something not listed in these pages? You can make your own Planter's and Picker's Pages for the plants you want to grow. Go to the library or use the telephone to get the information. Your pages don't have to be like the ones in this book. But they should try to include most of the same kinds of information. So you'll know where and when and how to grow it.

# A Dictionary of Garden Language

When you begin to talk with gardeners, nursery people, seed companies, and other plant people, they will speak a language that may sound foreign to you. It sounds foreign. But it isn't really. It's just garden language.

Here is a dictionary of words you may hear when talking with anyone about gardening. If you read or hear a gardening word you don't know, look it up here.

## A

*acid soil* Sour soil. Like lemons or vinegar. Opposite of alkaline soil. On pH scale, acid soils measure 6.9 or below.

*aerate* Opening soil for air. Improves the circulation of gasses through the soil.

*alkaline soil* Bitter soil. Like ammonia or baking soda or seawater. Opposite of acid soil. Alkaline soils measure 7.1 or above.

*annual* Any plant living for one growing season. Yearly.

*anther* Pollen-producing part of a male flower. Found on the end of a flower filament.

*aboretum* Large garden of trees, mostly. Some rare. Some native. Trees are respected, studied, and cared for. A quiet place.

*axil* Point on stem of plant where leaf is attached.

# B

*beds* Reserved planting spaces where nobody walks. Flowers, herbs, vegetables, and other tame plants can grow in beds.

*bedding plants* Plants best suited for growing in garden beds. Formal and semi-formal plants. Perennials, annuals, or shrubs. Anything can grow in beds.

*biennial* Any plant that lives for two growing seasons. Biennials flower in second year, not first.

*blanching* Method of turning plant parts white. Some people think they're easier to eat this way. Usually done by keeping sunlight off the plant part. Can be done by mulching, covering with cardboard, or mounding up soil.

*blood meal* Dried blood from butchered animals. High-nitrogen, high-protein fertilizer. Add to soil. Speeds up heating of compost piles.

*blue moon* Rare event. Second full moon of a month. Happens once a year.

*boll* A round capsule that holds seeds. Flax and cotton seeds are contained in bolls.

*bolting* Troublesome time when some vegetables begin to flower. Bolting is bad because the plant's energy goes to the flower, not to the part of the plant you eat. Then it doesn't taste as good.

*bone meal* Crushed bones from butchered animals. Used as high-phosphorus fertilizer. Also high in nitrogen and protein. Add to soil or compost.

*border plants* A long strip of plants marking off the border of something.

*botany* The science of plant life. People who study this science are botanists.

*botanic garden* Large garden for study of plant life. Usually open to the public. Many cities have botanic gardens.

*broadcasting* Tossing and scattering seed to plant a large area, after soil has been dug. Also called "sowing."

*bud* Tight bump on a branch or stem. Future leaves, stems, and flowers grow from buds.

*budding* A way of starting new plants by putting a growing bud of one onto another. A bud is grafted onto the bark or stem. See "grafting."

*bulb* A whole plant (flowers, leaves, stems) wrapped in one tight ball. Most bulbs bloom in spring. Tulips, lilies, daffodils are true bulbs. So are onions.

*bush varieties* Short versions of long, viney plants; usually don't need support or staking up.

# C

*calyx* Tough outside cover of flower.

*club root* Fungus disease found in acid soils. Infects roots of cabbage family plants.

*cold frame* Any sunlit, enclosed, and unheated plant house. Used to protect young vegetables, flowers, tender plants from wind and weather. A little greenhouse. A big terrarium.

*colloidal* Any half-solid material that will chemically change in soil and become soluable food for plants. Phosphate rock comes in colloidal form.

*community garden* Group garden with many people sharing space, tools, information, etc. Most community gardens are found in cities and other places where people have no room to garden at home.

*companion planting* Planting friendly plants next to each other. Done to save space, make plants happy, and control bugs. No one knows how or why it works for some gardeners, but not others.

*compost* Home-made fertilizer. The best soil builder there is. Compost is made out of table scraps, kitchen garbage, old weeds, broken leaves, anything that is dead or dying and ready to go back to the soil.

*compost heap* Any pole or pit of compost. Compost heats up and breaks down faster when it is heaped at least three feet high and covered.

*conservatory* Any public or private greenhouse or greenroom used to display plants. Some cities have fancy public conservatories.

*corm* An underground stem that looks like a squashed bulb. Gladiolus grow from corms.

*corolla* A flower's colored petals.

*cotyledons* The first two leaves that form from each half of the seed. Not true leaves.

*crown* Part of plant between roots and above ground stems or leaves.

*cultivate* To dig and fertilize the soil, and to grow things in it. Also to pull out weeds and aerate topsoil.

*cuttings* The growing points of a parent plant that have been cut and put in water or a rooting mix. Roots will come out of the cut end of stem. This is how many new plants get started.

# D

*damping-off* Fungus disease in soil. Causes seedlings and tender young plants to wilt and die. Big problem when starting plants in places with poor ventilation.

*deadheading* Pinching plants to prevent flowers and seeds from forming. A way to keep some food and spice plants producing longer. Also a way to force more flowers to grow later.

*deciduous* Trees and plants that drop all their leaves in fall and are dormant in winter. Deciduous plants "leaf out" in spring.

*deep soak* Watering plants very slowly, drip-by-drip, for a long time. Useful in very hot climates where some plants need constant moisture. Very little water lost through evaporation.

*diclinous* Separate male and female flowers grow on the same plant, like cucumbers, pumpkins, and melons.

*dioecious* Separate male and female flowers grow on separate plants, such as asparagus.

*division* A way of starting new plants from old ones by dividing up the roots of the plant, usually perennials, not annuals. Done when plant is dormant.

*dormant* Not growing. Asleep, like animals in winter hibernation.

*double digging* A method of deep digging. Opens up soil for air, water, and roots to circulate deeper.

*drainage* How water drains through a soil. Water backs up, forms puddles quickly in poorly draining soil.

*drills* Shallow trenches for planting seeds.

*dwarf varieties* Small varieties of large plants and trees, similar to "bush" varieties. Many fruit trees come in dwarf varieties suited for small gardens.

# E

*edging plant* Plants grown along the edge or border of something. See "border plants."

*"escaped from cultivation"* Phrase used in botany books. Explains how a garden plant from one country is taken to a place where it never grew before. The plant "escapes" from gardens into the wild and becomes "naturalized." Now it's a weed that can take care of itself. See "naturalized."

*evergreen* Plants like pine trees that remain green all year round. They don't drop all their leaves in fall, like oaks and other deciduous trees. Sometimes called conifers.

*everlasting* Flowers that last a long time after they're cut from the plant. Used for flower decorations and winter flower arrangments.

# F

*family* Every plant on earth belongs to a family. Usually the number, size, and shape of a flower's petals tell what family it's in. Plant families are a lot bigger than people families. (And a lot more quiet!) Hundreds of different plants can belong to the same family. Also see "species" and "genus."

*fertilizer* Anything you add to soil to improve the life there. Leaves, sawdust, moss, ashes, peanut shells, seaweed, manure, wood chips, grass clippings, cocoa bean shells are natural fertilizers. There are many others.

*flats* Any planting tray used to start seedlings. Most plants started in flats are later transplanted. Many long-season plants are started in flats indoors in early spring or late winter.

*frost* When air temperature drops below 32° F or 0° C. Plants, soil, everything else in the garden is in danger of freezing. Usually the first hard frost of fall kills back most gardens. After the last expected frost of spring, gardens are dug and planted.

*full moon* Time of month when sun is on one side of the earth and moon is on the other. On the night of the full moon, all the moon is lit up, when seen from earth. Full moon is the wettest time of the month. Begins a two-week cycle of root growth.

*fungus diseases* Sickness caused by microscopic plants in soil. Damping-off and club root are fungus diseases. Mildew, rust, smut, and molds are fungi. Fungus plants do not have the green coloring of chlorophyll.

# G

*genus* A plant's general name. Always capitalized. The first name in a plant's proper name. Usually tells why these plants are grouped together.

*germination* The sprouting of seeds. When they germinate, seeds come to life. Most plants need moisture to germinate. Some seeds (snapdragon, lettuce, petunia) need sunlight.

*grafting* Inserting bud of one plant into another plant growing in the soil. This method of propagation is how new fruit varieties are created. See "budding."

*greenhouse* A large enclosed planthouse covered with plastic, glass, fiberglass, or other transparent materials. Used to grow things that couldn't be grown outside.

*ground cover* Any low-growing plant used to cover the ground. Prevents loss of soil moisture by evaporation.

*growing season* The time between spring and fall frosts when garden plants can reliably grow outside.

# H

*half-hardy* Between hardy and tender. Plants that need some special attention and protection from weather.

*harden off* Getting young plants ready to be transplanted into garden. Get them used to sudden temperature changes and full sunlight.

*hardy* Plants that are healthy and can withstand rough treatment from weather. And gardeners.

*harvest* Time for picking food plants. Usually happens in fall, but many fast-growing plants are harvested throughout the growing season.

*harvest moon* The full moon closest to the fall equinox. Usually happens in September. Rises near sunset. Gives farmers and gardeners extra light in garden.

*heavy soil* Tight, thick clay soils that weigh a lot. Hard to dig. Hard for roots to get through. Bad soil for most gardens. OK for native plants that like it.

*herbicides* Poison used to kill weeds and other garden life. You don't need it. See also "pesticides" and "insecticides."

*herbs* Dense soft-stemmed plants used for scenting, flavoring, and spicing foods.

*hill* Any circle of seeds. Hill can be mound- or bowl-shaped. Squash, melons, cucumbers, and sometimes corn are planted in hills.

*horticulture* The science of cultivating plants, especially for ornamental gardening.

*humus* What compost and other organic matter becomes when it is in soil. Decomposed, fine material. It does not have a regular size or shape.

*hybrid* New varieties of plants created by crossing other plants and varieties. Used to improve taste, size, color of a variety, or otherwise improve earliness or hardiness of a type.

# I

*inflorescence* A plant's flowering parts.

*insecticides* Poison used to kill bugs in your garden. Unnecessary expense. And very dangerous. See also "pesticides" and "herbicides."

*intercropping* Planting two or more different plants together. See also "companion planting."

# L

*landscaping* Creating a complete garden around a home. Many people work as landscape gardeners, especially in places where people can afford it.

*layering* Several methods of propagating woody plants while the rooting branch is still attached to plant. Air layering, mount layering, trench layering, stool layering, simple layering are some of the methods.

*leaching* The washing away of nutrients through the soil. Usually happens when soil is exposed to heavy rains and lots of heat.

*leaf mold* A great fertilizer made by piling decaying leaves together and covering them. Can be worked into soil in spring or used as mulch.

*leafstalk* A thick main stem or stalk that supports leaves, as in celery.

*leggy* Young plants whose stems grow too long as they stretch for sunlight. Leggy plants aren't sturdy.

*lime* Not the citrus fruit. Lime is a crushed or powdered limestone, a soft rock that formed from dead seashells during many hundred-thousand years. Used to sweeten any acid soil. Lime makes soils more alkaline.

*loam* Perfect garden soil. Not too much clay, sand or silt. And lots of open spaces for air and water to circulate. Good loam is half empty space.

# M

*manure* Solid wastes from animals used as a basic fertilizer in gardens and farms throughout history. Contains minerals and microbic life necessary to the soil. Original meaning of manure: to work by hand.

*microclimate* Like a little forest. The whole climate from top of soil to top of tallest plants.

*moon phase* The 29½ day cycle of the moon around the earth. Moon goes from new moon to waxing crescent to new moon again. And on and on. Many people around the world plant according to the moon phase.

*mulch* Any "blanket" of decaying leaves, lawn cuttings, hay, sawdust, stable sweepings, spread on the topsoil around plants. Four to ten inches deep. Or more! Mulch reduces need for watering, weeding, fertilizing. Mulching is a duplication of the natural process that happens on forest floor when decaying leaves fall and blanket the ground.

*mutation* Any unexpected change in a new generation of plants, animals, or other life. Could be change in color, size, flowers, habit of growth, or anything else that's noticeable. Mutation is nature's way of surprising everyone. Not caused by people crossbreeding it with another plant.

# N

*naturalized* When a new garden plant becomes a weed, because it grows so well in the new place. The plant "escapes from cultivation" in gardens and starts to grow wild. Sort of like an African animal escaping from a zoo and learning how to live in Hoboken, New Jersey. See "escaped from cultivation."

*new moon* Time of month when the sun and moon are on the same side of the earth. On the night of the new moon, people on earth can't see the moon because it rises in the daytime. The new moon is the driest time of the month. Begins two-week cycle of leaf and above-the-ground growth.

*nitrogen* One of the main plant nutrients. Nitrogen is "fixed" by microbes and is slowly released into the soil. Nitrogen must constantly be renewed in soil. Usually it is added in the form of aged manure and compost.

*nurseries* Not the kind of nursery for babies. This kind sells plants, trees, seeds, fertilizers, soil-builders, and other garden supplies.

*nutrients* In soil, all the elements and minerals that feed plants need to make their own balanced meals.

# O

*open-pollinating* A plant that will produce seeds that you can save, because the seeds will reliably produce plants like their parents. Open-pollinating plants "breed true." Not a hybrid.

*ornamental* Any plants grown for color, fragrance, shape, beauty, or any other reason for displaying them.

*ovary* Female part of flower where future seed waits for pollen. Once pollinated, the ovary will expand to contain the growing seed. Just like a womb grows with an unborn animal.

# P

*peat moss* Decomposed remains of plants piled up over centuries in swamps, bogs, and other low, wet places. Used to lighten heavy soils and hold together light ones. Some types of peat moss can absorb up to 15 times their weight in water.

*perennial* Any plant or tree that lives for more than two years and usually a lot longer. Roses, asparagus, and mint are perennial plants.

*pesticides* Poisons that can kill bugs, birds, plants, and sometimes people. They are dangerous because they seem to be killing more things than they are saving.

*pH test* The common measure of how acid, neutral, or alkaine a soil or anything else is. A pH of 7 is neutral, 7.1 to 14 is the alkaline side of pH scale. Acid side is 0 to 6.9.

*phosphorus* One of the main minerals in soil. Phosphorus improves root, flower, and seed growth in plants. Phosphorus can be added to soil or compost in form of bone meal and crushed phosphate rock.

*photosynthesis* The way plants turn sunlight into energy for growth. Happens in green chlorophyll parts of plant. Plants take in carbon dioxide and release oxygen during photosynthesis.

*picking out* Taking plants out of flats and transplanting them to new soil.

*pinching* Pruning the growing tips off a plant by using fingernails. Done to force plants to become bushy and develop more flowers.

*pistil* Female parts of a flower. Produces seed after pollination. Pistil is made up of stigma, style, and ovary.

*plant breeding* Inventing and growing new plants for a reason. Any reason. Usually done by taking pollen from one plant and fertilizing another plant in the same family. Also done by grafting.

*pole varieties* Tall-growing viney varieties of plants that need poles to grow on. Pole beans need support of a pole. Bush beans do not.

*pollen* Fascinating dust-like seed-making stuff in the male parts of flowers. When pollen fertilizes the female parts of flowers, this is called pollination. Pollen can irritate your skin, eyes, or whole body. Hay fever is caused by some kinds of pollen.

*potash or potassium* One of the three major soil minerals necessary for strong healthy plants. Also protects plants in dry or cold weather. Potassium can be added to soil or compost in form of hardwood ashes, green sand, stable sweepings, and granite dust.

*propagation* The ways plants get started. Plants can be propagated by seeds, spores, layering, cutting, budding, grafting, root division, runners, suckers, offsets. Propagation of your own plants is an easy way to make more plants.

*pruning* Trimming away damaged, diseased, or dead parts of a plant. Usually done when plant is dormant. Important way to increase harvest from fruit trees and berries.

# R

*recycle* To wisely reuse something instead of throwing it away. Anything can be recycled, if you can find a use for it.

*rhizome* A thick underground stem of many perennial plants. Rhizome is also considered a rootstock.

*rock gardens* Style of gardening using small plants and big rocks. Creates an environment similar to mountains. Sometimes called "alpine gardening."

*rootstock* Part of a plant's root used to start another plant, as in berries and rose propagation.

*rotation of plants* Planting something different in a spot after other plants have finished growing. Done to maintain balance of soil and insect life in the garden.

# S

*seed catalog* A mail-order book full of different varieties of many plants. Mostly vegetables and flowers grown from seed. Catalogs are very helpful in telling the difference among varieties.

*seed house* A seed company. Usually has a catalog and allows mail ordering of seeds.

*seedlings* Young plants waiting to be transplanted into the garden.

*seedstalk* A stem that produces seed.

*selection* The way plants are bred and grown by choice. People select plants for a certain reason. Larger fruit, for example.

*self-sowing* Seeds that plant themselves. All weeds are self-sowing. So are native plants, some vegetables, flowers, and herbs.

*sepal* The usually green leaflike pieces of calyx. Sepals form the outside covering of flower buds. Later sepals form tough green parts at the base of the flower.

*sewage sludge* A soil fertilizer made form solid remains of treated and aged sewage. Activated sludge has been processed with air bubbling through it. Digested sludge is processed by settling and gravity, instead of air.

*soil* The stuff of life! Soil is a fertile mixture of air, water, minerals, and humus. Soil is not dirty.

*spotting* Transplanting very tiny seedlings from one flat to another place.

*stamen* Male parts of a flower. Produces pollen for female parts of a flower. Stamen is made up of a filament and an anther.

*stigma* Female part of the flower which captures pollen. Located on top of the pistils.

*stolon* An above-ground stem that wanders along the top of soil, like a strawberry plant runner.

*style* Slender female part of a flower between the ovary and stigma. The tube that pollen passes through on its way to the ovary.

*subsoil* The layer or layers of soil underneath topsoil. Not as fertile as topsoil, but a necessary layer anyway.

*succession planting* A system of planting usually used in good gardens and farms. Done to insure a steady supply of food will be available throughout the growing season. Many gardeners make succession plantings of lettuce every two weeks, for example.

*sucker shoots* A side shoot from the root or lower stem of a plant or tree. Sometimes suckers can be used to propagate a plant. Sometimes suckers are unwanted because they "rob" the rest of the plant of energy.

# T

*tamp* To snugly pat down topsoil around the base of newly transplanted plants. Does not compress deeper soil, but does make topsoil solid enough to support plant.

*tankage* A high-nitrogen fertilizer. Made from slaughterhouse and butcher shop refuse.

*taproot* The main root down into soil. All other roots lead out of this.

*tender* Tender plants need a lot of care and attention. They are easily damaged by sudden temperature change and wind. Hard to transplant. Not hardy.

*trace elements* Many minerals necessary for plant growth and health. Found in very small amounts in the soil. Usually measured in "parts per million." Very small amounts.

*thinning* Pulling out less healthy, less vigorous, slower growing plants soon after they germinate and form their first true leaves. Important step in transplanting, because plants would grow too crowded if they weren't thinned.

*topsoil* The layer of rich soil on top of the ground where seeds germinate and begin life. Good topsoil is fertilized and dug each year.

*transplanting* Moving a plant from one place to another. Or from one container to another.

*trenching* Any method of adding compost, manure, or topsoil to deeper layers of subsoil. Done to improve drainage and fertility of soils growing tender and heavy-feeding plants.

*tuber* Short, thick, fleshy underground (but not always) stems. Tubers have "eyes" where new plants begin. Jerusalem artichokes and potatoes grow tubers.

# V

*varieties* Different kinds of the same plant. Silver Sweet and Illini Xtra Sweet are two varieties of sweet corn. Some varieties are suited for your area, some aren't. Gardeners must know the best local varieties to have a productive food garden.

*vine* Any long-growing plant, like tomatoes or melons, that stretches and grows a lot in one growing season. Some vines, like tomatoes, are tied up on stakes because their flowers and fruits aren't heavy. Other vines, like heavy melons, crawl along the ground.

*verticillium wilt* A destructive fungus disease that lives in soil for many years.

*virus disease* Sickness in soil caused by viruses. Mosaic and curly top are virus diseases. Viruses live within cells. A virus can duplicate itself only inside a cell. See "fungus diseases."

*volunteers* Plants that come up by themselves from seed lost in the soil of an earlier garden. Volunteers usually grow fast and have a strong will to live.

*waning moon* Time of the moon's phase between full moon and next new moon. Middle of waning phase is called waning crescent. Some say this is the time to plant carrots and other "root crops."

*waxing moon* Time of the moon's phase between new moon and next full moon. Waxing crescent is halfway between new and full moon. Some say waxing moon is the time to plant vegetables growing food parts above the ground.

*weeds* Plants that grow where you don't want them to. The strongest plants in any place.

*winterkilled* Plants damaged by winter winds, low temperatures, and freezes.

# A Catalog of Seed Catalogs

Seeds are the best things in the world to find in your mailbox. But seeds will be too late to plant if you don't order before the year-end rush.

Best time to order is late September to mid-November. Pick seed houses near you and send for their catalogs.

Most catalogs include order forms with complete instructions for ordering. One pack usually has enough seeds for a few seasons.

These are the seed companies with the best catalogs for kids:

R. H. Shumway Seedsman
628 Cedar Street
Rockford, Illinois 61101

Gurney Seed and Nursery
2642 Page Street
Yankton, South Dakota 57078

Grace's Gardens
Autumn Lane
Hackettstown, New Jersey 07840

George W. Park Seeds
Box 31
Greenwood, South Carolina
29647

# Mighty Little Seeds

Shumway, Gurney, Grace's and Park seed companies all offer midget vegetable collections in their catalogs. These include small corn, tomatoes, cucumbers, lettuce, and watermelons. Other seed houses also sell midget vegetables:

Burgess Seeds
Box 3000
Galesburg, Michigan 49053

Farmer Seed and Nursery Co.
Faribault, Minnesota 55021

Earl May Seed and Nursery Co.
Shenandoah, Iowa 51603

Henry Field Seed and Nursery Co.
Shenandoah, Iowa 51602

# Selected Seed Traders

Many small seed houses are dedicated to a new idea of seed selection and trading. They sell seeds like flax, rye, alfalfa, and yucca that are used for more than just eating.

Johnny's Selected Seeds
Organic Seed and Crop Research
Albion, Maine 04910

The Natural Development Co.
Organic Seeds and Supplies
Bainbridge, Pennsylvania 17502

Abundant Life Seeds
Box 30018
Seattle, Washington 98103

J. L. Hudson's World Seeds
Box 1058
Redwood City, California 94064

The Redwood City Seed Co.
Box 361
Redwood City, California 94064

Vita Green Farms
Box 878
Vista, California, 92803

Nichols Garden Nursery
1190 North Pacific Highway
Albany, Oregon 97321

# Complete Seed Houses

These seed houses have lots of varieties of almost everything. Vegetables, flowers, fruit, herbs, supplies. Everything.

Stokes Seeds Inc.
Box 548 Main
Buffalo, New York 14240

Burnett Brothers Inc.
92 Chambers Street
New York, New York 10007

Stern's Nurseries
Lehigh and Avenue E
Geneva, New York 14456

W. Atlee Burpee Company
300 Park Avenue
Warminster, Pennsylvania 18974
or
6350 Rutland Avenue
Riverside, California 92502

Tennessee Nursery and Seed
Nursery Road
Cleveland, Tennessee 37311

L. L. Olds Seed Company
2901 Packers Ave.
Madison, Wisconsin 53701

Harry E. Saier Seeds
Diamondale, Michigan 48821

Ferdale Gardens
702 Nursery Lane
Faribault, Minnesota 55021

# Wildflower Seed Houses

Many people collect wildflowers and sell them through the mail. Here are just a few of them:

Francis M. Sinclair
RFD 1, Route 85
Exeter, New Hampshire 03833

Putney Nursery Inc.
U. S. Route 5
Putney, Vermont 05346

The Three Laurels
Madison County
Marshall, North Carolina 28753

Gardens of the Blue Ridge
McDowell County
Ashford, North Carolina 28603

Hi—Mountain Farm
Route 1, Box 29
Seligman, Missouri 65747

Merl Gunderson Nursery
Rapid City, South Dakota
57701

Frank Rose Seeds
1020 Poplar Street
Missoula, Montana 59801

Clyde Robin Seed Company
Box 2855
Castro Valley, California 94546

# Herb Farms

Many small seed companies sell herbs. Here are a few:

Capriland's Herb Farm
Silver Street
Coventry, Connecticut 06238

Hemlock Hill Herb Farm
Hemlock Hill Road
Litchfield, Connecticut 06759

Greene Herb Gardens
Herb Seeds and Bulbs
Greene, Rhode Island 02827

Indiana Botanic Gardens Inc.
Herb Seeds
Hammond, Indiana 46325

Pine Hills Herb Farm
Box 144
Roswell, Georgia 30075

Casa Yerba
Box 176
Tustin, California 92680

Sunnybrook Farms Nursery
9448 Mayfield Road
Chesterland, Oregon 44026

Wide World of Herbs Ltd.
11 St. Catherine Street East
Montreal, Canada H2X 1K3

Merry Gardens Herbs
Camden, Maine 04843

# Miniature and Alpine Rock Gardens

Plants for alpine gardens are sometimes hard to find locally. Here are some places where you can mail order small plants for miniature gardens:

Girard Nurseries
Box 428
Geneva, Ohio 44041

Lamb Nurseries
East 101 Sharp Avenue
Seattle, Washington 99202

Mayfair Nurseries
Route 2, Box 68
Nichols, New York 13812

Carroll Gardens
Box 310
Westminster, Maryland 21157

Siskiyou Rare Plant Nursery
522 Franquette Street
Medford, Oregon 97501

# Specialty Seed Houses

Some seed houses specialize in one or two things.

*For all kinds of bean seeds, from Adzuki to Wren's Egg:*
Vermont Bean Seed Company
4 Ways Lane
Manchester Center, Vermont
05255

*For more kinds of strawberries than you can imagine:*
Dean Foster Nurseries
Hartford, Michigan 49057

*For aloe, yucca, cactus, and succulents:*
Spring Hill Nurseries
Tipp City, Ohio 45366

*For seeds of vegetables from China and Japan:*
Kitazawa Seed Company
356 W. Taylor St.
San Jose, California 95110

Tsang and Ma
Box 794
Belmont, California 94002

*The official seed house of Great Britain:*
Suttons Seed Ltd.
The Royal Seed Establishment
Hele Road Torquay
Devon, England TQ2 7QJ

# A Directory of Botanic and Biological Bug Controls

The logical way to control bugs is with other bugs. And with botanic sprays prepared from plants.

You can mail order bugs, bacteria, and botanic sprays. But sometimes they are expensive.

Send a post card to any of the following addresses and ask for a price list. If you can't afford it, find another way to solve your problem.

# Where to Order Ladybugs

If your neighborhood doesn't have enough ladybugs, you can order them through the mail. When they arrive, don't let all of them loose at once. Save some in the refrigerator.

Bio-Control Company
Route 2, Box 2397
Auburn, California 95603

L. E. Schnoor's Sierra Bugs
Box 114
Rough and Ready, California
95975

Organic Control Products
Box 25382
West Los Angeles, California
90025

World Garden Products
2 First Street East
Norwalk, Connecticut 06855

Lakeland Nurseries
Biological Controls
Hanover, Pennsylvania 17331

Montgomery Ward
618 W. Chicago Ave.
Chicago, Illinois 60610

# Where to Order Praying Mantids

Order praying mantid egg cases in the spring from:

Eastern Biological Control
Route 5, Box 379
Jackson, New Jersey 08527

Mincemoyer's Nursery
New Prospect Road
Jackson, New Jersey 08527

Robert Robbins
424 North Courtland
East Stroudsburg, Pennsylvania
18301

Agrilite Systems
404 Barringer Building
Columbia, South Carolina 29201

Gothard Inc.
Box 332
Canutillo, Texas 79835

Organic Control Products
Box 25382
West Los Angeles, California
90025

# Where to Get Lacewings and Trichogramma Wasps

California Green Lacewings Inc.
Box 154
Banta, California 95304

Rincon-Vitova Insectary Inc.
Box 95
Oakview, California 93022

Organic Control Products
Box 25382
West Los Angeles, California
90025

# Where to Find Friendly Bacterial Diseases

Order *Bacillus thuringiensis* in powdered form from:

River Bottom Naturals
Route 2, Box 106
Stafford, Virginia 22554

Thompson-Hayward Chemical Co.
Box 2383
Kansas City, Kansas 66110

Galt Research
RR1 Box 245-38
Trafalgar, Indiana 46181

Nelome's By Organics
Route 2, Box 49
Castleberry, Alabama 36401

International Minerals and
Chemical Corporation
Crop Aids Department 5401
Old Orchard Road
Skokie, Illinois 60076

Order *Bacillus popilliae* from:

Fairfax Biological Laboratory
Electronic Road
Clifton Corners, New York 12514

Reuter Laboratories
Box 1058
Manassas, Virginia 22110

Hydroponic Chemical Co.
Biological Controls
Copley, Ohio 44321

# Digger's Guide to Soil Supplies and Garden Information

If you want a great garden, you have to dig for it. You can mail order minerals, fertilizers, soil conditioners, and other soil supplies. But they might cost more than you're willing to pay. Check the following lists for soil suppliers near you. Then send for their price lists.

You will also have to dig for garden information. Many articles, books, stories, poems, and songs are written about gardens every day. There is so much to read that it crosses your eyes. But to find the truth you have to dig through it.

Don't trust any "fact" about gardening until you've read it four places and heard it eight times. And don't worry if it feels like it's taking you forever to find out.

# Where to Get Soil Supplies

Find a supplier near you and send a post card asking about prices.

*For greensand, granite dust, phosphate rock, and other minerals:*

Hocking Granite Industries
Clark Island
St. George, Maine 04857

Odlin Organics
Lakeshore Drive
West Brookfield, Massachusetts 01585

Brookside Nurseries
Soil Improvement
Darien, Connecticut 06820

Alsmith Inc.
Box 275
Seaford, New York 11783

Kaylonite Corporation
Rock Minerals
Dunkirk, Maryland 20754

Vita Green Farms
Box 878
Vista, California 92083

*For other soil conditioners:*

Squanto Peat and Organic Fertilizer
Rutherford Road
Oakham, Maine 01068

Zook and Ranck Inc.
Route 1
Gap, Pennsylvania 17527

Nature's Way Products
3505 Mozart Avenue
Cincinnati, Ohio 45211

Eisman Organic Garden Supplies
6046 Benken Lane
Cincinnati, Ohio 45211

Key Minerals Corporation
Box 2364
Salt Lake City, Utah 84110

Farm Guard Products
701 Madison NE
Albuquerque, New Mexico 87110

New Life Soil Conditioner
Box 241
Lewiston, Montana 59457

Reindeer's Organic Company Ltd.
5307 Patricia Bay Highway, RR5
Victoria, British Columbia
Canada

# Where to Dig for Information

Some schools, institutions, and agencies of the government print booklets about many aspects of gardening. Send a post card and ask for a list of their publications. The best are printed by:

Bio-Dynamic Farming and
Gardening Association
308 East Adams Street
Springfield, Illinois 62701

Agricultural Publications
Superintendent of Documents
Government Printing Office
Washington, D. C. 20402

Texas Agricultural Experiment
Station
Texas A and M University
College Station, Texas 77840

Country Bookstore Bulletins
Garden Way Publishing
Charlotte, Vermont 05445

Brooklyn Botanic Garden
1000 Washington Ave.
Brooklyn, New York 11225

Agriculture Extension Bulletins
Building 7, Research Park
Cornell University
Ithaca, New York 14850

# Some Helpful Books

Ask for these popular garden reference books at your local library. They will help you make your own Planter's and Picker's Pages.

*Manual of Cultivated Plants* by L. H. Bailey. Macmillan, 1924 (for names, family, relatives, sometimes native land)

*A Gardener's Guide to Plant Names* by B. J. Healey. Scribners, 1972 (for names, family, and relatives)

*Vegetables and Herbs: an Encyclopedia and Gardener's Guide* by Victor A. Tiedjens. Garden City Publishing, 1943 (how to grow it and use it, some history)

*Encyclopedia of Organic Gardening*, edited by J. I. Rodale and staff. Rodale Books, 1959 (how to grow it and use it, some history)

*The Pfeiffer Garden Book*, edited by Alice Heckel. Bio-Dynamic Farming and Gardening Association, 1967 (for everything)

*The Complete Guide to Garden Flowers*, edited by Herbert Askwith. A. S. Barnes and Co., 1961 (for most popular flowers)

*Secrets of Companion Planting* by Louise Riotte. Garden Way Publishing, 1975 (for friends of plants)

# A Year in My Garden

# My Garden in January

# My Garden in February

# My Garden in March

# My Garden in April

# My Garden in May

My Garden in June

# My Garden in July

# My Garden in August

# My Garden in September

# My Garden in October

# My Garden in November

# My Garden in December

## Something Important to Remember about Gardens

Plants are wise creatures that we barely know. So are bugs and bees and other animals in our gardens. People have a lot to learn about how to live harmoniously on earth. Plants, bugs, and other garden creatures can teach us, if we are silent enough to listen.

Gardeners and garden books don't always agree on the best ways to run a garden, because there is no best way. Don't believe everything you read or hear about gardening. Find out for yourself first.

GOOD
LUCK